Inside Book Publishing

Third Edition

Book publishing today is a highly competitive and exciting international industry. *Inside Book Publishing* provides a wealth of essential information for anyone interested in a career in publishing, or in understanding how publishing works.

This fully revised, updated and extended edition covers:

- the history and current structure of the UK book trade
- the role of the author, authors' agents, packagers and booksellers
- copyright and contracts
- key elements of the publishing process: commissioning, editorial, design, production, publicity and promotion, sales and rights
- the business of publishing
- the impact of electronic publishing and online bookselling
- getting a job in publishing and career pathways
- information on organizations offering training for publishers, suggestions for networking opportunities, and an annotated guide to further reading.

Giles Clark is Deputy Manager of the Copublishing Department at The Open University

Visit the 'Inside Book Publishing' webside: www.insidebookpublishing.com

Inside Book Publishing

Third edition

Giles Clark

London and New York

First published 1988 by Blueprint
Second edition 1994
Reprinted 1995

Reprinted 1996, 1998
by Routledge

This edition first published 2001
by Routledge
11 New Fetter Lane, London EC4P 4EE

Simultaneously published in the USA and Canada
by Routledge
29 West 35th Street, New York, NY 10001

Routledge is an imprint of the Taylor & Francis Group

Typeset in Palatino by Keystroke, Jacaranda Lodge, Wolverhampton
Printed and bound in Great Britain by Biddles Ltd., Guildford and King's Lynn

British Library Cataloguing in Publication Data
A catalogue record for this book is available from the British Library

Library of Congress Cataloging in Publication Data
A catalog record for this book is available from the Library of Congress

ISBN 0–415–23006–3 (pbk)
      0–415–23005–5 (hbk)

Contents

Preface

In the 1980s, the Society of Young Publishers (SYP) asked me to write a book for the benefit of its members, giving an overview of publishing and the careers available. My employer, The Open University, supporting the project, gave me special leave to undertake the primary research and over 150 publishing managers were interviewed.

The publishing history of this book is indicative of the dramatic and sometimes fraught changes that have since occurred in the industry. My first contract was with Allen & Unwin, a long-established, family-owned publisher of medium size and diversity most noted for its general list, including the classic works by J. R. R. Tolkien of *Lord of the Rings* and associated titles. This publisher also had a respected school textbook list, and higher education and professional titles in the earth sciences and the social sciences. By the time I had pulled together my research, Allen & Unwin had been taken over by another privately owned company and became Unwin Hyman. My first editor Adam Sisman left the restructured company (later going on to write a well received biography of A. J. P Taylor), and my new editor cancelled my contract and paid compensation. Unwin Hyman was then bought by HarperCollins, the international book publishing imprint of Rupert Murdoch's media corporation, News International. The valuable Tolkien classics joined the ranks of other famous dead and living authors of HarperCollins, but the staff were surplus as were the more specialist titles. A few of the Unwin Hyman managers formed University College London Press later acquired by Taylor & Francis and the social science titles were acquired from HarperCollins by Routledge, the prolific and respected academic imprint of the International Thomson Organization.

I was thankfully saved from the wilderness of being unpublished by Gordon Graham, then President of The Publishers Association and Chief Executive of Butterworths (legal and technical publishers) who introduced me to Dag Smith of the Book House Training Centre who contacted Blueprint Publishing – a new small publisher spearheaded and owned by Charlotte Berrill who successfully focused on books on publishing and printing. My work was adapted to the brief they drew up. The first edition of *Inside Book Publishing* (1988) was energetically published and sold by Blueprint.

Blueprint Publishing was later acquired by Chapman & Hall, the scientific and professional book imprint of Thomson. In 1993, Vivien James (the publisher in charge of Blueprint) asked me for a thoroughly revised second edition, which duly appeared in the autumn of 1994. German translation rights were sold to Hardt Wörner which published their edition in 1996. During the summer of 1995, International Thomson conducted a re-organization which included combining the business and management lists of Routledge and Chapman & Hall into a new company, the International Thomson Business Press, and the transference of Blueprint to the media studies list of Routledge under the editorship of Rebecca Barden. By the autumn of 1995 the first printing of the second edition of *Inside Book Publishing* had fortuitously sold out, enabling the reprint to appear under the Routledge imprint. A management buy-out of Routledge occurred in 1996, supported by the venture capitalist CINVEN. Routledge acquired the journal publisher CARFAX. In 1998, the UK journal and book publisher, Taylor & Francis bought Routledge.

Thus since conception, my work has passed through six changes of outright publishing ownership and five imprints and editors. This story is not unique in publishing today.

My special thanks are therefore due on the first edition to all my friends in the SYP, to The Open University, Gordon Graham, Dag Smith and Charlotte Berrill; on the second edition to Vivien James; and on the third edition to Rebecca Barden (Publisher Media Studies, Routledge), Alistair Daniel (Editorial Assistant), Sarah Eden (Production Editor), Malcolm O'Brien (Marketing Executive), and to Penny Mountain for compiling the Appendix on publishing courses, to Iain Brown for 'Further Reading' and particularly to Audrey N. Clark for reading the manuscript and indexing. On this edition, I gratefully acknowledge the kind assistance of Jo Henry of Book Marketing Ltd for the supply of book trade data on p. 69 and to the Taylor & Francis Group for the reproduction of the book costing estimate in Chapter 5. Furthermore I am indebted to the many dozens of people who have helped me with *Inside Book Publishing* over the years.

About the author

Giles Clark, with a family background in publishing, works at The Open University, Milton Keynes, where he is Deputy Manager in the Copublishing Department. He organizes copublication arrangements between the University and a wide range of publishers from small to large, across most academic disciplines. The partnerships forged with commercial publishers extend the University's readership internationally, reduce its costs and give it entrepreneurial income. He also develops the University's best-selling own-published titles. In a private capacity, he facilitates the publishing of books of local interest to serve the community. Over the past 20 years he has made an extensive study of all aspects of commercial publishing at home and abroad.

Introduction

The aims of this book are twofold: first to give a broad overview of the activities of book publishers – to many, including authors, wrapped in myth and mystery; second to help those seeking their first job in the industry or wanting to enhance their career prospects. It should be stressed that the subject-matter relates to the highly competitive businesses concerned with developing and marketing books for profit, and this includes those university presses operating along similar lines. Commercial publishing is not a slow-paced genteel hobby to nurture literature or poetry without reference to the market, or a continuance of academic study, or a vehicle to express and propagate one's own particular views. Risk-taking is inherent in the business: while prepared for failures, a publisher, as an eternal optimist with a short memory, forever searches for and expects success – sure in the belief that future rewards will more than exceed past losses – the last mistake seemingly the worst.

Publishing involves working with (but not universally for) congenial people and provides opportunity for individuality, creativity, and considerable responsibility for the young. The work-force is fluid, there are many possibilities for changing jobs early on, scope to go freelance, and for some high-fliers, the building of empires. Even quite junior jobs call for the management of people, products and money. Such skills combined with ideas, effective communication and organization are marketable.

Starting salaries are low, staff work hard and long hours, formal career structures are uncertain, middle-ranking salaries are usually modest, and there is little job security in some firms. Yet there is intense competition to secure some of the most junior jobs, and many people are hooked for much of their working life though rarely in the same firm. The appeal and fulfilment lie in serving people's entertainment, educational and informational needs, and sometimes in influencing the future course of events, in discovering and moulding new writing talent, in creating new markets. Publishers are continually dealing with many new products, each of which presents its own challenge in the way it can be produced and marketed for a particular audience. All jobs include routine and boring work. It is the infinite variety that fascinates. Each book presents its own problems to be solved at both the macro and micro levels. And success depends on personal contacts with authors, illustrators, printers, customers and colleagues; and networking.

'To publish' is commonly defined as 'to make public'. Here we are concerned predominantly with the work of commercial book publishing (including the publishing of allied and digital products), as distinct from that of newspaper and magazine publishing.

The book is an enduring medium through which ideas and knowledge are communicated, and a society's culture portrayed; and as such it is a primary resource for the student, the general reader and sometimes for the media. The diversity of books and publishers is vitally important to a democracy.

The book in printed volume form scores over other communications media by its length, permanence, portability, robustness, browsability, re-readability, accessibility, overall general convenience, physical attractiveness, status in society and relative cheapness. It has no need for a power source, an after-sales service or maintenance and, unlike electronic media, it transcends ever-changing and dating technologies. Book publishing, as a long-established industry, has a worldwide distribution system through which its output can be traded profitably in a continuing and largely regulated and controlled way; but while book publishers have to compete vigorously against other forms of entertainment, other learning processes and information sources, they are in a strong position to take advantage of digital media markets.

Book publication attracts an enormous number of diverse authors who want to communicate their ideas, thereby gaining recognition. Book publishing serves the million-copy fiction writer and the most specialist author with under one thousand sales: books can be published profitably for tiny markets which though limited in scale are limitless in number.

Elements underpinning UK book publishing are copyright protection; a plethora of talented living (and dead) authors; the freedom to publish; the English language, fortunately shared by much of the world; and a multiplicity of varied micro-markets, as opposed to a few mass markets, that arise and change rapidly and give opportunities for a wide range of publishers.

Publishers are not mere 'middlemen' interjecting themselves between authors and readers. They commission authors (often before manuscripts are written), confer authority and add value to authors' works, finance the production process, and marketing, and promote and sell the works wherever possible. The publisher, aiming to make a profit for the owners/shareholders and to carry on publishing:

- researches in the markets in which it specializes and builds contacts;
- seeks authors (sometimes in competition with other publishers) and is sought by them;
- matches marketable ideas to saleable authors;
- assesses the quality of the author's work (sometimes externally refereed), costs of production and sales prospects;
- decides whether or not to risk its investment funds in particular authors/projects to appear under its imprint;
- edits and designs books to meet author/market/branding needs;
- specifies, buys and oversees the work of print suppliers (in the UK or abroad) which manufacture the books;
- exploits new technologies to reduce costs, to develop new marketing techniques and to exploit digital communication channels;
- builds a worldwide sales network;
- promotes and publicizes the books to their intended users, the media, and to the intermediaries (the retailers, wholesalers, and overseas firms) through which the books are mainly sold;
- sells the books face-to-face to the intermediaries;
- holds bulk stocks of titles to satisfy demand;
- fulfils orders, distributes the books and collects the money, paying royalties to authors on sales made.

Additional income benefiting publisher and author may be made from various licensing arrangements which enable other organizations at home and abroad to exploit the author's work in different ways, media and languages.

Although the specialist staff of large publishers carry out all the above activities, some work (such as the detailed editing of books) is often contracted out to freelance workers or possibly to other firms. Smaller publishers may not have the resources to employ their own sales representatives or to distribute the books themselves so they may use larger publishers, or specialist firms. Apart from the decision to publish a book and raising the finance, all the other work could conceivably be outsourced, under the publisher's direction, to freelances or separate firms. Publishers of all sizes have increasingly outsourced work in order to reduce their staff overhead costs. But there are potential drawbacks: the publisher may have less control over the way the books are produced; lose the marketing emphasis projected by its own employees committed solely to its books; run the risk of out-sourcing core competences; and contribute to profit margins of sub-contractors.

Publishers, of course, come in all shapes and sizes; but in order to give a comprehensive review this book concentrates on commercial publishing in medium and large firms with their specialist departments. Such firms account for most of the industry's sales. Small publishers are generally started up by people with particular expertise: the information contained here, covering the way in which larger firms with more resources tackle other areas, could be invaluable to them.

The industry was traditionally broadly based with many medium-sized firms, but by the mid-1980s and after a spate of mergers and acquisitions, ownership became far more concentrated. A handful of very large international publishing groups now control over half the home market and throughout the world in the English language. The breadth of choice for both authors and employees is narrowing.

Chapter 1 'Book publishers: from family houses to international media corporations', traces significant changes in the structure of publishing businesses and the market to the present day. The chapter looks forward to the emerging digital media markets that open new opportunities and challenges for book and learned journal publishers.

Negative impacts of the take-overs of smaller publishers include the cancellation of authors' contracts, staff redundancies and in some cases the virtual or actual demise of once respected imprints. On the other hand, some bought firms survive relatively intact, are rejuvenated, and take full advantage of corporate funds, management expertise, lower print production costs and greater worldwide marketing muscle provided by the larger enterprise. Some authors, too, benefit from increased sales and higher royalties on sales made by the constituent firms of an international group the senior staff of which can earn large salaries.

A sign of a vigorous industry is the frequent start-up of new firms – compared with many industries publishing needs only a little equipment (e.g. a personal computer connected to the internet) and a relatively small amount of investment capital. Some new firms arise from management buy-outs of lists or imprints surplus to a large firm; or are created afresh from their former employees. No professional qualifications are needed to be a publisher – entry is unrestricted.

While the trend is towards larger publishers, there will always be room for numerous innovative, imaginative and entrepreneurial small publishers which, with lower overheads, can move faster and more sharply than some large ones that are over-burdened with bureaucracy, complacent and unresponsive to innovation and to fast changing markets. The larger the giant publishers become, the larger the niches they leave open for smaller publishers to exploit. Small publishers tend to be more specific in the books they publish, and with less resources and small margin of error, must work hard at choosing and marketing their titles carefully, and at developing authors and books which endure on the backlist. They can offer a more personal service to authors, who may receive scant attention from larger publishers.

All publishers give most attention to their most important new books, especially in respect of marketing and sales effort. An author, or book, ranked lowly on a large publisher's list may be given greater prominence on a smaller publisher's. Small publishers may, however, ultimately lose their successful authors to larger publishers.

Publishing is intimately interwoven with society, touches on every aspect of knowledge, often reaches a worldwide market and produces books for tiny tots to high-powered lawyers. But most publishers specialize in marketing certain kinds of books. The main sectors of the industry are described in Chapter 2.

Fundamentally book publishing rests on copyright and the

creativity of authors. Chapter 3 'From author contract to market outlet', opens with a review of the importance of copyright and gives an example of the contractual relationship between author and publisher. Most publishers do not sell their books directly to readers. Publishers' main customers are the booksellers and others in the supply chain. The ever-widening sales channels making books available to the public in the UK are summarized. Furthermore, the supply chain of businesses from author to reader is undergoing change, especially in response to the effects of new communication technologies. Businesses owe their existence to their ability to charge, at a profit, for the added value they give to a product or service in the supply chain. During such periods of rapid technological change, some businesses (and that can include existing publishers) are prone to 'disintermediation' – removal from the food chain. Conversely, reintermediation can occur as new businesses appear or as old ones re-define their roles.

Whatever the size, a publisher's underlying strength lies in the quality of its staff: a group of individuals who, ideally, share similar aims and values and are committed to the core business of publishing and selling books and information, who establish a stable of authors and go from strength to strength over the years. Publishing is a complex interplay of the creative and economic.

The publication of a book is a complex activity demanding at every stage ideas, flexibility and great attention to detail, and the close liaison of many specialist staff from editorial through to sales and distribution. Chapter 4 'The process and the people', outlines the principal tasks performed, generally concurrently, by staff in various departments. The main skills ideally needed to perform the tasks are listed, but it would be a rare person indeed who was strong in all.

Chapter 5 concentrates on the central financial aspects of publishing a book, which in itself is a new and different business venture, and Chapter 6 offers career advice.

The publishing industry has successfully undergone many changes. But the pace of change affecting the publishers' businesses and the professional lives of their staff is quickening at an unprecedented rate. The application of new technologies to the production of printed books, to their marketing and selling – and the growth of the internet – are impacting on every aspect of the business, and are included throughout this edition.

A further step is to publish in digital form, variously called digital publishing, electronic or e-publishing, or as 'e-books'. The publishers of legal reference works and of scientific learned journals are arguably the most technologically advanced in this respect, and some of their techniques may in due course be applied to other sectors. Even so it should be stressed that the publishers currently earn most of their revenue and profits from selling printed books; and even in the case of learned journals, the printed form still co-exists alongside the digital form for many titles. (E-enthusiasts may refer to printed books as p-books or treeware or dead treeware.)

Most of the new media advances come from the United States. In the late 1990s, several first-generation proprietary e-books (handheld reading devices, like tablet computers) were promoted. The term 'e-books' subsequently came to embrace the downloading of books in digital formats from the internet into all kinds of computers. However, reading from screens generally was still headache-inducing, far slower than reading from the printed page, and hampering readers' comprehension. Nevertheless, once the technology can match the quality of print and 'open' de facto standards for e-books have been adopted, they may confer their own particular advantages for some readers, such as the immediacy to down-load books any place, to link to other books and information sources, and to enlarge type for aged or poor-sighted readers – and e-books may be 20–30% cheaper – publishers save on printing and distribution costs. For the publisher, the development of e-books offers another channel to disseminate their authors' ideas, stories and information – the fundamental point of publishing.

At the turn of the century many managers of book publishers were wedded to printed books and were dismissive of the emerging digital communication media. They could point to some publishers' ruinous ventures in the early 1990s into multimedia publishing on CD-ROM that all too few consumers wished to buy and to the continued loss-making nature of the internet companies (including Amazon). Running profitable businesses derived from trading in printed books; they imagined that to invest in digital formats would be seriously damaging to profits and to shareholders, or at least premature. Who would read an e-book in bed or on the beach? However, for those entering book publishing today, publishers of the next generation, there are going to be far-reaching changes to the ways in which books are published; though no-one can predict the nature, or the timing, of the course of events.

The survey of publishing provided here necessarily excludes much detail but it should give you sufficient insight of what is to many an exciting and satisfying way of life.

In this third edition, some company names are given (along with their corporate owners where appropriate). But it should be noted that individual publishers are rising or falling and are subject to changing ownership. The web site *insidebookpublishing.com* associated with this book provides links to other sources of useful information.

SALIENT FEATURES OF BOOK PUBLISHING

By commercial standards, book publishing as a whole is a small but profitable and influential industry which turns over around £3 billion and is thought to employ around 14 000–20 000 people. Detailed statistics on employment structure or salaries are not available, though it is estimated that full-time job losses at the peak of the recession in the early 1990s were around 10% of the work force. However, there were very few outright company failures. Publishing companies can usually generate high turnover with relatively small numbers of full-time employees, say sales of £150 000–180 000 each. Whitaker lists 3500 'most active' publishers but this includes many small publishers and those for which publishing is a sideline.

Compared with other industries book publishing is unparalleled in the number of new products launched each year. In 1999, Whitaker recorded 110 155 new books published in the UK, up from 62 102 in 1993, 45 652 in 1987, 37 382 in 1980, and 27 247 in 1975. In 1988 the number of titles in print was 444 000; by 1993 it had reached 600 000; and by the century end it was nearly one million. It should be noted that these statistics include books originated in the USA but published in the UK, especially in the academic and professional fields, and those produced by thousands of small publishers or 'non-profit publishers'. But within the 1999 total of 110 155, Whitaker includes 26 150 'revised and new editions' many of which are books re-issued in paperback or merely repackaged by commercial houses; and only 1968 titles which were translated imports. Generally speaking the number of copies sold has not grown apace. Print quantities per title have declined, and the expected effective sales life of titles has shortened, often to under a year.

Critics of book publishers perennially complain about publishers' 'over-production' of new books; that so many new books, they argue, do not allow sufficient advertising or high-street bookshop display of each one; that by publishing fewer books, better books (even though such a term could be subjectively defined) would result. But would, for example, a fiction publisher qualitatively improve the work of current great writers by publishing fewer new writers, or would it by publishing fewer third-rate writers cause more of them to turn into second-raters, and second-raters into first-raters? Would the curtailment of academic publishing aid poetry publishing? A publisher could ask each editor to cut the number of new books signed up with a view to sharpening the editors' judgement of quality or somehow to reducing their fallibility. If that were possible a publisher could increase its sales and reputation by critically reducing the size of its list every year. Some publishers (particularly during recessions) cut their lists and may claim that they increase sales and profits by concentrating their efforts on marketing properly a smaller number of titles, while others continue to expand title output and may claim that they are increasing their market share. Authors want to be published. Publishers constantly try to find new ones, and meet the ever growing diverse leisure and professional interests of readers; and there is fierce competition between publishers in every field. Furthermore, technological advances enable printed books to be produced more economically in smaller and smaller quantities, and e-books are just getting started. New title output and reader choice increases.

For company size, each publisher annually launches a large number of untried and untested products. Few new books could support the cost of retaining a market-research company to pre-test the market; thus their publishing is a high-risk decision. Books like any commodity need a clear perception of the product and buyer and vigorous marketing to bring them together, but the marketing techniques deployed by other consumer goods industries are not wholly appropriate. Books are not a basic life necessity; the reader usually buys a single copy, only once, not repeatedly; company brand name identification, with some exceptions, is of little consequence to the reader (but can be important to authors and booksellers); and readers are confronted by a multiplicity of choices to satisfy their interests. Books are borrowed free from libraries and from other sources.

In comparison to faster moving industries such as music, video, software and consumer magazines, book publishers take a long time (some would say an inordinately long time) to produce a book from author's manuscript through to publication. Production schedules of 4–12 months (or more) are typical – to allow adequate time for worldwide promotion and sales. Most of a publisher's cash is tied up in stock. The turnover of a publisher's complete stock of all books commonly takes more than a year. Typically 20% of the titles account for 80% of the revenue but the uncertainties of estimating demand make the success of such books initially difficult to determine. Publishers service an enormous number of small orders, often of low value, but totalling considerable sums.

A report in 1998 by KPMG addressing the costs of book distribution in the UK, revealed that only 3% of titles accounted for 50% of the total volume of retail sales. The other 50% consisted of thousands of slower moving titles selling in small quantities. Fewer than 40 of 15,000 publishers were responsible for 56% of bookshop sales, and 4 bookselling chains accounted for 42% of all retail sales. Despite the consolidation of publishers through mergers and acquisitions, no one publisher had a market share of more than 9% at that time.

The publishers that prosper in good times and bad are those which have developed and maintained a core group of long life titles delivering handsome margins, which are not too overdependent on such past successes and which focus on producing high quality books which are good of their kind. Provided a project has a genuine reason for being, reflects quality in its conception, content and production, and is made available at the right time and price to a well-targeted market it will sell, sometimes prodigiously. Many of the most interesting and successful books are those that are exceptional, not a slavish imitation of other books or even a product of market research.

Much of UK publishing depends for its survival on exporting. Nearly 30% of UK publishers' sales are exports and additionally publishers receive royalties from editions licensed abroad. (Exports are nearly double imports.) The major markets are the countries of Europe (39%, especially Germany, Netherlands and Ireland), North

America (20%) and Australasia (8%). From the mid-1980s to the early 1990s, sales to mainland Europe grew and supplanted North America as the main export destination, and sales to Americanized Australasia declined. East Asian and Asia/Pacific rim countries are growing in importance.

UK industry exports approach those of the much larger US industry. Both countries dominate English language exports, but face increasing competition from indigenous publishers, some of which publish in English. Piracy in developing countries is a considerable threat and is the enemy of UK publishers, legitimate indigenous publishers and authors alike. The growth of the bulk photocopying industry, especially in the Middle East and the Far East, hinders exports. The British Council is the major government agency promoting books, journals, digital publications and authors abroad.

Chapter 1

Book publishers: from family houses to international media corporations

Book publishing was traditionally broadly based with around 50 medium-sized firms employing around 50 or so staff and issuing, say, several hundred titles per year, usually in hardback. The publishers were owned privately, usually by family members who held majority share stakes. They concentrated on fiction and non-fiction (termed 'general' or 'trade' or, more recently, 'consumer books') though they also developed educational (i.e. school text-book) and academic lists, subservient to the general side.

Throughout the 1960s and 1970s (other than in the recession of the early to mid-1970s), much of the publishers' fast growing prosperity was based on readers' affluence and increasing public expenditure. The consumer book publishers of hardback adult and children's books were underpinned by generous government funding of libraries, as were the rapidly expanding educational publishers, and the academic publishers responding to heady growth in higher education. Expansion in science, technology and medicine (STM), and ample funding of UK and US university libraries stimulated the publishing of high-priced academic monographs and of immensely profitable learned journals, produced especially by the STM book publishers. During this period many of the main educational, academic and STM publishers moved out of London to cheaper offices in the New Town ring in order to house their burgeoning staff numbers.

While the first overseas subsidiaries had been opened in the late nineteenth and early twentieth centuries in Australia and Canada, in the 1960s the educational and academic houses opened subsidiaries in the newly formed African Commonwealth countries and exported massive quantities of UK-based textbooks. The Commonwealth countries' educational systems were based on

UK curricula or examinations, and many professors were UK-educated.

The British publishers enjoyed their traditional export markets: the USA, Commonwealth and northern Europe. The giant American publishers with their much larger home market gave little emphasis to exports, the major exception being the college textbook publishers (especially in STM). These opened subsidiaries in the UK after the Second World War and came subsequently to dominate the English language major 'first-year' textbook adoption markets worldwide, Commonwealth countries included.

Mass-market paperback publishing grew substantially and was carried out by separate firms which in the main acquired reprint paperback rights from the famous general firms that originated titles in hardback. Literary agents who increasingly began to represent the interests of fiction and non-fiction authors, were resented by some traditional publishers who saw them as unwarranted intruders into the publisher/author relationship. New publishers arose producing in large quantities highly-illustrated non-fiction books in full colour at low and affordable prices – these books were cynically described by traditionalists as 'down-market' or as 'non-books'.

Paul Hamlyn, the greatest exponent of affordable illustrated books, self-made a series of fortunes from illustrated book publishing. First by selling his Paul Hamlyn imprint to the magazine company IPC, then by founding Octopus, by buying back the Paul Hamlyn imprint for a nominal sum, plus liabilities, and then by selling his imprints to Reed Consumer Books for an enormous sum. In his lifetime, he founded the Paul Hamlyn Foundation (see Appendix) to give greater access to the arts and also to aid the training of publishers. (Robert Maxwell similarly made a fortune in publishing from learned journals through his Pergamon Press but he went bust and overboard.)

The publication of *The Reader's Digest Great World Atlas* (1961) with its opening of double-page spreads displaying superb full-colour graphics, with extended captions not unlike magazines, and the *Treasures of Tutankh-amun* (tied-in to the British Museum exhibition) (1972) were inspirational to some embryonic book packagers. The packagers went on to produce highly illustrated full-colour information books which they pre-sold to publishers around the world to market and distribute under the publishers' imprints. In the late 1970s, the highly illustrated publishers broke colour books into the supermarkets by producing 'own brand' books for them at very low prices.

By the end of the 1970s the era of the 'gentleman' publisher was fast disappearing. (The phrase 'gentleman' has been used historically to describe grand publishers of literary fiction or belles lettres, or derided as gentlemen who ran their companies by the seat of their pants, who adopted a paternalist management style, or who according to some literary agents exhibited very ungentlemanly behaviour indeed in their contractual arrangements with authors.) Some of the foremost publishers who had personally built great publishing companies had reached the end of their careers. Some of their descendants, given senior management positions, were either incompetent or quite ill-prepared for the changes to come.

The stable and expansionary publishing world of the 1960s and 1970s was rudely shattered by the recession of 1980 which forced publishers to cut their lists and overheads (e.g. by making redundant the older staff and the weaker staff sucked in during the fast growth era). From then on progressive cuts in public expenditure throughout the English-speaking world would be the order of the day. Reductions in public expenditure adversely affected the publishing and availability of some kinds of books, such as hardback fiction written by new and minor authors destined for public libraries, certain categories of children's books supported by public and school libraries, high-priced academic monographs for university libraries, and school textbooks produced for underfunded UK state schools. A further factor of the 1980s and early 1990s was high book-price inflation and the appreciation of sterling against the currencies of countries to which UK publishers traditionally exported. This led to a continued decline in export sales and aided competition from US publishers benefitting from American dominance of the world's media. For instance, American general books, particularly mass-market paperbacks and college textbooks, were more competitively priced in mainland Europe and Australia. Both US and UK textbook publishers' export sales suffered from the near collapse of the economies of developing countries, especially the African.

The 1980s was the period of mergers and acquisitions which restructured the publishing industry. A handful of large international publishing groups eventually came to control over half the home market: long established independent medium-sized firms were to become a rarity – a good example being Faber & Faber. The deregulation of the financial markets led to increased availability of long- and short-term equity and debt financing allowing large publishers or their parents to take over medium-sized publishers, and small publishers to expand or start-up. Book publishing was attractive to investors who could see that the industry had consistently, that is until 1987, returned pre-tax profits and return on capital above the average level of all industries.

At an earlier time some industrial conglomerates had begun to buy up and amass publishing companies of different types (e.g. general hardback and mass-market paperback, educational, academic and STM) though they tended to keep such companies as separate, sometimes prestigious entities rather than parts of an overall corporate industrial logic. Unlike today, book publishing had traditionally been linked to printing. Some book publishers either owned printers or were owned by printers. The idea that general book publishing was part of the larger media leisure industry evolved slowly. Early examples included the acquisition of general publishers by magazine publishers and by independent television companies which wanted to control television tie-in books (the BBC usually licensed its best-selling television series tie-ins to publishers).

Throughout the 1990s, the international consolidation of the main English language publishers continued. But the boardroom strategies switched from acquiring publishers across the range of different market segments (e.g. consumer, educational, academic/ STM) to focusing on the leadership of such segments.

CONSUMER BOOK PUBLISHING

The 1980s restructuring of UK book publishing affected all types of publishing but its effects were most dramatic in consumer book publishing, the fault lines having appeared in the 1970s. As mentioned above, the ownership and character of consumer book publishing (both adult and children's) was traditionally divided between many hardback publishers and around a dozen separate mass-market paperback houses. (The so-called mass-market in publishing terms ranges from the big authors who sell in mass-market paperback hundreds of thousands of copies down to minimum print runs of 25 000 copies in the 1970s, subsequently reduced to nearly half that number in the early 1990s, and more than halving again by the late 1990s.)

The publishing strategy was (and sometimes still is) to first publish and establish a book in hardback at a high price and subsequently to re-issue it, a year later or less, in a paperback format at a lower price in greater numbers to a wider audience. Hardback fiction and non-fiction lists were, and to some extent still are, published in half-yearly seasons (the spring/summer, and autumn/winter) headed by major 'lead titles' and sold to booksellers, to libraries (mainly via library suppliers) and sometimes to book clubs. Whereas the mass-market paperbacks were fast-moving, small 'A format' or 'pocket' or 'rack-sized' books published in monthly batches, each month headed by lead fiction and non-fiction titles, with various category titles forming the remainder. Such paperbacks were usually straight reductions of original hardback sizes (i.e. pages of the hardback edition were photographically reduced down to the size of the paperback edition), were printed overall in much larger quantities on cheap paper, reached a wider retail market beyond bookshops such as in the display racks of the confectioner/tobacconist/newsagent (CTN) outlets; and were sold in a way more akin to that of magazines.

The respective character of hardback and paperback publishers was very different. The hardback general publishers inhabited their fine but slowly decaying Georgian houses in Bloomsbury, around Bedford Square, and in other high-class central London locations. The palatial former reception rooms, with Adam marble fireplaces and hung with chandeliers, were impressive settings for the managing director or the editorial director. The editors were very much in control. The production staff who hired the printers to produce the books, and the marketing and sales staff, were crammed in the former secondary bedrooms and servants' quarters, the basement and the attics. The mass-market paperback reprinters occupied concrete office blocks in cheaper London locations. Theirs was a sales-driven operation.

The hardback publishers played their traditional role of nurturing new writing talent and working closely with authors on manuscripts. Their backlists were complete with great and loyal authors, and some enduring money-spinning books. Their formidable reputation ensured that their new books were reviewed (literary review editors ignored paperbacks), that the public librarians would automatically order sufficient quantities, and that the compliant independent booksellers would display and stock their titles. The advent of book clubs supplied another outlet. The booksellers complained that the book clubs by offering their members new hardbacks at discounted prices by mail-order were undermining their business. The publishers were pleasantly surprised by the paradoxical increased sales through bookshops stemming from a book club's large-scale consumer advertising campaigns. However, by the early to mid-1980s, hardback publishers found themselves making hardly any profit from selling copies themselves. They derived their profit and laid off risks by making rights and co-edition sales to others: to the paperback publishers, to book clubs, to US publishers and foreign language publishers etc. While the hardback publishers employed highly talented editors, some of whom had immense egos and a passion for books, they included editors who favoured pet projects and authors who produced books which few wanted to buy.

The false dichotomy between hardback and paperback publishing could not survive. The book market was rapidly changing, readers' expectations were altering, competition between publishers to secure best-selling authors was intensifying and literary agents were far more adept in extracting from publishers maximum advance payments against future royalties for their authors' works.

The hardback publishers were used to acquiring the exclusive right to publish an author's work for the full term of copyright in hardback and paperback, even though they had no mass-market paperback publishing capability, and similarly to acquiring US rights which they in turn licensed to US publishers. The hardback publisher would then sub-license the UK paperback publisher, for a fixed period (say eight years), the right to publish the paperback on which it would pay the hardback publisher a royalty of say 7.5% on published price, rising to 10% or more after specified large quantities had been sold. The hardback publisher would share the royalties received with the author (e.g. 50/50, 30/70 respectively). The paperback publisher would want to acquire its main titles two years ahead of paperback publication. The originating publisher would secure at that time a large advance payment from the paperback publisher, similarly shared with the author.

Paperback publishers facing escalating reprint advances increased their output of original titles, sometimes licensing rights to hardback publishers. In that some authors derived most of their income from paperback sales (and sometimes US sales), it was prudent for agents to cut out the hardback publisher's royalty share from such sales. Agents, for example, might have licensed the book directly to an independent hardback publisher, to a separate paperback publisher, and to a US publisher, thereby obtaining advances from each party and full royalty rates for their authors (less the agent's commission). The general publishers which came to own both hardback and paperback firms (termed vertically integrated) paid authors full royalty rates on each edition and were therefore better positioned to capture the leading authors. Paperback and hardback publishers without a hardback or paperback arm were increasingly desperate – sometimes they entered into alliances in order to bid for the big books jointly.

Another strand leading to the amalgamation of consumer book publishing, again reaching back to the late 1970s, was the weakening polarization between the traditional formats. The mass-market paperbackers, with increasing competition between themselves, as well as higher title output, recorded lower unit sales per title. Paperback prices rose and the ownership of paperback houses became more concentrated. Furthermore readers' expectations created a new market for certain books and authors to be published in 'quality' or 'trade paperback' or 'B format' books printed in larger size to higher standards, and published in quantities lower overall than the 'A format' but at higher prices, mainly for the bookshop. Such books could be reprints from hardbacks, reissues or originals. Both mass-market paperback and hardback houses started up trade paperback literary imprints (publishing titles in monthly batches or less regularly) and some hardback houses ventured into the 'A format' field as well, usually with near fatal consequences. Over time, the use of the trade paperback to publish original fiction (including new writers) and non-fiction has grown apace as has the greater use of larger paperback sizes. For while the mass market A format (178×111 mm) still commands much shelf space in Smiths and supermarkets etc., the B format (say 198×129 mm) has been supplemented by larger sizes often referred to as trade paperbacks – the C formats – which can be typically 216×138 mm (i.e. the demy octavo, 8vo, size) or 234×156 mm (i.e. royal 8vo). Many trade hardbacks, as well as academic titles, are produced in these latter 'standard' sizes.

By the end of the 1980s and early 1990s, most of the formerly independent hardback houses were part of the major publishing corporations. Each had the capability of publishing in all formats, mass-market paperback, trade paperback and hardback. Their imprints were gathered together in modern London offices usually under one roof. The new owners combed through the old reprint paperback contracts entered into by their hardback publishers with the paperback publishers and noted the titles which had, from other take-overs, fallen into the hands of rival paperback imprints and the termination dates of such licences. In due course they would claw-back the paperback rights to those books for their own paperback imprints much to the consternation of the bereft paperback reprinters, and some authors and agents.

The main financial assets of a publishing company (other than buildings etc.) are its intellectual property assets (IPA). These are enshrined in the contracts it holds with suppliers (i.e. contracts negotiated directly with authors or via their agents; book packagers, US publishers and foreign languages publishers) and with companies to which it has sold rights, such as to book clubs, US publishers and foreign language publishers. The original IPA derives from the author to which the publisher adds value; but ultimately the value of the IPA is affected by the consumer who may, or may not, buy the product in book or other form. The pressure to control rights internationally prompted US general publishers to acquire UK imprints, and vice-versa, and both UK and US publishers were attractive to expansionist mainland European publishers, especially to the German and privately owned media corporation Bertelsmann. However, although virtually all the major consumer book publishers had sister imprints on both sides of the Atlantic, their ability to acquire world English rights in the works of best-selling authors was constrained by the US and UK literary agents who, on behalf of their authors, continued to license UK and US editions to imprints in competing ownership.

The hardback general book publishers had taken years to develop, held valuable IPA, had an increasing rarity value and at the peak of the merger boom commanded high prices.

As for the staff of the taken-over general publishers, the outlook for many was rather bleak. Other than the staff made immediately redundant, those who were transferred entered the world of corporate publishing. The editors, especially, who had been brought up in the culture of smaller companies who had enjoyed considerable autonomy in their publishing decisions over the kinds of books they wanted to publish and their work with authors, carried with them a set of values quite often at odds with their new employers who emphasized sales and profit motives and sometimes clean and tidy desks clear of manuscripts and books, a world apart from their former houses. Some editors blamed the accountants for preventing them from doing the books they wanted to publish. It was not the accountants *per se*; the publishing socio-economic culture had changed. Editorial status was no longer conferred by access to the cellar of fine wines, but by the size of their work stations. The nature of consumer book publishing had changed from being 'product-led' to being 'market-driven'. Furthermore, some publishers have the ability of leading the market by introducing new authors, publishing books in different formats, and marketing and selling them in different ways. Editorial individuality and innovation are still present in the large corporations.

Although consumer book publishing appears to be dominated by the existing majors, there are quite large publishers, for example in the highly illustrated information book field, medium-sized independents, fast-growing new entrants, and many dozens of smaller specialist publishers producing adult or children's books. The smaller publishers cannot compete against the large corporations in terms of advances paid to agented, established authors. Thus, for example, they concentrate on bringing forward new writers, or those overlooked who may not have agents, or they build a stable of authors who will work for one-off fees instead of royalties – common in the highly illustrated book fields.

While general or 'consumer book' publishing was being restructured, the increased availability of finance in the 1980s also aided the transformation and concentration of UK bookselling. Traditionally, UK bookselling had been characterized by the dominance of the major chain WH Smith (which had its roots in station bookstalls and high-street stationery outlets), smaller independently owned chains and a great number of independent and small bookshops. But the arrival of new chains, such as Waterstone's and Dillons, established large well-stocked bookshops (e.g. stocking c.50,000 titles, three to four times the size of many independents) around the country. The enhanced professionalism in bookselling spread to the existing larger independents which had to compete. The small independents lost market share. The new chains aggressively expanded but also argued with publishers that they needed higher discounts (i.e. the bookseller's percentage margin between the retail price of a book and the price bought from the publisher) and extended – or very extended – credit periods (i.e. the time to settle invoices) to operate. The consumer book publishers benefited from the new well-stocked and style-branded bookshops displaying their books, but they gave them better discounts and credit. The power relationship between publishers and booksellers, for so long weighted in the publisher's favour, began to tip towards the major retailers, as is common in most consumer goods industries. Furthermore by the mid-1990s, the major supermarkets were devoting more space to books and were intent on driving down book prices to the consumer, and their costs of supply.

Another factor impinging on consumer book publishers' margins, pushing up the average discount on sales made to UK customers, was the rise of the trade wholesalers supplying the declining and fragmented independent bookshop sector. From the early 1980s to the early 1990s, a proportion of a publisher's sales passing through such wholesalers grew from say 10% to 20%+ at the expense of direct supply to bookshops. While the growing bookselling chains argued for discounts from the publishers of well above 40% off the published price, the small independents were stuck with the traditional discounts of 33–35%. The trade book wholesalers argued they needed at least a 15% margin between the price they bought the books from the publisher and the price they sold them to an independent, thus they pressed for a 50% discount or more from the publisher. WH Smith and the bookseller chains, meanwhile, ratcheted up the publishers' discounts still further. Overall, from the mid-1980s to the late 1990s, publishers' average trade discount to their UK customers increased by 10–15%.

The major publishers also locked themselves into a battle of paying rocketing levels of advances for lead titles in order to maintain or increase their market share of the limited number of such titles available. Consumers' expenditure on books peaked in 1993, yet by the time those books were published, the consumer book market was declining. The return of unsold books from booksellers, a long-time feature of consumer book publishing (especially of paperbacks), surpassed more than 25% of the publishers' sales as booksellers destocked hardbacks and paperbacks. On some lead titles, the actual sales fell far short of the expected number on which the author's advance against royalties had been calculated – the advance was thus unearned. A publisher which may have budgeted an author's royalty rate of between 15–20% of the publisher's revenue, may have paid an advance (in effect a non-returnable fee) which equated to an effective royalty rate of 30% of sales income, or more in disastrous cases. The consumer book publishers emerged from the recession leaner and fitter – three hour publishing lunches had been curtailed – but with low levels of profitability.

The Net Book Agreement (NBA) or the resale price maintenance (r.p.m.) of books which had endured throughout the twentieth century, collapsed in September 1995. Up to that date, the publishers set the retail prices of books (termed the 'net price'). Retailers were not allowed to sell such books to the public below the stated net prices, or in practice to offer sales incentives commonly used on other kinds of products. In that virtually all the main consumer book publishers were members of their trade organization, The Publishers Association (PA) and were voluntary signatories of the NBA, the PA was highly successful in enforcing r.p.m. among retailers, and defending the NBA against critics. The PA regulated the operation of the market in other ways, such as negotiating the rules governing the operation of book clubs, which offered books at discounted prices to their members by mail order. Also libraries, under a special licence, were allowed to purchase books at 10% off the net price.

The purpose of the NBA was to create a well-ordered book market in which a large number of dedicated booksellers could afford to stock a wide range of new and backlist titles, and to offer free customer services, sure in the knowledge that they could not be undercut by predatory retailers taking the cream off the narrow range of current bestsellers and fast-selling backlist stock titles.

Prior to the demise of the NBA, consumer spending on books continued to fall, and pro and anti arguments on the NBA raged among publishers and among booksellers. More publicly, some retailers, such as the bookselling chain Dillons and the supermarket chain Asda, presented themselves in the press as championing the consumers' right to low book prices, by selling books at deeply discounted prices from publishers who had abandoned the NBA – these retailers and publishers such as Hodder Headline and Reed Consumer Books appeared to be gaining a competitive advantage. The pro-NBA publishers and booksellers also faced expensive and uncertain legal proceedings to defend the NBA in the courts, threatened by the government's Office of Fair Trading and the

European Commission. Then in September, the announcement of a cut price promotion by major trade publishers Random House and HarperCollins with WH Smith triggered the collapse. With no consensus among publishers and booksellers, r.p.m. on books passed into UK trade history. But various forms of r.p.m. continued in some mainland European countries.

In the immediate aftermath, the UK consumer spending on books bottomed out in the spring of 1996, and then staged a steady recovery to a new peak in 1998 – a vintage year for bestselling titles. Retailers' heavy discounting to the public of the new, most popular titles became the norm. Publishers increased their 'recommended retail prices' above the general rate of inflation to accommodate the higher discounts offered to the public and the higher discounts they gave to the retailers caused by the NBA collapse. Each year in January, the *Guardian* newspaper calculates the UK unit sales of the top 50 best-selling paperbacks. The 1986 cumulative total of 14.07 million copies was the peak of the decade. By 1998, the total had fallen by 9.5%, prompting the view at the time that the heavy discounting and increased sales of the hardback editions being published at higher prices – making them easier to discount – might be eroding the subsequent paperback editions' sales.

In consumer publishing, the first wave of new media excitement – the publishing of highly illustrated multimedia titles on CD-ROM – occurred in the early to mid-1990s. At that time there were large numbers of US imports. Analysts pointed to the rapid rise of computers fitted with CD-ROM drives being purchased by UK households. This would lead, it was argued, to an exponential rise in the consumer purchase of content titles. Some of the major trade publishers, such as HarperCollins, Penguin and Reed, and the illustrated book reference publisher Dorling Kindersley, established new media divisions. The world's main encyclopaedia publishers converted their voluminous works to CD-ROM (except *Encyclopaedia Britannica* which it was said did not want to upset its door-to-door sales force); and Microsoft created *Encarta*, localized successfully around the world. Major entertainment companies such as Disney exploited their character properties on the new medium. UK start-up multimedia producers arose. But by 1996, most of the UK trade book publishers, with the exception of Dorling Kindersley, withdrew from the market place bearing large losses. It was said that a typical multimedia title had cost 10 times the cost of producing a book and its sales were one-tenth of that of a comparable book. No mass-market arose to cover the high development costs and the US was resistant to imports. The booksellers did not stock the titles sufficiently and the publishers were left to compete in the computer stores, an alien and hostile setting for their business. By the late 1990s, the remainder dealers had extensive stocks of life-style titles from around the world to sell off for a few pounds per title. Nevertheless, the publishing of multimedia titles on silver disk (CD-ROM and DVD) continued mainly in the educational (home and school), cartographic and text-based professional reference fields, while *Encyclopaedia Britannica* was available for free on the net, competing against *Encarta* which also appeared in print through Bloomsbury.

The failure of multimedia publishing re-inforced many publishers' sceptical view of the new media and negatively coloured many senior managements' response to the news of e-books in the USA in the late 1990s. If the business model for multimedia publishing on silver disk was loss making, they argued, what hope would there be for publishing on the internet, a generally free medium devaluing the price of information, with few business models, other than, for example, using content to attract advertising revenue?

The low company valuations of the consumer book publishers in the 1990s were in marked contrast to the boom of the 1980s. While most of the owners persevered, Reed decided to sell its consumer imprints to concentrate on professional publishing, recording a massive write-off in the process. Nevertheless, newer independent UK publishers, such as Bloomsbury, Fourth Estate, Orion and Piatkus grew strongly, while some others failed. Another source of new publishers were the book packagers, many of which apart from the main exception, Quarto, decided to publish their illustrated books in English under their own imprints in the UK, and sometimes the US, rather than license them to publishers.

By the end of the century, the main consumer publishers had mostly recovered their levels of profitability, and WH Smith paid what was considered by some competitors to be a perceived high price for the UK publisher Hodder Headline. The leading publishers dominating sales through the UK general retail market at the turn of the century and vying for the top sales rankings were the Bertelsmann companies of Random House and Transworld (which in 1999 together accounted for 15.5% share of book sales), the Pearson companies of the Penguin Group and Dorling

Kindersley, and HarperCollins (part of News International). The other main contenders in the home trade book market included Hodder Headline (WH Smith); Macmillan (owned by the German private company Holtzbrinck); Orion (in which the French media group Hatchette had invested); BBC Worldwide; and Little, Brown (OAL/Times Warner). Other significant publishers included the children's book publisher Scholastic, Faber & Faber, Simon & Schuster UK Trade Division (part of US media group Viacom), UK publishers Bloomsbury and Fourth Estate (acquired by HarperCollins in 2000), AA Publishing and the trade division of Oxford University Press, and Reader's Digest selling its books by mail-order and via the trade.

Children's publishing

By the late 1970s the outlook for some publishers of children's books, especially those producing quality hardbacks, appeared grim. Many bookshops other than the major multi-product stationery chain WH Smith were hardly enthusiastic buyers, public and school libraries (traditional major markets) were cutting back, and the birth rate was forecast to fall. In that the vitality of children's publishing creates the book buyers of the future, there were serious worries about the end of book reading, foreshadowing the end of publishing itself. Between 1981 and 1990 the population of five- to fourteen-year-olds did indeed fall by 13% but the inventiveness of authors and illustrators, of the existing publishers (other than those which closed or sold off their imprints), of new publishers, such as Walker Books, and book packagers transformed children's publishing during the 1980s into arguably the most dynamic sector of the industry. Retail sales per child rose by nearly three-times, and the number of new books and new editions (including reprints and re-issues in paperback) increased from 3009 to 5879. The sales of children's book publishers from 1985 to 1990 rose in real terms by 26% while their adult general book publishing counterparts managed only 7%.

The publishers found new ways of reaching the home market via supermarkets (from the mid-1980s selling them books appearing under the supermarket's own brand label), toyshops and direct selling distributors/book clubs/school book fairs etc. They sold international co-editions to US and European publishing partners, enabling picture books and highly-illustrated non-fiction or information books to be published at low and affordable prices worldwide. Paperback sales grew enormously and in volume terms came to dominate the market. Teenage fiction lists were established.

The recession of the early 1990s saw a reversal in sales of around 13% yet the publishers continued to increase their title output through to 1995 when it stabilized at around 8,000 titles. The UK market for children's books declined from 1990 through to 1997, as other new products competed for children's attention and parent's spending. However, in 1998–9 the market staged a substantial recovery. Government policy to give greater emphasis to literacy in primary schools was a fillip to some children's publishers, which gained widespread school and library sales. Their books became more answerable to the needs of the National Curriculum, though it did create a tension between the book as entertainment and the book as a learning aid.

By the end of the century an explosion in new children's fiction was apparent, most notably led by J K Rowling's Harry Potter series which not only rocketed the medium sized independent publisher Bloomsbury up the charts for retail sales in the UK, but which became international bestsellers and widely translated – attractive to a children's *and* adult readership – stimulating interest in children's books across the board. The major children's publishers included, for example, the children's imprints of Puffin, Ladybird and Dorling Kindersley (part of Penguin, owned by Pearson) and of the other adult consumer book publishers such as Hodder (owned by WH Smith), HarperCollins (owned by News International), the Bertelsmann companies of Random House and Transworld, Macmillan (owned by Holtzbrinck), Oxford University Press and BBC Worldwide. But, there are other specialist children's publishers, which are not part of adult book publishing groups. Some of these are larger in terms of sales turnover than some of the children's imprints listed above – Egmont, Scholastic and Walker Books for example. It is important to note that the children's publishers sell their books through many different distribution channels beyond booksellers, thus publishers' sales ranking by general retail market sales recorded by BookTrack (which are listed occasionally in *The Bookseller*) need to be viewed conservatively. For example, there are high sales of children's books to the religious market, served for instance by Lion and John Hunt Publishing.

NON-CONSUMER BOOK PUBLISHING

These publishing sectors encompass the educational, academic, STM (scientific, technical and medical), learned journal and professional book publishing companies. The two major university presses are very active in these fields. In that the main publishing sectors vary in profitability at different times, management try to spread their portfolios of companies in the UK and abroad. Some private-sector publishing groups are more weighted towards the consumer market while others are weighted in the more specialized areas. The latter, especially publishers producing high-level books and associated information and reference products for professionals (e.g. in STM, business and law), are highly profitable and strongly cash generative.

Educational publishing

During the 1980s, school pupil rolls declined, and the number of significant educational publishers decreased from around 30 to 15. Sales volumes fell from 1986 to 1990 reflecting in part the gross underfunding of UK state schools, the poverty of some Commonwealth countries and the more nationalist approach abroad to curricula diminishing export sales. By the early 1990s, the top three publishers commanded 50% of sales to schools, the top seven over 75%. The remaining publishers concentrated in specialist areas or subjects.

The home market used to be characterized by little central government intervention and a variety of examination boards setting curricula. A diversity of books and ancillary materials were published by a variety of publishers. The books were purchased through local authorities and supplied to schools via specialist suppliers, local authority purchasing organizations and bookshops. However, the effects of the Conservative government's 1988 Education Reform Act were profound. The new National Curriculum was far more prescriptive and defined. At first, the publishers tried to salvage their old backlist textbooks (from which they earned most of their profits) as best they could. Nevertheless many of their products were obsolete. The race was on to produce new materials, especially schemes or programmes of study in core subjects, quickly and at great cost. Speed and quality were of the essence as each school had to be locked into the publisher's programme ideally for say three to five years. Slow publishers risked being knocked out, as indeed some were.

The government responded to the campaign mounted especially by the Educational Publishers Council, for increased school funding but only in the short-term; the sales in the early 1990s rebounded to their 1986 levels as did the publishers' profitability. Moreover, the local management of schools gave schools cheque books enabling them to order books themselves; and schools turned out to be faster payers than local authorities. Many in the former supply chain which received discounts of 17–20% thought that publishers' distribution systems could never cope with supplying books directly to so many schools. They were wrong. Direct supply by publishers grew fast from 15% to 45–50% in the secondary market, and 80% in the primary. While publishers gave schools, if necessary, initial incentive discounts in order to secure their programmes, subsequent orders were supplied at full price. The publishers thus maintained their former discount levels and the direct supply route provided valuable marketing information to help fend off competitors.

The incoming Labour government of the late 1990s made successive changes to the National Curriculum necessitating new teaching materials to be produced at very short notice. The Examination Boards in England were merged down to three: the treatment of subjects narrowed further. The boards, which receive a fee per candidate, competed vigorously to secure schools' choice of their syllabus and accreditation (secondary schools usually pay a greater sum to the boards than they spend on textbooks). The degree of closeness or otherwise of some publishers to the boards became somewhat of a grey, if not contentious issue.

Curriculum changes, somewhat erratic central government funding earmarked to particular key stages and subjects favoured (and the competing demands on schools to strengthen ICT learning), created sales revenue volatility in the home market for publishers in general, and in particular for those publishers which published in the favoured sectors or not. But by the end of the century, the educational publishers were benefiting from increased investment by government.

In December 1999, educational book publishing was con-solidated again. The leading educational publisher of the decade – Heinemann Educational Books (owned by Reed) – was challenged by the creation of Nelson Thornes, the combination of Stanley

Thornes and Thomas Nelson. Wolters Kluwer nv, the owner of
the former, purchased the latter from the Thomson Corporation.
Thus secondary school textbook publishing was dominated by
seven publishers – the others being Cambridge University Press,
CollinsEducational (part of HarperCollins: News International),
Hodder & Stoughton Educational (part of Hodder Headline:
WH Smith), Longman (part of Pearson Education) and Oxford
University Press. The other publishers tended to concentrate on
specialisms, and a somewhat different range of publishers served
primary schools, including the children's publishing imprints, for
instance Scholastic.

From the early 1990s, the use by schools of multimedia on
CD-ROM (more recently going online) has grown from a very low
base. At the start, the market was filled by US imports not designed
for UK curricula and cultural needs. UK multimedia producers,
publishers and distributors arose. Some of the book publishers
produced CD-ROM titles, or commissioned them from multimedia
producers: but only to a limited extent. In 2000, three players
deriving from television interests led the silver disk/online market:
Anglia, BBC and Granada. (When selling silver disks to schools,
some publishers adopt a simple licensing model, such as pricing
the purchase of the first disk at say £60, and each thereafter at say
£10.) Other important publishers included the Pearson companies
of Logotron and Dorling Kindersley. Meanwhile, computer software companies, such as Microsoft, hardware companies, such
as Research Machines (serving primarily UK schools) extended
their range of software products and systems designed for schools.
In such a fast changing and difficult market complementary
partnerships and alliances between different kinds of companies
became evident.

Another possible pointer to publishing futures occurred in the
trade educational market concerned with curriculum revision
books. These are sold to concerned parents and to worried students
via bookshops, though may also find their way into schools. Such
educational content, designed for home-based self-learning, can
be a source for adaptation for delivery by silver disk, internet and
digital TV. Furthermore, publishers may extend their services by
offering online tuition to families as a remedy for failings of state
education, as occurs in the USA. In September 1999, Granada
Learning was strengthened by the acquisition of Letts Educational
(the leading curriculum revision book publisher) and of BlackCat,

an educational software company. Educational content was seen as attractive 'sticky content' for the internet drawing in advertising, subscriptions and e-commerce.

Some of the educational book publishers, such as Collins-Educational, Hodder & Stoughton Educational and Nelson Thornes specialize in publishing for the colleges of further education ('A' level and GNVQ vocational qualifications). There are instances of their leading 'A' level texts selling into higher education at the sub-degree first year level, whereas it is far more difficult for the academic/college textbook publishers to sell their introductory texts down into the highly prescribed 'A' level market.

ELT publishing

The publishing of English Language Teaching (ELT) course materials and other materials engages very large investments and a worldwide marketing strength for this export-orientated field. The publishers enjoyed strong growth from export sales through the 1990s but in 1997/8, it faltered. Though the quantity of books exported rose, prices fell in sterling terms and the real value of turnover decreased. The strength of sterling, the Asian economic crisis, and the problems in Brazil and Argentina (important ELT markets) took their toll. ELT publishing continued to consolidate. In 1998, Reed sold Heinemann ELT to Macmillan. By 2000, four publishers dominated the global ELT market. In respect of the two leaders, Pearson had added the important American English lists of Addison Wesley and of Prentice Hall, to its original mainly British English Longman imprint; and Oxford University Press ELT accounted for much of the profits of OUP and maintained a market leadership in British English, most notably through its general English course *Headway*, while also publishing in American English – essential for all major publishers. Macmillan Heinemann ELT was part of the German and family owned company Holtzbrinck, while Cambridge University Press was ranked fourth in the major league having built its own business on its own account without acquisition. However, there are smaller UK ELT publishers, which specialize in niches and packagers also offer editorial, design and production services to the majors – often their former employees.

From the standpoint of the majors, ELT publishing is a distinct field of publishing needing its own publishing operations, typically based in the UK and the US to produce British and American

English materials; plus other publishing centres such as those in Spain, the Far East, Latin America and Eastern Europe to fulfil national or regional markets; and marketing sales offices elsewhere. The strategic importance of ELT is that it provides the publisher with a local or regional foothold in non-English areas of the world, either through the opening of local companies or marketing offices or through the acquisition of local publishers. Although the major publishers dominate the international provision of teaching materials, they face increasing competition from indigenous local publishers (which in many European countries are the national market leaders in schools); private language school chains venturing into publishing; new entrants such as Microsoft, Disney and English First; and start-up online publishers serving the adult corporate training markets. Nevertheless, the majors expect their own growth to continue.

Academic, STM and professional publishing

The internationalization through ownership of academic, STM and professional book publishing occurred earlier than that of consumer book publishing, and is far more extensive. High-level books and journals, especially in STM, in the English language, have an international currency, mainly throughout the developed world. Such publishers rarely have to contend with literary agents' retention of territorial rights and other rights. They invariably acquire all rights in authors' works worldwide.

Major publishers with an international outlook dominate these fields on a world scale. Indeed, the publishers which inhabited these markets at the century end took many of the top ten world rankings: Pearson, Reed Elsevier, the Thomson Corporation, Wolters Kluwer, McGraw-Hill and Harcourt.

The USA market, by far the world's largest and richest, is their most important market in terms of sales turnover, be it from the publishing of learning materials, of primary research through learned journals, or of information and reference materials for business and professional users (e.g. law and tax). However, the focus of their publishing varies markedly. For instance, the publicly quoted UK media group Pearson, was the world's largest *education* publisher (i.e. of learning materials). Not withstanding Pearson's ownership of Penguin, *Financial Times* (newspaper and business information), and television interests etc., Pearson Education

Europe embraced the UK-founded textbook imprints (mainly in higher education) of Longman and Financial Times Management and the major US-founded textbook imprints of Addison Wesley and Prentice Hall. Whereas the Anglo-Dutch group Reed Elsevier, in sales turnover, was mainly focused on publishing high-level professional *information* products (e.g. science learned journals and reference products for lawyers under the Butterworth imprint etc.). The enormous Thomson Corporation is another major financial, professional and legal information publisher predominantly serving the US market (though with some education publishing) – and is represented in the UK by International Thomson Business Press; as is the very large mainly European publisher Wolters KIuwer, headquartered in Amsterdam.

In respect of UK-originated publishing in addition to Reed mentioned above, the main STM book and learned journal publishers include Blackwell Science, Harcourt (especially medical), John Wiley, Taylor & Francis and Wolters KIuwer. Academic publishers concentrating on the humanities and social sciences include Blackwell Publishers, Macmillan – rebranded as Palgrave (Holtzbrinck), Routledge (Taylor & Francis) and the social science publisher Sage Publications. And there are the university presses. In 1998, Oxford University Press, with annual sales approaching £300m, was of such size to be ranked just inside the world's top twenty largest publishers (just ahead of John Wiley). It is the largest university press in America, and is far bigger than Cambridge University Press with sales around £100m. However, both OUP and CUP are major academic and STM publishers measured on a world scale. The London office of Yale University Press is a significant publisher of art, architecture and humanities books. There are many other smaller commercial publishers with turnovers below £10m and other university presses, which specialize in publishing for a limited range of disciplines.

The first stage in establishing a worldwide publishing network involves opening sales and distribution offices or subsidiaries to market imported books. Thus in the post-war period the major US publishers such as Addison Wesley, Harcourt Brace, John Wiley, McGraw-Hill and Prentice Hall established offices in the UK and elsewhere, and UK publishers did the same in the US, but to a more limited extent, and elsewhere. Such offices then usually grew into publishing offices in their own right, feeding their originated books into the international network. The American STM giants and university presses quite often used their UK firms to handle international sales not only in Europe, but sometimes further afield.

In the world of international publishing, it is somewhat invidious to describe companies as US, UK, German or Dutch, other than on patriotic feelings. These majors are transnational in their approach to publishing. However, the location of the operational headquarters can be significant.

In the 1960s and 1970s, publishers in the UK enjoyed heady growth, but it slowed in the 1980s and UK sales in real terms fell after 1988 and flattened from 1989 through to 1991, as did title output. During the 1990s, publishers grew their sales revenue only modestly, mainly through increased prices. Publishers' unit sales of books remained static despite the rapid rise of student numbers in UK higher education – mainly at the sub-degree level and concentrated on vocational courses (e.g. computing and management studies), while book sales to libraries declined. The fortunes of these publishers and the kinds of books and other products they produce are inextricably linked to institutional spending on research, especially in relation to library budgets in the developed world, to the numbers and wealth (or lack of it) of full-time and part-time students (particularly in UK higher education), and to the behaviour of librarians, researchers, teachers and students.

A near casualty of the virtually worldwide library cutbacks has been the publishing of high-priced academic hardback monographs, for so long a cornerstone of commercial academic publishing and of the university presses briefed to disseminate works of scholarship. For the scientists, the publication of research in a learned journal became more important than publication in the form of the monograph, whereas academics in the humanities and social sciences still needed to publish in full-length monograph. Throughout the 1980s selling just 1000 copies was progressively more difficult. Publishers reduced the costs of typesetting, and author royalty rates sometimes to zero, but even so, profitable publishing of potential monographs was increasingly problematic. By the turn of the decade academic libraries had moved from self-sufficiency in their collections to sharing copies through inter-library loans; and document suppliers copied individual chapters and journal articles for users, potentially cannibalizing book sales and subscriptions. While some publishers withdrew from monograph publishing, the remaining hard core of publishers (e.g. OUP, CUP, Palgrave, Routledge and Sage, and some of the STM publishers) continued to publish large numbers of titles, sometimes in tiny quantities of say 500 copies, or below, by applying low cost production techniques.

A further difficulty affects the smaller UK publishers without a US publishing arm in common ownership. In order to access the important US library market, such UK publishers may enter into a copublishing link with a US publisher, whereby the latter places a firm bulk quantity for a book and receives a high discount of, say, 70–85% off the UK published price. The US print order enables the UK publisher to spread the book's development costs (such as editing and typesetting) over the combined quantity thereby lowering the per copy cost and increasing its margin on its edition sold outside the USA.

On some books, a US order could be essential to the book's viability. The contract between them would exclude the US publisher from exporting copies but cannot preclude a third-party, such as a US exporting library supplier or internet bookseller buying the books from the US publisher and exporting it overseas. Acquisition librarians and their suppliers in the major markets of northern Europe, Australia and the Pacific rim have online bibliographic databases listing the prices of the US and UK editions of the same book. If the US edition is significantly cheaper and there is a US exporting supplier offering them a discount off that lower price, they will order the US edition, other factors being equal. Thus the UK publisher would find copies supplied to its US partner at a very high discount entering markets to which it expected to sell its own edition profitably at lower discounts. It is estimated that about one-third of UK academic library expenditure is spent on books directly imported into the UK mainly by UK branches of US publishers, but some imports might be UK-originated books making a round trip from America.

The international publishers which invariably control world rights in their authors' works and which have a worldwide publishing capability through their own offices, can control pricing in markets throughout the world. However, they often set different prices on the same title on either side of the Atlantic. The transparency of such differences evident on the internet prompted some publishers to adopt 'world pricing' on their titles, i.e. parity pricing on UK/US editions. By 'world' price they mean that prevailing in the developed world. (In some cases special, lower price editions may be published for sale in the developing world.)

The academic publishers, especially, during the period when monograph publishing was under increasing pressure, turned to publishing supplementary texts in paperback for second and third level, and post-graduate students. However, from around the mid-1990s that market became problematic thus they turned to textbook publishing. But these 'high level' publishers were up against the established UK and US textbook publishers.

Textbook publishing is very different. It demands greater concentration of editorial effort on a small number of more thoroughly researched titles, far greater investment in product development, and sustained marketing and sales, and today after-sales effort in the form of web site support. The publishing techniques deployed by the commanding giant US college textbook publishers began to enter UK publishing, albeit more modestly.

US first year college textbook publishing is characterized by a small number of mass-selling titles, in high enrolment and arguably 'defined' academic subjects, such as in human biology, chemistry, psychology, economics, computing and management. The US publishers locked themselves into a battle of investment, the thousand plus page hardback printed in full colour with expensive artwork covering the subject. That was not enough to secure the college adoptions. They competed on the free 'supplements' or ancillary materials: e.g. test-banks of questions; instructors' guide including slides of illustrations; videos; a CD-ROM inserted in the book; and more recently the books' web sites. The US publishers globalized the teaching of subjects by publishing such texts at very low prices overseas, including the UK, where publishers were still struggling to afford two-colour text printing. US textbooks were adopted in the UK, but rarely vice versa.

However, the US college textbook publishers face some challenges. In their home market the campus bookstore chains, such as Follet, re-cycled used books to students prompting the publishers to re-issue new editions more frequently than they would have liked. The US content became less acceptable to overseas markets which opened opportunities for UK publishers to produce texts mainly for UK and northern European markets, or the UK sister companies of US imprints to produce versions of US-originated texts. Moreover, by 2000 the internet booksellers in the US began heavily to discount college texts, and the publishers' overseas pricing was exposed on the internet. In the US, a college text might be published at \$90 while in the UK it might be sold for under £30 (the UK parity price could have been nearer £55). Some US commentators (and students) criticized the weight of books: e-book and online study were proposed as alternatives. The publishers pondered on their warehouses stacked with tons of big books and planned the next generation of teaching materials supported to a greater extent by e-publishing – a potential weapon against the used book re-cyclers by time-limiting passwords.

The rapid growth in distance learning through independent self-study (or open or direct learning) is worldwide. It was kick-started on a mass scale by the founding of The Open University (OU) in 1969. The OU deployed mixed media: print; broadcast television; video and audio – and more recently multimedia on CD-ROM and online materials – and provided students with tutorial support, assessment and accreditation. The worldwide driving forces behind the growth in distance learning are: governments' desire to increase student participation in higher education; flexibility of home-based part-time learning; scalability and economy in that institutions can increase student enrolments without investment in real estate and can gain economies in staff/student ratios; and the convergence of media through the internet, digital TV and mobile phone. Furthermore, private sector internet universities such as Phoenix, and corporate 'universities' for staff training emerged.

From a publishing perspective, direct learning affords many opportunities. Institutions adopt their books etc. and better-off older students are usually better buyers than younger ones. Large student enrolments provide greater scope to establish partnerships with institutions. For instance, the OU through copublishing marries its core competencies in producing excellent self-study materials for its large internal market with those of publishers to market and sell them for profit to non-OU markets. On the other hand, publisher-driven direct learning initiatives may also be used to create 'closed' markets shutting out competitors' products and sometimes book trade intermediaries, and possibly even conventional institutions.

Publishers at first entered the high value professional and corporate training markets, exemplified by BPP training of accountants in the UK, by the Harcourt company NetG supplying ICT training via CD-ROM and online through corporate intranets, and the

McGraw-Hill company Xebec offering management skills training through digital products. Financial Times Management (Pearson) in the UK married its materials in post-graduate management learning to partner universities which carried out the tuition and accreditation.

The prospect of publishing media corporations using converged media for direct learning *and* themselves awarding recognized qualifications to students is sending a shiver through academia. Governments typically protect universities from private sector take-overs and maintain regulators which set higher education quality assurance standards and which confer award-bearing status on institutions attaining these standards: such standards usually derive from the established order – and may be under-pinned through state funding which may make private sector entry too expensive. However, in the USA in the late 1990s McGraw-Hill considered purchasing an established university, and Harcourt announced the establishment of its own university and entered the maze to win accreditation approval. Meanwhile, competing publishers argued that such moves were beyond their core competencies, would antagonize their main institutional customers, and that the more profitable route was to offer institutions learning materials and to form partnerships. The institutions should be left to carry out the high cost activities such as student recruitment through consumer advertising, tutorial provision and student assessment.

In the corporate training market internet intermediaries have arisen – the Learning Service Providers (LSPs) which offer learning management and training delivery software usually on a hosted/rental basis. They may offer the opportunity for the HR departments of corporates to develop their own learning portals gathering content from a range of courses provided by training companies and publishers.

The growth in the 'granularization' of learning – i.e. the splitting of content into smaller chunks, enabling students to learn what they need to learn more exactly, when they need it – features in corporate training down to the micro level of specific learning objectives. However, this trend is also evident in higher education where institutions, both classroom and distance, are chunking courses into shorter modules.

A parallel trend is the need for the customization of content. Throughout the 1990s, lecturers increasingly created their own course packs for students including chapters from books and journal articles, at first photocopied and then digitally copied. In 1982 the Copyright Licensing Agency (CLA) was set up by the Publishers Licensing Society (PLS) and the Authors' Licensing & Collecting Society (ALCS). The CLA on their behalf issues copying licences within stated parameters to the educational, business and government sectors, collects the fees and proportions them to the PLS and ALCS, each of which distributes the fees to their members. The CLA's Rapid Clearance Service (CLARCS) is designed to ease the arduous task of lecturers in applying for copyright clearance from individual publishers to copy materials for inclusion in course packs, and to distribute the fees to the copyright holders.

While the CLA operates at a national collective level and negotiates fees payable, for example with the universities acting in concert, various kinds of retailers may also customize content for institutions and organizations. The likely outcome of these trends, is that publishers may receive an increasing proportion of their revenues from licensing bits of their content held in re-usable digital form: potentially high volume, low sales of extracts.

Professional publishing and learned journals

The term 'professional publishing' is used variously but may be applied generally to the publishing sectors providing information, for lawyers and accountants etc. and for researchers in universities and industry. The information may be conveyed in printed form (e.g. books, loose-leaf format, newsletter, and serial journal); and/ or in digital form, on silver disk, and increasingly on the internet.

The publishing of refereed (or peer-reviewed) learned journals is a major adjunct to academic and STM book publishing – indeed for the latter it may far outweigh the publishers' subject-related book operations. Historically, the higher profits (of say 25–30+%) derived from journals have in effect cross-subsidized their book publishing which earned lower profits (of say 10–15%). Among the significant publishers are Academic Press (Harcourt), Blackwell Science, Cambridge University Press, John Wiley, Oxford University Press, Taylor & Francis, Reed Elsevier, Springer Verlag (Bertelsmann), and Wolters Kluwer. The learned societies and associations also publish their own journals (e.g. Institute of Physics Publishing and Institution of Electrical Engineers), or may have their journals produced and marketed for them by the publishers (e.g. by Blackwell Science, CUP etc.). In STM, there are at least 50,000 titles published worldwide of which single title publishers publish around 25% – the largest publisher Reed Elsevier has around 1,200 titles. Although during the 1980s academic libraries were under financial stress, their journal collections were generally maintained at the expense of book purchases. However, continued library cutbacks from the early 1990s on the one hand, and the enormous expansion of the volume of published research articles (estimated in STM to be doubling every 15 years) on the other, appeared to be inducing a negative feedback loop. The volume increases of articles and the proliferation of research topics led to price increases, to cancellations of subscriptions of particular journals by libraries, and hence to further price rises. Moreover, libraries and researchers began to change their behaviour. The acquisition policies of libraries increasingly moved from that of self-sufficiency in collections to that of co-operation between libraries through the use of interlibrary loans and of remote document (e.g. journal article) supply. In the USA, the commercial document suppliers (sometimes as an extension to their abstracting/indexing publishing operations) at first faxed articles to researchers. In the UK, the British Library rapidly expanded its photocopying of articles at its Document Supply Centre in Boston Spa to supply academic, government and business markets.

A further, far-reaching impact on journal publishing has been the internet which originally in the 1960s grew out of a US Defense Department network project before it was taken up by academia under a public service ethos to allow free and unrestricted movement of information; and subsequently in the late 1990s by commerce into the general population. The first examples of electronic publication on the net occurred in research dissemination, published by authors themselves, research institutions and by publishers. Some commentators argued that within a few years the main intermediaries that profited highly from the research communication process – such as the publishers – and the subscription agents (which handle the supply of journals to libraries) and the libraries themselves would be dis-intermediated – removed from the process. Researchers would be able to communicate their research instantly and directly among themselves for free.

In reality, the extent of change, though considerable, has been far slower than anticipated and reintermediation occurred – existing businesses re-invented themselves and new intermediaries arose. Some of these have developed from well-established publishers seeking to migrate their content to an online environment, either in consortia with other publishers, or alone (e.g. Science Direct, owned by Reed Elsevier). Others have derived from originally not-for-profit initiatives such as Ingenta, which grew out of the Bath Information and Data Services (BIDS) offering free summaries of articles to academics. ISI – bibliographic publishers of journal citation reports used to evaluate journals' ranking – offers click-through from references to full texts via Web of Science and ISI Links. The aggregators/subscription agents offer their own solutions too (e.g. Blackwell's Electronic Journal Navigator and SwetsNet – which have recently merged). All of them offer additional functionality over the printed page (such as search engines, click-throughs to other articles via references etc.). In many cases, the concept of the journal itself is being eroded both as the unit of currency is becoming the *individual paper* and as services develop to serve discrete subject areas (known as portals, or communities) drawing material from different journals and/or publishers.

By the end of 1999, the publishers still operated relatively strong businesses and continued to commission new journals. The great majority of journals were still issued in printed form but many were also available electronically. Some publishers, which tried to increase subscription charges for the electronic version, were disappointed. They had to bear the additional cost of producing the electronic version themselves, another factor impinging on profits. Some reasons advanced for the endurance of print were that authors wanted to see themselves in print and publishers found electronic-only journals difficult to market. The electronic-only market place had become clouded by often non-peer-reviewed journals of uncertain quality; and the librarians who do not usually trust publishers saw the archiving of such journals as a major problem. It is vital for the publishers to maintain the quality of articles submitted; and for the authors to try to have their work published in the top-ranking journals which take years to develop.

From a user's viewpoint, however, having an article online from their desktop is a virtue in that they expect, for example, to be able to link easily to other information sources and to access the full text of articles referenced in an article. But in moving between different publishers' servers, the user would encounter barriers. At the end of 1999, some STM publishers collaborated to facilitate direct links between their journals though collaboration with the International Digital Object Identifier Foundation, potentially posing another challenge to the intermediaries.

The above developments are affecting the publishers' conventional business model which is essentially based on charging the reference libraries an upfront annual subscription to each journal. The journal publishers are entering a more complicated and a far less predictable world of a multiplicity of distribution channels, and of different payment systems (such as pay-per-view) which may lead to a shift from upfront income to its being more spread throughout the year, and possibly a lowering of their former substantial profits.

Chapter 2

Sectors of publishing

Although there are common themes in all book publishing there are marked differences in the ways different kinds of books are published for different markets. Publishers specialize in reaching particular markets. The skills of their staff, the activities they perform and the structure of the business are aligned accordingly.

All kinds of publishers can be described as serving niche markets. Attaining a critical mass in a particular field, right down to a list of books on the narrowest subject area, is vital to publishers of every size. It allows the employment of editors who understand and have contact with authors and associates in a particular field, and who can shape projects for their intended markets. A respected list attracts authors. Furthermore, a list of books needs to generate sufficient turnover to allow effective and focused marketing and selling which in turn feeds new publishing. At the broadest level, the main sectors of publishing are as follows.

CONSUMER BOOK PUBLISHING

The consumer book publishers (sometimes called 'trade' or 'general' publishers) are the most visible part of the industry. Their adult and children's fiction and non-fiction hardback and paperback titles are displayed prominently in high street bookshops and other outlets, receive considerable mass-media coverage and are aimed mainly at the indefinable 'general reader', sometimes at the enthusiast or specialist reader. They form (in hardback though increasingly in paperback) the mainstay of public libraries and book clubs, and in some cases penetrate the student/academic markets. In 1998, such books accounted for about 56% of the industry's sales value, of which exports accounted for 16% (represented especially by highly illustrated colour books and international fiction). The most active UK book buyers are 66% female, who are better readers, heavier purchasers of children's books and spend more time shopping in terrestrial stores rather than buying books on line – in the 25–44 age group, from the better-off social classes, and located in the south rather than the north. While about 20% of book sales are made to the highly educated, often metropolitan, AB social grades, 80% of new paperback buyers and 78% of new hardback buyers come from the C1/C2/DE socio-economic grades.

Most publishers (including the majors and most medium-sized independent firms) are in London giving them ready access to authors, authors' agents, other publishers, social venues, journalists and producers of the mass-media, and other influential people who decisively affect the life of the nation. The remaining publishers are spread around the country, in Scotland, and tend to be more specialized.

Consumer book publishing is the high-risk end of the business: book failures are frequent but the possible rewards from 'best-sellers' – some of which are quite unexpected – are great. The potential readers are varied, spread very thinly through the population, expensive to reach, difficult to identify and to locate, and have tastes and interests that can be described generally but are not easily matched to a particular book. These publishers bet to a great extent on their judgement of public taste and interests – notoriously unpredictable. Sometimes the publication of a book creates its own market. And the authors whose work arouses growing interest can develop a personal readership, thereby creating their own markets – perhaps attaining a 'brand name' following, especially in fiction. Publishers compete fiercely for their books.

Publishers are opportunistic – they must respond fast if they want to capture a well known author or personality, or take advantage of current fashions, media events or topical issues on which to hang a book's promotion. Additionally, some firms want to fulfil the traditional role of publishing literary works, and of developing authors who may in the future be recognized as having written a great work. But only a few authors and books become part of the eternal backlist. The public libraries aid, albeit to a declining extent, the hardback publishing of some serious fiction and non-fiction, and there are novelists who are heavily borrowed but not bought.

Few other consumer goods industries market products with such a short sales life. Generally speaking for a book's sales life to survive, it is vital for the publisher to secure advance pre-publication 'subscription' orders from booksellers and for the response to the book to be good in the opening weeks post-publication. The peak sales of most new books occur within a year of publication. Most adult hardback fiction and paperback titles are dead within three months or just weeks, while hardback non-fiction and paperback fiction written by famous authors may endure longer. Compared to the non-consumer book publishers, the trade publishers tend to earn a higher proportion of their revenues from their frontlist publishing. Nevertheless the main trade publishers earn c.58% of their revenues from backlist sales. Some publishers are very frontlist weighted (such as television and film tie-in publishers), while others keep strong backlists alive from their new book programme and by relaunching old books in new covers, re-issuing them in different sizes and bindings, adding new introductions or revising them. An energetically promoted back-list provides retailers with staple and more predictable stock, should earn good profits for the publisher, and keeps authors in print.

Many readers mistakenly believe that the large price differential between hardbacks and paperbacks is due to the extra cost of binding a book in hardback. The considerable price gap does not represent that cost (which is low): rather it reflects the ways in which publishers try to maximize the revenue from a title by segmenting the market through the use of different formats and price points, often sequentially. For example, a fiction title could be launched first in hardback at a high price to satisfy eager readers, libraries and sometimes a book club then subsequently at a lower price to reach a new and wider market of readers in trade or mass-market paperback; or it might be originally published in A, B or C format paperback. Furthermore some titles of minority appeal could not recover their investment if first published in a lower paperback price range established for books with higher sales potential over which the costs could be spread.

In comparison with other publishers consumer book publishers tend to operate in the following ways:

- They pay their authors advances of a half to two-thirds or more of what they expect the author to earn from royalties from sales of the first printing – paid in instalments (e.g. on signature of contract between author and publisher, on delivery or acceptance of manuscript, on publication).
- They tend to give much greater emphasis to their top authors in terms of promotional expenditure, sales effort and publication dates to maximize sales. However, it is possible for them to gain great free media coverage on other books.
- They depend to a far greater extent on retail exposure to sell their books, and on gift buying of adult and children's books (the pre-Christmas period is of immense importance); but they suffer from returns of unsold books from retailers and wholesalers. While their main customers are the bookselling chains, these publishers have a wide range of other retail, wholesale, and book club distribution channels available to them. The choice of books by centralized buyers of retail chains and of wholesalers determined to satisfy their differing customer profiles inevitably influences publishers.
- They have greater scope to sell rights in the author's work to other firms, and to set up co-edition deals with others (e.g. book clubs, overseas publishers etc.). The co-printing of two or more editions together allows the originator to use the other partner's cash to spread high development and printing costs (especially on highly illustrated adult and children's colour books) over several markets, thereby making the book affordable to the readers in each market. Adult and children's publishers specializing in books which sell on the strength of the illustrations (including art book publishers) make great use of this technique.
- They are squeezed to a far greater extent by agents (on behalf of their authors) negotiating higher royalty rates and advances, and by large retailers ratcheting up their discounts granted by publishers. The major trade houses tend to pay out on average 30% of their sales revenue to authors (more than twice the percentage the non-consumer publishers pay out); and the discounts granted to the book trade, including those overseas, are around 50% of the published price of a book, at least 10% higher than those granted by the non-consumer book publishers.

Some publishers producing mass-market low-priced illustrated hardbacks and paperbacks sometimes pre-sell bulk quantities of own-brand books to large retailers, thereby obviating risk.

Children's publishing

Children's books are published by the specialist children's divisions of the major consumer book publishers with both hardback and paperback lists and independent children's book publishers. The vitality of children's publishing creates the book buyers of the future. As on the adult side, there are a number of book packagers creating books for publishers, typically on an international co-edition basis.

An unusual feature of children's publishing is that although the text and illustrations of these books must excite and appeal to children of different age groups, at different levels of reading skill and comprehension, they must also appeal to adults in the supply chain (the major non-book and book retailers, wholesalers, book clubs) and to adults who buy or influence choice (such as parents, relations, librarians and teachers). Furthermore, in that many titles include much colour yet have to be published at low prices, such titles often need co-edition partners in the USA, in Europe and elsewhere in order to attain economies in printing.

The books are usually aimed at age bands reflecting the development of reading skill. The 0–5 age group from babies to toddlers may be described as the parent pointing stage. Included here are the so-called 'novelty books' (which extend above the age group), a category of book of ever-widening inventiveness, such as board books and bath books (introducing page turning), sound story books with electronic panels, colouring and activity books, question and answer books, pop-ups etc.; and the lower end of picture books. Books for the very young need to be very durable and often use cloth, plastic or hardback binding.

The 5–8 age group may be described as the starting to read, as well as reading to children stage. Picture books figure prominently. These books, invariably in full colour, tend to be 32 pages long (12–14 double-page spreads), display strong narrative and may include just a few words up to possibly several thousand; they may be created by an illustrator or writer (or one controlling mind), and invariably need co-edition partners. Story books for younger fiction tend to have more text, say 2000–7500 words and may be published in paperback in smaller formats, with black and white, or colour illustrations; and are designed for children reading their first whole novels. There are major series produced by many of the main trade publishers as well as reading schemes by the educational publishers. Moving up, and through, the 9–12 age group, longer length novels of up to 35 000 words come into play as well as the more recent mass-market genre series. Above 11–12, there are the teenage or young adult, fiction titles. As school and library budgets are cut, many of the traditionally hardback publishers of middle and young adult fiction (such as Oxford University Press and Faber & Faber) have moved to B format, following on with mass market paperbacks, and in many cases omitting hardback editions altogether.

Non-fiction, sometimes highly illustrated, spans the age groups as do home learning series, reference titles (e.g. dictionaries), anthologies and character books (some which are tie-ins to films etc.) and so on.

Broadly speaking, in comparison with adult consumer book publishers, authors' advances tend to be lower (reflecting the lower published prices which are several pounds lower than the price points of adult titles, owing to consumer expectations that books should be low cost/good value, compared to say, computer games and videos); rarely receive window or promotional space in general bookshops; and children's publishers of quality books earn a higher proportion from backlist sales – the thirst for established favourites is constantly assuaged. The children's/young adult's (YA's) market is subject to huge – often advertising- or character-led – crazes.

Children's publishing in the UK continues to push out the frontiers of book availability into a wide range of retail outlets, including grocery, toy and garden centres etc. reached directly, or indirectly via wholesalers and internet suppliers. Such retailers, and some of the book clubs, tend to concentrate on books for the younger age groups. Internationally, the Bologna Book Fair held in the spring is the world's meeting place of children's publishing with over 1500 exhibitors from nearly 100 countries. The UK publishers and packagers have for long dominated the international trade in the selling of overseas co-edition rights though, like their adult counterparts, they import far less.

Consumer mail-order publishers

A few publishers, the prime example being Reader's Digest, sell enormous quantities of books to readers predominantly by mail order: retail sales are additional. Examples of their output include condensed fiction, and highly illustrated information titles (including atlases, dictionaries and other reference titles) published individually, or in series, for UK households and, where appropriate, abroad. Their strengths lie in their mailing lists containing discriminative information on millions of households, their expertise in selling by mail order and (on information titles especially) their use of the mailing lists for scientific market research on projects before publication (e.g. the testing of concepts, content, price etc.) and their development of complex books to suit the market.

Promotional book publishers

Bargain books (sometimes referred to as 'manufactured remainders' or 'promotion books') are primarily aimed at the gift buyer, like so many consumer books; but more specifically not so much at the hardcore regular book buyers frequenting bookshops but at the great majority of people thinking of buying something of enduring value keenly priced and on impulse. The nature and low price of these books compete head on against other gift choices. Bargain hardbacks and paperbacks are usually mainstream, slow-dating non-fiction preferably international subjects such as cookery, gardening, do-it-yourself, children's reference, leisure, hobbies and art through to classic fiction.

Bargain books, some of which are reprints of successful remainders (e.g. overstocks of publishers' full-priced editions sold off cheaply to clear warehouse space), are produced by promotional book publishers, an American term applying to publishers which primarily promote their books on price – low retail price. A prime example occurred in the early 1990s when start-up publisher Wordsworth issued public domain classic fiction titles at £1, against the established series of the big publishers, such as Penguin, the prices of which were creeping towards £5. Such publishers can be in part remainder dealers; or they are predominantly concerned with reprinting, repackaging or originating material. They may be independently owned with their own specialities, or are divisions of the major consumer book publishers drawing on their former hardback and paperback full-priced editions. Promotional publishers may repackage material in book form which first appeared in magazines or in part works, scour through publishers' lists of suitable out-of-print books, find out-of-copyright works, or originate new bargain books themselves, or commission book packagers to produce books for them. Payments to authors, if any, have to be minimized through one-off fees. These books must offer overt perceived value for money – big and chunky, bulked up on thick paper if necessary, with lots of colour and powerful, straightforward non-intimidating jackets or covers. In order to achieve very low prices the books must be printed in large quantities, say more than 15 000 copies. A promotional house sells them to the UK bargain chains and bookshops, to UK direct selling operations, and pre-sells large English language firm orders to promotional houses abroad (e.g. in the USA, Australia, South Africa, New Zealand, Canada) which sell to their own bargain chains etc.; to overseas trade publishers if possible at higher prices; and to foreign language publishers, as an international co-edition.

NON-CONSUMER BOOK PUBLISHING

The educational, academic, scientific, technical and medical (STM), and professional book publishers have a great advantage in that:

- the markets for which they publish are more defined;
- their authors and advisers are drawn mainly from the same peer groups as the readers who strongly influence the choice of books bought;
- these groups can be reached through their place of work;
- backlist sales, especially if textbook and reference, account for a major proportion of their business, say 80%.

Educational publishing

The educational publishers provide materials for schools: chiefly textbooks bought in multiple copies, sometimes supported by ancillary printed materials for class use or for teachers (and where appropriate audiocassettes, atlases, software, CD-ROM, web sites), published individually or as a series (e.g. representing a progressive course of study). Publishers concentrate on the big subject areas. School publications represent about 9% of home market sales value. The main publishers are located in and around London.

The books are market-specific (i.e. precisely tailored to the National Curriculum, examinations, academic levels and age groups). While to some extent the broad content is pre-determined, publishers with their external advisers and authors give great attention to the pedagogy, influence curriculum development, and also cater for more conservative teachers. They help raise the quality of teaching. Many books are highly illustrated, increasingly printed in colour, and involve a publisher in much development work. Yet they must be published at very low prices. Book provision in state schools is always under-funded.

Compared with consumer book publishing, educational publishing is long-term. Most publishers derive most of their sales revenue from established backlist books. Schools can ill afford to dump adopted texts frequently. New books are published in the hope that they will be reprinted and revised in following years, but in practice may fail. Educational publishing calls for a large amount of working capital invested over a long time. These features make life very difficult for small publishers or those wanting to enter the field.

New and backlist titles are promoted by mail directly to teachers and by publishers' sales representatives in schools and at exhibitions. Teachers scrutinize bound copies before adopting a book. Textbooks are supplied directly to schools or via booksellers, specialist school contractors and local authority direct purchasing organizations, and may be stocked by booksellers for parental purchase.

Some educational publishers produce books for further education (especially for vocational qualifications), self-education, reference, and curriculum revision aids which are sold through bookshops.

UK-orientated school textbooks generally have drastically reduced export potential though there can be scope, for example, to produce specially prepared textbooks, such as in science and mathematics, for less-developed countries dependent on aid agency funding.

In contrast, the publishing of English Language Teaching (ELT) or English as a Foreign Language (EFL) course materials is export-orientated (say above 90% of sales) to better-off countries and has to some extent offset the overall decline in exports of UK school books. The main markets, in addition to the UK, are Europe (Spain, Greece, Italy, France, Turkey), Japan, the Far East and South East Asia (Hong Kong, Taiwan, Korea, Thailand), Latin America (Argentina, Brazil and Mexico) and the Middle East intermittently. The ELT publishers have set up companies or opened offices or acquired publishers in such areas, or have copublishing links with local publishers, or local marketing arrangements.

The mixed media ELT courses are major investments and may be orientated or versioned to regional cultural distinctiveness and are sometimes produced for ministries. The courses serving primary, secondary and adult sectors are backed up with supplementary materials (such as reading books, dictionaries and grammars) with a broad international appeal. They are sold to the Private Language Schools (PLS) (from primary to adult), primary and secondary state schools, sometimes to universities. In the UK there are specialist booksellers supplying the local and export markets.

Academic, STM and professional book publishing

The publishing of high-level school books may cross over to college courses. Academic publishing can refer to books published in all subjects from first-year university/college students and above, but the term is sometimes restricted to the humanities and social sciences alone in which some imprints of large publishers, or smaller independent publishers, specialize. Scientific, technical and medical (STM) publishing is a relatively distinct area undertaken especially by large publishers. UK academic and STM publishers associated with US firms import numerous US originated titles.

These publishers are mostly outside central London with a high concentration in Oxford, and their output (representing about 29% of the industry's sales) includes first-year introductory textbooks (mainly the preserve of larger publishers); higher level textbooks for more advanced students through to postgraduate; edited volumes of reprinted or commissioned articles for students or academics; research monographs; books for professional use; reference titles (some on CD-ROM or online) and learned journals. These broad categories are not clear cut (e.g. high-level 'textbooks' may incorporate original research).

Broadly speaking textbooks are published in paperback, though some for professional training (e.g. medicine, law) may be hardback. The high-level textbooks occasionally have a short high-priced print run for libraries, issued simultaneously with the paperback. Monographs are usually short-lived high-priced hardbacks published mainly for libraries and to a far lesser extent for personal purchase, and are printed in small quantities (e.g. 500–750 copies) once only, though a few are re-issued in paperback. Short-run publishing is not risk free – the profit may come from the sale of the last fifty copies. Conversely, textbooks, printed in larger quantities, may become established and are reprinted for annual student intakes and revised through new editions when appropriate – unlike US publishers, UK publishers do not suffer from large-scale re-cycling of their books among students a year following publication. Competitors constantly attack the market share of successful books. The successful sale of a textbook entails persuading the lecturer to adopt it, the bookseller to stock it and the student to buy it. Students and lecturers are becoming far more demanding. Publishers producing major textbooks for subjects with high student intakes adopt US practices, such as higher design and production standards, with possibly a CD-ROM in the back of the book, or increasingly a periodically updated web site carrying data, activities and web site links, and lecturers' guides. Many of the campus bookshops are owned by the bookselling chains. Nevertheless, publishers have been more successful than the consumer book publishers in resisting booksellers' demands for higher discounts, and in containing author royalty rates, and advances if any. Trade wholesalers find it difficult to enter the supply chain.

These publishers promote (and sometimes sell directly) their books to lecturers, researchers and practitioners (mainly by mail, telephone and e-mail) and compared with consumer book publishers usually have smaller sales forces calling on a limited range of booksellers. However, some firms publish titles of wider general interest and of bookshop appeal in which case booksellers may be granted higher 'trade' discounts. These include more titles in the humanities, especially history, than the social sciences, some technical books (e.g. on computing) and medical works (e.g. personal health) supplied through specialist wholesalers. They are sometimes bought by specialist book clubs.

Not even the largest publisher could claim to be equally strong in all disciplines, or even those in science alone. Publishers concentrate on particular subjects, and vary in the emphasis given to different categories of book.

The books for professional or practitioner use which have a wider market beyond teaching institutions, tend to be those in the applied sciences for researchers or practitioners in industry and government agencies; and those serving professional sectors (e.g. law, medicine, management, accounting, finance, architecture). Such high priced titles are bought by the wealthy (offices, commercial libraries and individuals). Special sales channels include training companies serving corporations, agencies and individuals; dedicated business, computer and medical book distributors or book clubs reaching end-users directly; conference and exhibition organizers; and companies which take bulk orders of titles as promotional items.

The legal and financial publishers, especially, have traditionally used loose-leaf publishing for some of their reference titles. The purchaser, having bought the initial volume, receives updated pages at intervals on a standing order. However, some major reference works are completely updated regularly and supplied on standing order. Such publishers, as well as those producing books for business, sell a high proportion of their materials by mail order to end-users, not via booksellers. Sometimes, reference products (including directories, sometimes dependent on advertising revenue) are written in-house. Publishers issuing voluminous and/or time sensitive information are shifting their businesses to digital information services, either alongside printed products or in lieu of print. Their products may be available on silver disk, though increasingly online, and are usually licensed directly to libraries and businesses etc. on subscription or by site licenses governing usage on local area networks (LANs) or intranets. Key abilities of such publishers are to identify information needs and the way that information is used, and to translate that knowledge into the creation of products and services using the appropriate media and technologies.

Typically nearly 40% of the output of these publishers is exported. As English is the world's scientific language, STM publications are often more exportable – e.g. above 60%.

Western Europe and North America account for more than 50% of export sales, followed by the Far East and Southeast Asia, and Australia. For many publishers, mainland Europe is the single most important market but one which is diverse and growing. The

Scandinavian and Benelux countries can be significant markets for English language textbook adoptions, and for professional lists. Holland in terms of sales often ranks third after the USA and Australia, and is dominated by a few major bookselling chains, while Germany, another large market, is served by a variety of regional and local chains. Southern Europe, such as Spain and Italy, is a market for high-level professional texts, especially in STM; undergraduate texts exist in translation or are published locally.

High-level textbooks and professional titles are sold to the USA, the largest and richest market, via the UK publisher's US counterpart. A UK firm without a US presence may develop a copublishing link with a US firm, or license rights to a variety of publishers, or sell through importers.

Sales to less developed countries tend to be dependent on aid agency funding. Publishers may on their own account arrange for special low-priced editions of some of their textbooks to be published in less developed countries, either through their own local companies or through sub-licensing editions to local publishers. At the minimum, such editions have different covers in order to reduce the possibility of their penetrating developed markets through conventional and internet traders.

Journal publishing

The content of learned journals, as distinct from magazines, is not predetermined (commissioned or written in-house), rather contributors submit papers of original research to an academic editor for refereeing and inclusion. As such, refereed journal articles are a primary information source, establish or enhance academic standing of authors (counting towards their personal and institutional research funding and their promotion prospects), and serve the research community. Generally speaking, learned journals are not dependent on advertising for their viability; their revenue is derived from subscriptions.

Journals are published by not-for-profit societies and research institutes (a few of which run substantial journal and book publishing operations), and by divisions of academic and STM publishers including the university presses. The commercial journal publishers initiate journals, or produce and market journals for societies and others.

The key people in a journal publisher are the commissioning editors who bring in new journals, the production editors who organize and produce them, direct marketing specialists who market them directly to academia etc., and subscription service specialists; plus, where appropriate, advertising sales staff.

There are more STM journals than academic, and nearly two-thirds of sales are exports. Many journals are printed in the 500–3000 copy range. They are promoted by mail and at academic conferences, supplied on subscription, sold mainly to academic libraries worldwide (often via subscription agents) and to a lesser extent sold direct to individuals (more so in the USA). Journals of applied science, management, economics and law also sell to industrial and commercial libraries. (Members of societies may receive a journal free as part of their membership fee, or at a reduced rate.) Journal academic editors may be paid (some only expenses), but contributors and referees are not. Limited offprints are usually supplied to authors for their private distribution. Authors normally assign their copyright to the journal publisher or society.

The great advantage of their conventional business model is that annual subscriptions are received in advance of production and can be used for other acquisitions. But new journals take a long time to break even (e.g. more than five years for some STM journals). Once established, the sales pattern is more predictable than books, the demand for capital lower (as are staff overheads), and the value of sales per employee is higher.

Journal publishing, unlike book publishing, does not require a sales force or a complex network of overseas agents. The discounts granted to subscription agents may be from 0 to 10%. The credit risk is low, and the return of unsolds rare. Other income can arise from advertisements and inserts (especially in STM), from sales of back issues and of additional offprints, from copyright fees from commercial document suppliers and from subscription list rental. The lists and journals can be used to advertise and sell the publisher's books. There is cross-fertilization of contacts and ideas between book and journal publishers. However the migration to electronic publishing and the consequent transition from a physical product industry to an electronic service information industry is causing publishers to re-evaluate the added value features of their business.

Reference publishing

Reference works (spanning words, pictures, numbers, maps etc.) are sold by all kinds of publisher from consumer book to professional. Although some are ephemeral, reference publishing is usually for the long-term backlist. Major works (such as dictionaries) can take years to compile and can involve investments of millions.

Reference publishing is most amenable to the application of new technologies in terms of aiding the product development and the publishing of a family of products in different media (e.g. on paper and/or on silver disk or online), of different sizes and prices for various markets. For example, in dictionary publishing the lexicographers (and in bilingual works, translators) no longer have to rely on the manual identification and retrieval of words in primary sources. Typically they use electronic text corpora holding a vast range of primary and diverse sources from which evidence of word meaning and sentence contextual meaning can be retrieved, manipulated and to an increasing extent analysed electronically. Once the main dictionary database has been built and coded, spin-off shorter or special purpose dictionaries can be subsequently published. Generally speaking, the publishers of online databases, such as in law, try continually to enhance their functionality, for example, by improving their web browser interfaces and analytical research tools for users.

Chapter 3

From author contract to market outlet

This chapter opens with a review of the importance of copyright to authors and publishers, and gives an example of the contractual relationship between them. In that literary agents represent many of the professional writers of fiction and non-fiction books, agents' work is described, and the ways in which it may affect the scope of the publisher to sell the author's work in various forms worldwide are covered. Also included here is the role of book packagers, an important source of highly illustrated books for some publishers. Most publishers do not sell books directly to readers. Publishers' main customers are thus the booksellers and other intermediaries. The ever-widening and changing channels of distribution in the UK book trade market are outlined in the last section.

COPYRIGHT

Book publishing today rests on copyright. In general terms, copyright is a form of protection, giving authors and other creative artists legal proprietorship (ownership) of their work – that is, it establishes their work as their personal, exclusive property; and because it is their property they have the absolute right to sell or license it to others, or not.

It is these exclusive rights that make author's works attractive to publishers. What the publisher wants from authors is the sole, exclusive right to publish their work and sell it as widely as possible. Without the protection of copyright, authors would not be able to grant this exclusive right and could not demand payment for their efforts; and publishers would not risk issuing a book which, if successful, could be instantly copied or plundered by competitors. Copyright stimulates innovation in a market economy, protects the author's reputation and is the common foundation for publishing and the other cultural industries.

For copyright to subsist in a literary work (one which is written, spoken or sung) it must be 'original' (i.e. some effort, skill or judgement needs to have been exercised to attract copyright protection) and it must be recorded in writing or otherwise. There is no copyright in ideas: copyright exists in the concrete form of expression, the arrangement of the words.

Copyright protection endures for the author's life plus seventy years from the year end of the author's death. After that period the work enters the public domain. Publishers compete fiercely on the pricing of public domain classics on which no royalties need be paid.

Through the European Commission (EC) authors' statutory rights are strengthening and include the moral rights of **paternity** (the author's right to be credited as the author of the work) and of **integrity** (the author's right to be protected from editorial distortion of the work). Such moral rights are likely to grow in importance in the age of electronic publications which frequently involve substantial adaptation of authors' and illustrators' work, greatly ease the manipulation of authors' works and facilitate the risks of non-attribution and of plagiarism.

Works created by employees in working hours (and covered, as a further safeguard, by their terms and conditions of service) are the copyright of the employer. Publishers who commission freelance editors, technical illustrators, indexers and software engineers ensure that copyright is assigned in writing to the publisher through an agreement. The publisher's typographical layout of the page is the copyright of the publisher and that lasts for twenty-five years from publication. Copyright exists in compilations, such as databases, provided that there is an adequate degree of originality in the selection and arrangement of the information.

AUTHOR–PUBLISHER CONTRACTS

Each publisher draws up its own contract (or agreement) and each contract differs with the book and the author. Commissioning editors negotiate contracts with authors or their agents. The contract defines formally and in detail the relationship between author and publisher.

Items covered in a typical contract between author and publisher

- Date, names of the parties (their assigns and successors in business) to the contract, and the book's title.
- Author's grant. The author usually grants the publisher the sole and exclusive licence and right to publish the book in volume form (printed and electronic) in all languages, for the full-term of copyright (author's life plus 70 years), throughout the world. By granting a licence, the author retains ownership of the copyright. Sometimes, however, authors (e.g. contributors to multi-authored books or to highly illustrated general books) assign their copyright, thereby passing ownership and all control to the publisher. Such authors may be paid one-off fees instead of royalties.
- Author's warranty. The author warrants that he or she controls the rights granted, that the work is original (not a plagiarism), does not contain defamatory, libellous or unlawful matter; and will indemnify the publisher for loss or damages etc.
- Competing works. The author agrees not to write a directly competing work for another publisher.
- Manuscript length, delivery date and form (e.g. disk plus two hard copies, double spaced), and the responsibility for supplying illustrations and the index etc., and for obtaining and paying for third-party copyright material (often the author's responsibility unless otherwise agreed). The publisher reserves the right not to publish if the delivered manuscript is overdue or does not conform to a previously agreed brief.
- Corrections. The author is constrained from making extensive corrections to proofs (other than those attributable to publisher or printer) and is charged if author's corrections exceed a specified percentage (e.g. 10%) of the cost of typesetting. The author must return proofs within two to three weeks.
- Publication. The publisher entirely controls the publication (its production/design, publicity, price, methods and conditions of sale etc.). In practice authors may be consulted. The author is given say 6 gratis copies and may purchase more, not for re-sale, at a discount.
- Payments to authors: publisher's own-produced edition(s). Authors are normally (but not always) paid a royalty expressed either as a percentage on an edition's published price ('list' or

'retail' price) on all copies sold; or, preferably from a publisher's viewpoint, as a percentage of the publisher's net receipts – its income (i.e. the sum of money received by the publisher after discounts have been deducted) on all copies sold. The author's earnings are thus proportional to price (or net receipts) and sales. Royalty rates are quoted for the publisher's own-produced edition(s) (hardback or paperback, generally lower on paperback) on sales made in the traditional home market (the UK and Ireland) and in export markets (export rates are lower to take account of the higher discounts involved).

A scale of royalties rising by steps of 2–2½% when certain quantities have been sold may be included (especially on home market sales). Royalty rates on published price range from say 5 to 15% (many authors never surpass the lower base rates). If an author has attained a higher rate and a new edition is produced, the royalty reverts to the base rate. When the book is remaindered, no royalties may be paid. Other provisos where lower royalties apply are stated, e.g. if the publisher sells the book to a large retail chain at a very high discount of say 50% or above.

- Payments to authors from rights sales. The contract lists further rights granted to the publisher (unless otherwise agreed) which it could license to other firms, and the percentages (e.g. 50–90%) payable to the author on the publisher's net receipts from such sales. If the publisher is granted, for example, US, book club and translation rights, the firms to which these rights could be licensed may print their own editions and pay royalties to the publisher to be shared with the author. However the publisher may print bulk quantities for them to appear under the licensees' imprints. The publisher sells such copies at a high discount and the author's royalty may be inclusive of the sum received (e.g. 10%). There are many other rights such as serial and extract rights; dramatization rights on stage, film, television and radio; broadcast reading rights; quotation and anthology rights; digest condensation; mechanical reproduction rights (e.g. on audiocassette); electronic media publishing rights etc. All or some of these rights may be termed 'subsidiary rights'.

- Accounting. The publisher's accounting period to the author is usually 6 months for general books, or sometimes annual for educational and academic books, with settlement 3–4 months after.

- Revisions. The author agrees to revise the book when requested or to permit others to do so at the author's expense.
- Termination. The rights revert to the author (e.g. if on request the publisher fails to keep the work in print).
- Arbitration in dispute.
- Option. The author may give the publisher the right of first refusal on his/her next book.
- Author's moral rights.
- Special provisions, such as an advance on author's royalties.
- Signatures of the parties.

In the above example, under author's grant, the publisher's 'volume rights' or 'primary rights' encompass print and electronic. Some of the far-sighted educational, academic and STM book publishers included electronic rights in their contracts with authors during the 1990s, even in the 1980s. The learned journal publishers are also free to publish electronically since the contributing authors usually assign their rights to the publisher, or society. Similarly, many of the book packagers and highly illustrated publishers own the copyright in the text, and in the commissioned artwork and photography, through assignments. But the trade publishers do not generally hold electronic rights in their backlist books. Agents have withheld them. Agents may not agree with the publisher's view that the publisher's volume rights must include e-books (i.e. read-only version of the printed book), and license them separately, possibly to another publisher, as well as licensing other kinds of electronic rights, such as turning the book into an interactive game. The exploitation of various forms of electronic rights in trade publishing is in flux.

The inclusion of third party material (e.g. text extracts, photographs, data) in many books across most sectors of publishing is another impediment to the e-publishing of the backlist and of new books. The rights holders (e.g. printed book publishers and picture agencies) can be resistant to granting electronic rights or charge exorbitant fees – in effect a refusal. Thus e-books may be devoid of third party material. E-publishing is likely to benefit most those publishers and rights owners who control very pure products, comparatively free of third party content.

THE DIVISION OF ENGLISH LANGUAGE RIGHTS

Traditionally, the UK and US publishers (especially consumer) have been in separate ownership and have divided the world English book market between them. For books published on both sides of the Atlantic, the UK and US publishers seek exclusive market areas (closed markets) from which the other's competing editions of the same book are excluded. The US publisher's exclusive territory was essentially the USA; the UK publisher's the Commonwealth, Ireland and South Africa and a few others, the remaining areas being non-exclusive to either (the open market, such as mainland Europe) where UK and US editions of the same book are in direct competition. Canadian rights were exclusively retained by UK publishers on their own originated books, and by US publishers on theirs. For some books this broad division still persists and can affect the way agents and packagers grant rights to publishers, and the way publishers trade books between themselves. For example, a UK publisher holding world rights could either sell its own edition to the USA through its related US firm (or by a distribution arrangement); or license the rights to a US publisher, in which case the US publisher's exclusive, non-exclusive, and excluded territories would be negotiated. Conversely a UK publisher may buy a US originated book from a US publisher or author represented by an agent, and its rights and territories, too, would be so defined.

This traditional territorial split in English language publishing of exclusive, non-exclusive (open market) and excluded territories is threatened by actions of governments, consumer pressure groups and internet traders. By the late 1960s, India became an unofficial open market, Singapore legislated itself into the open market in the mid-1980s, in 1996 Australia required local publication (e.g. by the UK publishers) to occur within 30 days of first publication (in effect from the publication date of the US edition to allow for the UK publisher to maintain its exclusive rights), and in 1998 New Zealand declared itself an open market. Nearer home, the advent in 1992 of the EC single market principle of free movement of goods is in conflict with the traditional UK/US publishers' contracts whereby the UK is an exclusive territory and mainland Europe is open. The greatest fear of UK publishers is that the UK itself might potentially become flooded with cheaper US editions of general paperbacks imported from mainland Europe, negating the UK publishers' exclusive contractual and territorial rights. Such 'parallel' importation is unlikely to occur from direct breaches of contracts by US publishers, but at the hands of third party traders in the USA or mainland Europe.

Thus UK publishers argue with agents and US publishers that the European Union and additional countries joining it should be treated as a single market and that it should be the exclusive territory of UK publishers, in the same way as the US unified market is treated.

The development of internet bookselling in the late 1990s enabled UK consumers to purchase easily a US edition from US-based internet booksellers; and US consumers to purchase a UK edition from UK-based internet booksellers if, for instance, the UK edition were published ahead of the US edition. (Some of the major internet booksellers in the UK have agreed to list only the UK editions, based on territorial rights information provided by the bibliographic database supplied by Book Data.)

Most of the major UK and US consumer book publishers are in common ownership and aim to be strong enough in all main countries to be able to acquire exclusive world English language rights in authors' works thereby overcoming legislative difficulties anywhere in the world and ameliorating 'buying around' practices of third-party traders. However, the authors' agents may still believe that they can secure better offers from different international publishers by dividing exclusive territorial rights among competing publishers.

The collapse of territorial rights is not a foregone conclusion. If they are in the interests of the US media corporations, the US government would defend their continuance. The major power blocks of the USA and European Union also have to grapple with the related issue of the potential loss of tax revenues from off-shore internet traders escaping the conventional tax nets. On the internet, the consumers' choice of internet bookseller is affected by the cost of shipping the physical book and the timing. Once books are available online those factors will be removed: world publication date would need to be instantaneous.

Apart from price differentials between competing editions (which are influenced by £/$ exchange rates with the Euro and other currencies), the time of the release of different editions of the same title is another factor. US and UK consumer book publishers deploy the strategy of maximizing earnings through the sequential publication of a particular book in different formats and prices. For example, first publication would be in a higher priced hardback, followed by a paperback, and possibly by accident or design, by a remainder or bargain book edition. In export markets, especially the growing mainland European market, UK and US publishers attempt to pre-empt the other's competing edition in paperback while maintaining their home markets for a period exclusively in hardback. Hence UK export editions of mass market paperbacks are available earlier on mainland Europe than in the UK, and can be bought on the air-side of UK airports. Mainland European paperback importers may hedge their bets by simultaneously ordering their stock from both US and UK publishers to ensure they receive stock from whichever is the earliest. Importers also compare the prices of competing editions, and scout around for bargain priced editions.

AUTHORS' AGENTS

Literary agents, now called authors' agents (reflecting the broad range of writers they represent), are mostly located in the London region giving them close proximity to their main customers – fiction and non-fiction editors, mainly in adult but also in children's book publishers and other media industries. Their business is selling and licensing rights to a variety of media (not just book publishers) at home and abroad on behalf of their client authors with whom they have a contract. Agents receive a commission on authors' earnings, at the bare minimum 10% but rising to 15–20%, especially on deals made abroad. Owing to increased administrative and sales costs, minimum commissions have crept upwards to 15%. The prevalence, power and influence of agents is very much a feature of the Anglo-American media worlds – in mainland Europe and elsewhere there are few agents, and they are usually 'sub-agents' of English language agents or publishers, not of local authors.

Agents represent many of the established professional writers (i.e. those who derive much of their income from writing). While some agents are prepared to review unsolicited manuscripts from aspiring novelists for which they may charge a reading fee, others discourage this practice and take on new clients only on personal recommendations from credited sources, such as publishers. Rarely is it worth while for an agent to represent academics unless their work appeals to a wide readership.

An agent manages a writer's career primarily from a commercial viewpoint, for example by placing the author's work with the right publisher or fuelling competition between publishers (on major books by holding auctions); negotiating deals to secure the best terms; by submitting their own contracts to licensors weighted in the authors' favour; checking or querying publishers' advance payments against royalties, royalty statements and chasing debts.

The example of the author–publisher contract summarized above, and weighted in the publisher's favour, shows the author granting various world rights to the publisher. Because most authors are unable to market the rights on their work worldwide they mainly allow publishers to do so on their behalf. But an agent representing an author may limit the rights granted to a publisher, and their territorial extent, and license the rights retained on behalf of the author to other firms at home and abroad. For instance, the UK publisher's licence may apply to the English language only, and the territory (the countries) in which it has the exclusive right to publish (e.g. the Commonwealth and Europe) are listed, as well as those from which it could be excluded (e.g. the USA, including/excluding Canada). An agent could then license the book in the English language to a US publisher directly. A UK publisher, within its exclusive territory, could for instance be granted the following rights: the right to publish a hardback and a paperback; and to license to others book club, reprints, second and subsequent serial (i.e. extracts appearing after book publication in newspapers etc.), quotation and anthology, mechanical and reproduction, broadcast reading rights etc. (the income from which is shared with the author). An agent retains, for instance, foreign language translation, first serial (extracts appearing before book publication giving a newspaper scoop), stage/radio/television/film dramatization, merchandising, electronic rights etc. However, there is no clear-cut division of rights or territories covered – each book differs. A publisher which has the idea for the book and contributes much editorial and design effort, or which is investing a large amount, for instance in a new writer on a two book deal, has a strong case for acquiring wide territorial rights and the sharing of other rights. Adult and children's publishers and packagers producing highly illustrated books for the international market need world rights in all languages. Book packagers and some highly illustrated book publishers often try to acquire the copyright outright from minor authors enabling subsequent re-packaging and recycling of authors' material without further payment or author contract.

UK agents retaining rights may sell them directly to, for example, US publishers or film companies or mainland European publishers, or use overseas agents with whom they have arrangements. Conversely, UK agents may represent well known American authors on behalf of US authors' agents, and sometimes US publishers via their rights sales managers. The selling of rights from a publisher's viewpoint is described in Chapter 4; an agent's work is similar except that an agent solely represents the author.

The additional dimension of agents' work falls under an editorial heading. For instance, agents send out synopses and manuscripts for external review, comment on manuscripts and advise authors on what they might write and the media they might write for, and develop ideas with them; or be asked by publishers to supply authors; or initiate projects themselves for sale to publishers. In such ways, some agents increasingly take on roles which were once the province of publishers' editors. They can reflect trade realities back to authors, and arbitrate on arguments between their authors and publishers.

Agents can provide a degree of continuity in the face of changing publishers and editors. However, some authors decide to change agents. The former agent continues to receive commission on existing contracts which can conceivably endure for decades after the author's death. The long established agencies manage the literary estates of classic authors whose work remains in copyright.

Many agents operate from home as single person companies. There are medium sized agencies consisting of several agents plus assistants, and a few large agencies such as Curtis Brown, or Peters Fraser & Dunlop. The large agencies consist of a range of agents each of whom specializes in broad areas of books or the selling of particular rights, though each agent usually looks after a particular primary group of authors. Some of their assistants show sufficient aptitude to develop their own list of authors, and new agents arise from one-time rights sales staff and editorial staff of publishers. There are also agencies which specialize in selling particular rights, such as translation, or film and television, on behalf of publishers and authors' agents.

BOOK PACKAGERS AND MULTIMEDIA PRODUCERS

Packagers, usually small and founded by an editor or designer or sales person, tend to produce mainly highly illustrated and saleable, expensive to produce, informational colour hardbacks which are published and marketed under the imprints of other firms (chiefly adult and children's general publishers, and book clubs). They may supply own-brand books for bookselling chains and supermarkets; bargain books for promotional publishers; and books and colour brochures for other businesses. A few packagers produce illustrated school textbooks, or mixed or multimedia English language teaching courses, or dictionaries, encyclopaedias or atlases etc. Packagers are discreetly named on a book's copyright page.

They provide a customer with creative editorial, design and production expertise which would be too difficult or expensive to sustain in-house. Sometimes packagers are commissioned to produce the books, for instance in ELT publishing, up to the point the books are ready for printing by the publisher. But more frequently packagers initiate projects and try to pre-sell bulk quantities of printed books to publishers usually on an international co-edition basis, often restricting the exclusive territorial rights granted to a UK publisher and other rights. For example, before the book is written and created, the packager shows publishers the book's synopsis, specimen material, mock-ups of printed pages, dummy and cover. Their aim is to secure orders for sufficient quantities and up-front payments from a UK publisher (sometimes with book club support), and usually from a US publisher to cover the direct development costs spread over the first printing of several imprint editions. Further English language reprints and foreign language co-editions printed for publishers should bring in the profit.

Packagers may become frustrated by the lack of sales effort given to their books, which they have created and sold to UK publishers, and the tight margins they are put under. If the book flops, the publisher blames the packager. If the book is a success, the publisher takes the credit. Thus some packagers take the risk of becoming publishers in their own right in the UK and US markets while continuing to sell co-editions elsewhere. Packagers, like some publishers, may overstretch themselves and go bust.

The selling of international co-edition books by packagers and publishers can be a volatile market depending as it does on the vagaries of American, Australian and European publishers, and on fluctuating exchange rates.

The business techniques adopted by book packagers and highly illustrated book publishers can be extended to the new media. Multimedia producers face very high development costs which usually need spreading over several partners by segmenting the market through licensing customized editions (with up-front payments) to different kinds of publishers and distributors around the world, in the English and non-English languages. At the outset, they try to pre-sell projects on concept demo disks or web templates. Outright copyright ownership of the content (e.g. text, artwork, animations, photography and video) is fundamental to the reversioning of material. Some of the former book packagers and highly illustrated book publishers which own their copyrights are offering to re-package it for web-based presentation on internet portals and company web sites. In the educational field, some of the multimedia producers are reversioning or customizing their own assets for publishers' digital presentation (often to supplement the printed textbooks) and are redesigning publishers' printed textbooks into 'dynamic' e-books.

THE UK BOOK TRADE

The sales success of consumer books, especially, depends on retail exposure. *The Impulse Buying of Books* (1982) survey found that about half the books sold over the counter were on-the-spot impulse buys, and in the confectioner/tobacconist/newsagent (CTN) outlets, about three-quarters were impulse buys. Of possible factors prompting impulse purchase, 30% bought on the name of the author (higher with fiction buyers), 30% liked the look of the book, and only 13% related to the impact of publishers' marketing and recommendations by the bookshop. Over 40% of impulse buys were made without any prior knowledge of the book or author.

Conventionally above 80% of books have been sold through terrestrial (or 'bricks and mortar') shops. The remainder were sold directly by mail order, mainly through book clubs. However, the founding by Amazon of internet retailing (e-tailing), if not of e-commerce, in the USA in 1995, transformed mail-order book-selling. In the UK, 1999 was the year internet bookselling began to take off. Though by 2000, internet bookselling was still loss-making, its growth was so fast as to prompt expectations that within five years it might account for from 12–20% of the overall UK book market. Whatever, the booksellers (terrestrial and internet, and in combination – 'clicks and mortar') are the consumer publishers' most important customers at which they aim most of their marketing and sales effort, along with the very significant inter-mediaries – the wholesalers. Around half of publishers' total sales passes through the home book trade, the balance is accounted for by book clubs, direct supply routes and by exports.

Booksellers

The UK book trade, in its great variety, underwent enormous changes during the 1980s and 1990s – especially in the growth of the bookselling chains and that of the main trade wholesalers – and continues to do so. Booksellers' well-known brand names disappeared as some were taken over in the late 1990s (Dillons by Waterstone's, John Menzies by WH Smith). Waterstone's and WH Smith were the dominant booksellers, accounting between them for around 20% of the total UK book market, estimated at around £3bn.

Book Marketing Limited, a market research company special-izing in the book industry, in its report *Books and the Consumer 1999*, gives the following breakdown of the consumer book market, i.e. excluding sales to institutions and schools etc.:

Percentage share of consumer book market, 1999
Data taken from *Books and the Consumer 1999* (BML, 2000)

	Volume	Value
	%	%
Chain bookshops*	17.5	25
Independent/bargain bookshops	20	16
Books & stationery stores**	19	21
Supermarkets	7	5
Other shops***	14	10
Book clubs	14	14
Other direct	8	9

*Blackwell's, Books Etc./Borders, Hammicks, Ottakar's, James Thin, Waterstone's
**includes WH Smith, Sussex Stationers
***includes department stores, CTNs, toy shops etc.

NB Internet sales are included in the relevant section, i.e. purchases from Waterstone's online are included in Waterstone's, purchases from amazon.co.uk in other direct.

Throughout the 1990s, in contrast to the private sector bookselling chains which were characterized by new store openings, larger investments in the numbers of new titles stocked, longer opening times and increased sales, the local authority funded public libraries were prone to branch closures, lower new stock investment, shorter opening times and declining borrowings.

The retail outlets differ greatly in their character. For example, WH Smith is described as a book and stationery store or as a multiple retailer selling many different kinds of products. In 1998, it selected 10 000 titles from the 50 000 trade titles published, predominantly from the large publishers but its suppliers included 1500 small publishers, right down to local history publications. Waterstone's is described as a 'range' or 'stockholding' bookseller with more than 200 shops. During the 1980s Waterstone's and Dillons competed fiercely with each other, opening well-designed branded stores, throughout the country, typically carrying 50–70 000 titles, many times bigger than traditional bookshops. They tended to be called 'up-market' booksellers, exemplified by their wide range of hardback and trade paperback titles and the depth of backlist titles stocked. However the size of these stores eventually became dwarfed in the late 1990s by the opening by Waterstone's and Borders of flagship superstores carrying upwards of 150 000 titles. In late 1997, the fast-growing London based chain Books Etc. with some stores stocking up to 50 000 titles was purchased by the US book and music superstore chain Borders. (In America, Borders has over 300 superstores, while its main rival, the world's largest bookseller Barnes & Noble has over 500. During the 1990s these chains were credited with transforming US bookselling.)

The medium sized chains usually operate smaller stores than the range booksellers and tend to be weighted to fast-moving frontlist titles, concentrating on the top-selling 5000 titles. However, amongst them are the academically orientated stores of Blackwell's, which together with Waterstone's, dominates the ownership of campus-related bookstores, and the Scottish based chain of James Thin. For publishers of high level academic and professional titles, Blackwell's is a major customer owing to its UK retail and library supply businesses, as well as its leading position in exporting specialist titles.

Many of the independent bookshops stock from 12000–20000 titles. Most of them select and purchase much of their own stock from the two largest trade wholesalers Bertrams and Gardners stocking up to 250 000 titles, and from the third-placed wholesaler THE. (In comparison, the big supermarkets typically stock up to c.20 000 general product lines.) From the late 1980s, the trade wholesalers revolutionized the speed and efficiency of book distribution by supplying, at first, the independent bookshops which faced dealing with a myriad of publishers' invoicing systems, and their warehouses which were often slow and inefficient. The wholesalers' growth was grounded on their focus on customer service to booksellers. To the bookseller they offered the convenience of dealing with just a few wholesalers' invoicing systems, rather than those of dozens of publishers; of online bibliographic information systems (including marketing and purchasing advice); of online ordering; and of consolidated orders with fast and reliable delivery. The wholesalers became the booksellers' stockroom. If the trade wholesalers had restricted their ambitions to the independent booksellers they too would have faced eventual decline. But they extended their reach into serving some of the retail chains and supermarkets, entered the school library supply market (for long restricted to specialist suppliers) and began to export. At the end of the 1990s, they received a fillip from the emerging internet booksellers such as Amazon UK and Bol.com (owned by Bertelsmann) which initially at least drew their stock from the wholesalers. The wholesalers developed internet bookselling packages for terrestrial booksellers wanting to enter that market. Moreover, in 2000, a novel deal was announced between the wholesaler Bertrams and the publisher The Stationery Office, whereby Bertrams became the exclusive distributor to booksellers of the trade part of that publisher's list.

WH Smith is its own wholesaler in that it operates centralized buying from publishers and its own warehouse at Swindon which receives the stock from the publishers and which distributes the books to its branches. The system relates each title and quantity to a scale determined by the size and character of its branches.

Some other chains operate centralized buying, that is the chains' highly knowledgeable book buyers at head office select titles presented to them by the publishers' sales managers, thereby usually precluding the publishers' sales representatives (reps) from selling titles directly into their branches. Conversely, some chains place the book purchasing decisions mainly in the branches – the publishers' reps call on the branch departmental buyers, and the publishers deliver stock directly to the branches. In some cases, chains mix centralized buying with some discretion for the branches to purchase stock locally. The ways in which the chains manage their purchasing decisions are in a state of flux.

The major bookselling chains have central marketing departments which organize, often in collaboration with publishers' sales and marketing staff, consumer advertising, and instore promotion (including window displays etc.) of particular books or of publishers' brands, author promotions and other instore events etc. in the branches.

Other book outlets of significance to particular kinds of publishers included airport terminal shops, especially at Heathrow and Gatwick, which sell enormous quantities of paperback fiction, travel and business books (flight delays are a boon for book sales); and specialist bookshops, such as religious.

Bookshops, however, are a narrow channel to reach the general public – BML's *Books and the Consumer 1996* report found that only 33% of the population buy books from bookshops (and 20–25% of the population never buy books from any kind of retailer). There are around 1500 bookshops of reasonable size, of which some half significantly influence the pattern of book buying, and a smaller number, say 500, are the main retailers of non-fiction. There is a view that regular book buyers when presented with a wide range of interesting books in an attractive bookshop facilitating browsing will buy more books, while people not used to book buying would be baffled by choice and intimidated by the setting. But if such people were presented with a very narrow choice, in a non-bookshop setting, they would be more likely to purchase a book on impulse. (Focusing the public's attention on a selected and small number of recommended titles has long been the fundamental strategy of book clubs.)

Non-book retail outlets

Other kinds of big retail chains, such as the supermarkets, buy centrally and receive their stock either directly from publishers or via wholesalers. The supermarkets often offer (in their stores and on their web sites) massive discounts on a narrow range of bestsellers, usually of female interest, as a way of impressing on their customers (most of whom probably never enter a bookshop) the value for money they offer. Other kinds of non-book retailers can use books as a cut-priced commodity as a lead into the customer purchased of other kinds of product, provided that is they order large enough quantities from the publisher.

Books are also available in many other kinds of retail outlets, which the publishers reach through wholesalers. For example, the merchandising wholesalers serving CTN outlets with mass-market paperback fiction buy centrally from the publishers and scale out the books in relation to the number of 'pockets' in the outlets, some of which may be bookshops. They regularly replenish the outlets and remove slow-selling titles for destruction. Such merchandisers may also service many other kinds of outlet such as convenience general stores, ferry port outlets, and motorway service stations (with male interest titles, except at holiday times) etc. There are ethnic wholesalers (e.g. Asian and Irish) serving their communities, and wholesalers dedicated to supplying garden, DIY and leisure centres, and specialist shops and chains (e.g. computer stores, toy shops, chemists, alternative medicine, wine, food and gifts etc.).

Children's books

The children's book market has undergone radical change with under a third of sales through retail bookshops. Children's books sell well when displayed face out alongside other kinds of products such as in the multi-product WH Smith chain, or among groceries or toys especially where parents or relations have children in tow. The books are supplied through library/institutional suppliers, children's and school book clubs, school's leisure market suppliers, supermarkets, toyshops and retail learning centres, specialist wholesale merchandisers, direct selling operations into the home and workplace, internet retailers and to a minor extent trade book wholesalers. Like the educational textbook publishers, children's publishers also supply their books directly to schools when their books are used to support the National Curriculum.

The school with its parents is an important outlet for children's books. The school provides a setting where children's books leap through the adult sales barrier and in which important word-of-mouth recommendations among children themselves take place. School book fairs have grown enormously and involve the supplier providing the school with upwards of 300 titles displayed face out, the school benefiting from a sales commission or free books. Moreover, school bookshops run by teachers and more linked to in-school reading acquisition, provide deeper access to publishers' backlists.

Bargain bookshops

The recession of the early 1990s witnessed considerable growth in bargain bookselling chains, selling remainders (UK and US titles) and bargain or 'promotional' books specially prepared for this market. Some of the chains are owned by remainder dealers. They occupy high-street positions, sometimes on short-leases granted by stressed landlords. Conventional 'full price' booksellers also incorporated bargain book tables in their product mix, thereby helping to widen their customer profile among non-regular book buyers. The collapse of the NBA in 1995 which triggered the discounting of new books, had little discernible effect on the bargain book trade.

Publishers have a long history of ridding themselves albeit quietly of their mistakes in overstocking, of printing too many copies. When a title's sales are insufficient to cover the cost of storage, it may be pulped or remaindered. Some publishers never remainder in the home market, or at all. A publisher having sold a book to a book club is restrained from remaindering. Remainders commonly stem from speculative or poor or disastrous publishing decisions on new books, or from the one reprint too many of good books. While a title may no longer sell in hardback or paperback at full price, it may sell well when released at a bargain price. The publisher needs to convert its dead stock into cash.

A publisher's sales manager sells the titles either directly to bargain chains or to a remainder dealer usually at a price well below the cost of manufacture. The dealer sells them on to bargain booksellers and to conventional booksellers, at say three times that price. The booksellers, who cannot return such books, sell them to the public at any price. Dealers also export remainders. A publisher may remainder only part of the stock (partial remaindering); if the publisher has a one-year stock plan and holds two years' stock, the balance is off-loaded to free warehouse space. A dealer may purchase from a publisher's warehouse, or distributor, pallets of mixed titles which have been returned from bookshops.

The promotional book publishers provide the bargain chains with a ready supply of newly created low-priced books. Such publishers and the remainder dealers are well represented at the London and Frankfurt Book Fairs, and have their own London fair, Ciana, in September.

Retail book market information

The outlets summarized above account for most of the UK terrestrial retail sales of books. The publishers sell their new titles directly to the retailers (or via wholesalers). But the data of actual sales made by the retailers to their customers is of critical importance to the retailers, wholesalers and publishers. The installation by retailers of Electronic Point of Sale (EPoS) systems reading the bar codes on covers when sales are made, enables the retailers to monitor the rate of sale of titles and to control their inventory (i.e. by re-ordering the titles which sell or by returning the titles to the publisher which do not). The effect of EPoS installations was that booksellers placed smaller orders more frequently (provided that a title was stocked in the first place) and expected faster deliveries.

Whitaker's market research company BookTrack collects the sales data by title from almost all of the different kinds of book retailers from across the country and from internet booksellers, and produces various bestseller charts which are published in *The Bookseller* weekly. BookTrack sells its data to interested parties. Thus, for example, publishers (and authors' agents) can not only monitor the volume sales performance of their own titles – their rise and fall – but also that of competitors. WH Smith supplies BookTrack, but also operates its own management information system, data from which it makes available to major publishers. Publishers armed with that information are in a far better position to respond to the needs for quick reprints or not. However, Book-Track data cannot help publishers' sometime over-optimism or misjudgement of printing too many copies of a new title at the outset, or that of booksellers' stocking of too many copies.

The returns of unsold books to publishers from retailers and wholesalers is an expensive and wasteful characteristic of the book business, which was estimated by KPMG in 1998 to cost a bookseller £0.50 and a publisher £1.00 per book returned. In 1995, 20% of consumer publishers' home sales were returned, but by 1998 that had dropped to 12%; conversely the returns of academic and professional books leapt from 11% to 18% over the same period (*Book trade yearbook 1999*, PA).

The BookTrack retail sales data gives a partial picture of some publishers' home sales. A proportion of children's publishers' sales and a very high proportion of educational publishers' sales do not pass through retailers. Furthermore, some publishers, especially those issuing specialist academic and professional titles, sell them directly to end-users by conventional or internet means, and there are other sales channels available, such as those used by the highly illustrated and promotional book publishers.

Library suppliers

The public, academic and corporate libraries are supplied by booksellers and library suppliers. The UK public library market has, at best, been static. There has been a continued consolidation among the main library suppliers. Following the collapse of the Net Book Agreement, the public libraries sought higher discounts through collective regional purchasing consortia, while still demanding a large amount of bibliographic selection support and book processing from the suppliers such as Askews, Books for Students, Cawdor Book Services Glasgow, Cypher (in common ownership with trade wholesaler Bertrams), Holt Jackson and Peters (especially children's books). Blackwell's and Waterstone's serve the academic markets. There are dozens of small and specialist suppliers.

The library suppliers export, especially academic and STM titles, sometimes under tendered contracts, to national and regional governmental libraries, university and corporate research libraries etc. They may also offer subscription services worldwide.

Publishers' discounts

Publishers sell their books to these firms at different discounts off their recommended retail prices. They try to keep their own particular discounts secret. The main factors affecting discount levels are: the type of book; the role and value the intermediary plays in the supply chain; the balance of power between the buyer and seller; historical precedent; and size of order on a particular book or group of books.

From some publishers' viewpoint, the best discount is zero, the intermediaries are cut out of the supply chain entirely or are dealt with on low, or 'short', discounts. For example, the learned journal publishers may grant a discount to the subscription agents of 0–5%. The highly specialist publishers producing very high priced information products sold directly to professional markets may grant a discount of say 10–20% on an order received from a bookseller. The school textbook publishers may grant a discount of 17–20% to a school supplier such as a bookseller, specialist school contractor or local authority purchasing organization. In such examples, the publishers generate the demand themselves, are able to supply end-users directly – the intermediaries provide a convenience service to the end-users, preferably at their own expense.

The college textbook publishers tend to offer discounts to booksellers in the range 30–40%. The publishers argue that they have achieved the adoptions through their own promotion. The terrestrial booksellers argue that they are physically stocking the titles for student purchase and displaying other titles that they might buy. Textbook discounts have risen from the pressure exerted by the chains, especially Waterstone's.

In consumer books, the discounts are more varied and are probably the highest in the world. The terrestrial retailers argue that their expensive display space generates the sales for the publishers. The so-called standard discounts granted to booksellers for hardbacks were generally in the range 35–40%, with the chains receiving more than 40%. The trade wholesalers sought rates of 45 to 50% plus, while the library suppliers received around 40%. The mass-market paperback wholesalers received 50–60%, or more. But WH Smith always argued its special case, that its centralized distribution saved publishers cost, and its retail pre-eminence in books warranted the highest discounts. Subsequently other chains, such as Waterstone's and Borders, argued their cases, especially in respect of special promotions on particular books as well as the supermarkets ordering large quantities of paperbacks discounted to the public by say 20–40%, on which they too required massive discounts from the publishers.

The term 'high discount' appears in the royalty clauses in many of the author–trade publisher contracts. For example, when the publisher grants a high discount of 50% or higher on a hardback or trade paperback, or 52.5% or higher on a mass-market paperback, the author's royalty, when expressed as a percentage of the published price, is reduced (e.g. to four-fifths of that percentage, or is expressed as a percentage of the publisher's net receipts, i.e. price received from the bookseller). Authors find that an increasing proportion of their sales are made above such high discount thresholds.

Book clubs

Book clubs have conventionally occupied a major segment of mail-order sales to consumers. The general hardback book clubs have the largest memberships but there are many small specialist interest clubs. Broadly speaking, book clubs recruit their members (who are required to buy a minimum quantity of titles at separate times) by large-scale consumer advertising offering massively discounted premium offers, especially on reference titles. Their biggest problem is retaining members, and they face a challenge from discount retailers and the internet booksellers which are building individual customer interest profiles. However, a fundamental strategy of a club is focusing the members' attention on a selected and small number of recommended titles which are deeply discounted, and clubs are migrating to the net too. Publishers supply the clubs with non-returnable bulk quantities of the books at very high discounts, or the clubs reprint their own copies, paying a royalty to the publisher.

Book Club Associates (BCA) is the UK's largest book club operation with some 2 million members and over 20 clubs. It is owned by Bertelsmann.

Display marketing companies

Around half a dozen companies sell books (and other products) directly to customers in their workplaces or homes. They employ hundreds of 'agents' who receive a percentage on sales, and who allow customers time to examine the colourful books before they purchase. The companies order very large quantities of titles from publishers on a non-return basis, and sell them at say a 70% discount off the publisher's price, usually six months after publication.

THE IMPACT OF THE INTERNET

By 1999, the internet booksellers believed that the general public's home connection to the net was approaching a critical mass. Yet most of their orders were received during working hours from people ordering computing, business and academic titles. Moreover their (mostly male) customers, rather than progressing as the sites encourage, from the home page through to a subject page and then to a choice of book, arrived on the site seeking a known book, used the search engine to buy it and left. The major internet booksellers such as amazon.co.uk and bol.com (Bertelsmann), presented themselves as the ultimate range booksellers, listing up to 1.5 million titles available in the UK (usually drawing on the bibliographic databases provided by Book Data and Whitaker) to which they created added-value features. The major terrestrial booksellers such as WH Smith and Waterstone's opened internet sites, as did Blackwell's to compete against start-up internet booksellers aimed at student purchasers of college texts. Some commentators believed that UK terrestrial bookselling had over-expanded and was exposed to contraction from the challenge of the internet.

All the internet booksellers ran at significant losses while they built their market share and their brands: the cost of consumer advertising was enormous. Furthermore Amazon UK, for instance, invested heavily in software development, merchandising editors (who relate to the publishers' marketing staff), 24 hour customer services (not least to handle orders from overseas), and in 2000 built its own distribution centre.

From a publishers' viewpoint, the internet booksellers' massive discounts to the public on bestselling hardback titles – made at the booksellers' expense – appeared to be becoming the norm. Some publishers feared that such pricing policies would eventually affect the public's view of the pricing of books, and that in due course the publishers themselves would have to pay for such discount practices. On the other hand, publishers saw that internet bookselling opened a new channel to increase the sale of backlist books, which had long ago disappeared from terrestrial retail display, that their book return rates were much lower than from the terrestrial shops, and that it was preferable for the booksellers to fulfil low value single book orders – often prohibitively expensive for a publisher's distribution system geared to supplying the book trade.

While at the turn of the century internet bookselling is still in its infancy, the impact of the internet and other potential new digital media channels of book distribution and of reading are beginning to affect the ownership and connections between the content providers (e.g. the publishers) and the media distributors (e.g. internet booksellers). To give some indicative examples which occurred around 2000. In the USA, the bookseller Barnes & Noble sought to purchase the largest trade book wholesaler Ingram, and Bertelsmann (the world's largest publisher and book club operator) acquired a 50% share in Barnes & Noble's internet bookselling business, which was pressing up against the market leader Amazon. The world's major internet portal AOL merged with the media corporation Times Warner, which included some book publishing imprints, such as Little, Brown. The reading of books on screen was enhanced and encouraged by Microsoft's Reader ClearType software through a launch with barnesandnoble.com and participating publishers. The proprietary hand-held e-book reading devices into which books were downloaded from enthusiastic US publishers Random House (Bertelsmann) and Simon & Schuster (Viacom), were sold through Bertelsmann's internet bookselling arm Bol.com. In the UK, WH Smith at first bought the small multimedia reference publisher Helicon (which enabled WH Smith to offer free content on its internet site), and more startlingly, bought the major UK publisher Hodder Headline; and then signed agreements to sell books via the digital TV provider Telewest, and via BT's internet portal. It appears that some of the content providers and internet retailers are positioning themselves through mergers, acquisitions and alliances in order to take charge of the main channels of distribution from author to reader – to vertically integrate the entire process, be it in the form of printed or electronically-read books.

The definitions of what constituted a publisher or a distributor or a retailer became blurred from the late 1990s as a result of the development in the US of many e-commerce companies, such as Fatbrain and NetLibrary, which concentrated on the supply of electronic content, for example, at first to education, academic and to corporate communities. They adopted various business models and proprietary technical solutions to the supply of content in secure environments. In that they download content into handheld readers, laptops and desktop computers, they may be called 'e-book downloaders or distributors or retailers'. Some reached out to UK book publishers (and authors), presenting themselves as e-publishers (not unlike the paperback publishers of an earlier era) wishing to acquire electronic rights exclusively under a royalty agreement. Whereas some UK publishers saw them as non-exclusive e-tailers or distributors through which their books could be sold under their own e-book ISBNs on a discount basis.

ı ne process and the people

FINDING AND DEVELOPING THE BOOKS: THE COMMISSIONING EDITORS

Under the editorial director are commissioning editors (sometimes termed sponsoring or acquisition or senior editors; or in web publishing, 'channel mergers'), each responsible for finding, developing and matching marketable ideas with good authors, and for new editions (especially in reference and textbook publishing). Each editor, the main contact between author and publisher, builds a list of books (and/or associated products) that is part of, or composes, an imprint, constituting a publisher's brand.

In consumer book publishing, editors may cover adult fiction and non-fiction, or either, or specialize in hardback or paperback lists, or in non-fiction areas, or children's books etc. In educational, academic and STM houses, an editor concentrates on several subjects spanning a variety of academic levels and markets or concentrates on product types, such as high-level books or textbooks, which may have associated silver disks and web sites. While editors work within a brief, the style and identity of each list are the outcome of the editor's attitudes and effort.

A publisher depends on these editors to provide a sufficient flow of publishable projects to maintain its planned level of activity (say 15–30 new books annually per editor, sometimes far less or three times more). Moreover, editors are assessed on the overall profit-contribution of their books. Editors out of tune with senior management regarding the character of the books, or who fail to produce a profit, leave voluntarily or are fired.

Some major exceptions apart (most notably in fiction) editors do not assess titles for publication on their thorough reading of complete manuscripts. Most books (including some fiction) are commissioned from authors on the basis of an outline or specimen material, or are bought from agents. Furthermore most editors do not edit in detail the author's work – that is usually done by freelances or possibly by junior in-house staff. However, the senior editors may structurally edit by giving authors substantive criticisms and suggestions to help them produce their best work and to shape it for the intended market.

Editorial contacts and general market research

Good personal contacts are paramount. An editor's in-house contacts are the members of senior management who accept or veto projects; the people who produce the books (copy-editors, designers and production staff); and, most importantly, those who promote and sell them. But more significant are the editor's external contacts.

Prime sources of new books are the firm's previously published authors. They often have new ideas, or editors suggest ideas to them which are developed jointly.

In consumer book publishing, editors try to establish a mutual trust with authors' agents (over lunch). Agents may send fiction manuscripts or non-fiction proposals to selected editors one at a time, or usually, to many editors simultaneously, or sometimes conduct auctions on highly saleable titles. Conversely an editor may contact an agent if she or he is after one of the agent's authors, or has an idea and wants an agent to find an author.

Fiction editors may also try to find new talent by spotting people who can write well, not necessarily fiction, or who are journalists or who are being published poorly or in an uncommercial medium.

The non-fiction editors who develop contacts in a variety of fields, constantly keep an ear to the ground, notice people's enthusiasms, review the media for topical subjects, try to predict trends or events which will be in the public's interest, monitor successful book categories and authors by understanding what makes them good and why are they selling, and either avoid the competition, imitate it, or attempt to find unfilled niches by developing a new twist. They may write speculatively to people who have or may capture the public's imagination (as do the agents). In specialist fields, clubs and societies and their magazines and internet sites can be sources of ideas and authors, and indicate level of interest. Editors interested in television and film tie-ins keep abreast of new productions and monitor audience ratings.

Editors forge links with other firms from whom they might buy or sell to, for example at the Frankfurt Book Fair or if in the highly illustrated field with packagers. UK editors are in contact with or visit US editors and rights sales managers in their sister companies or not, in order, for example, to gather market intelligence on agents' new projects. Children's book editors have contact with agents, packagers, teachers and librarians, and if producing illustrated colour books know US and foreign language publishers' editors and rights managers with whom they might trade.

The educational, academic, STM and professional book editors publish for more defined markets on which more statistical information is available (e.g. student enrolments, and numbers of researchers or professionals working in specific fields). However, these editors, apart from reading school syllabuses, college prospectuses and the relevant journals, are essentially engaged in direct market research and product development, especially in textbook publishing.

The academic and STM publishers may retain for each discipline exclusive advisers (senior academics or professionals with worldwide contacts) who direct new writers to their publishers. These publishers and educational publishers also enlist external expert general or series editors (also deployed by consumer book publishers) whose task is to help publishers' editors develop and edit the books. They usually receive a small royalty.

But the main thrust is understanding the current and future market on the ground. Educational editors see local education subject advisers, inspectors, examiners and lecturers in teacher training colleges; school heads and teachers using the materials in the classroom; and attend conferences. ELT editors, in addition to UK contacts, travel abroad and visit the Ministries and Institutes of Education, major Private Language Schools, offices of the British Council, local publishers and distributors etc. in order to fulfil the educational needs within specific cultures, and to assess market potential and credit-worthiness.

Academic, STM and professional book editors, may spend say several days a week visiting institutions and interview teaching staff in order to discover subject trends and market size, to find out their activities and views on books available, to flush out any ideas and contacts they have and to sell the firm's books. They may forge links with institutions, societies, industrial organizations etc. for which they could publish or distribute books or journals. When large US sales are anticipated, editors shape the material in conjunction with their US counterparts and visit their sister companies. All editors attend relevant conferences and receive in-house feedback from the marketing and sales departments.

Unsolicited ideas and manuscripts

Hopeful authors bombard all publishers with unsolicited manuscripts and book proposals. Consumer firms, which may reject over 99%, may wish to direct them to agents or may employ part-time readers who sort through the 'slush' pile, write reports on possible ones and refer them to the editors. Most academic theses, too, sent direct to editors are unpublishable as they stand, but a fraction can be turned into monographs. It is very unlikely that an unsolicited textbook manuscript would be structured commercially, but occasionally unsolicited ideas can be developed.

The decision to publish

Many factors influence an editor's decision to pursue a new project, including:

- Suitability for list. A title has to fit the style and aims of the list for which it is known (or sometimes branded) so that it is compatible with the firm's particular marketing systems. Furthermore, editors assessing new titles with other titles are concerned with the list's overall balance, direction and degree of innovation.
- Author assessment. The author's qualifications, motivation and time available to write the book, public standing, reliability to deliver on time, and responsiveness to suggestions.
- Unique sales proposition (USP). What makes this book different from others or special (e.g. top author, new subject treatment, first illustrated book, differentiated by price)? What are the special marketing opportunities on which the book could be promoted (e.g. author celebrity, publicity angles, especially consumer books)?
- Market. Understanding the main audience for which the book is intended, who would buy it, the possible take-up at home

and overseas. (The sales records on the author's previous books or those of similar books may be used as a guide.) Sometimes the rights sales potential is assessed (e.g. licensed book club, US rights).

- Competition. The title's USPs and advantages compared with the firm's own and competitors' books (e.g. especially textbooks and reference titles).
- Frontlist/backlist potential. Is the book expected to have a short life on the frontlist, or does it have potential to endure on the backlist thus ameliorating the vagaries of the frontlist?
- Investment and return. How much time and money needs to be expended on acquiring the book (such as the size of advance expected by the agent) and on developing and marketing it through to publication, in relation to its expected earnings and profitability? Would its earning power justify its place on the list?
- Risk and innovation. What are the external factors at play affecting the risk investment, such as the timing of publication in relation to optimum time to publish, the link to events and their perceived popularity, and the actions of competitors? What are the downside risks if the expectations are not realized? To what extent is the project experimental in terms of taking on a new author, or publishing in a new area or format (print or electronic), or price? Without taking risks and innovating, the publisher is overtaken by competitors.
- Content. The editor's judgement on the quality and appropriateness of the content is aided by others. Fiction editors may use junior editors, or external readers, to supply plot synopses or to offer first or second opinions. Non-fiction editors may ask specialist external readers to comment on specialist titles. Other publishers rely heavily on experts (e.g. teachers, academics, professionals) sometimes worldwide to comment by e-mail on material initially, during or after the book has been written. (All these external readers are paid small fees and remain mostly anonymous to the author.)
- Book's physical appearance and price. The editor envisages a proposed title's desirable physical form (e.g. its word length, illustration content, size, binding style and production quality), the likely cost and the price range within which it could be sold.

Some ideas are rejected, especially on unfavourable reports; some authors are asked to re-submit in the light of editors' suggestions; others are pursued. An editor cannot offer a contract without the agreement of the senior management. Editors sound out and lobby senior colleagues, such as the marketing and sales managers, over possible prices and sales forecasts and the production manager over the production costs. The editor prepares a publishing proposal form (circulated) which covers the scope of the book, its form, its market and competition, readers' reports, publication date, reasons for publication etc. Additionally, a financial statement sets the expected sales revenue against the costs of producing the book and those of author's royalties to give the hoped-for profit margin – provided the book sells out. Different combinations of prices and sales forecasts, and of print-run production costs and of royalties, may be tried. Many publishers hold formal meetings at which the main departmental directors hear editors' proposals – most get through, but some are referred back or rejected.

The editor, given the go-ahead, negotiates the contract with the author or agent (agents present their own contracts weighted in the author's favour), agrees or invents the book's title (important for sales success), and on commissioned books ensures that the author appreciates what is expected (e.g. content, length, deadline). There may be an optimum publication date which would maximize sales (e.g. a consumer book that is topical or published for the Christmas market; or textbooks of which bound copies are needed for inspection by teachers ideally around the new year to secure autumn adoptions in the northern hemisphere and April–June for the southern). Some authors submit chapters for comment; others deliver the complete manuscript on time or later, an inherent trait of many authors (or never). The manuscript is checked for length, completeness and quality (may be again externally reviewed), may be returned or accepted and is then handed down the line. The book is costed again.

Editors brief and liaise with junior editors, designers, production, promotion and sales staff and may write the blurb (the first twenty words of which must grip the reader). Although editors have no managerial control over other departments, they endeavour to ensure their books receive due attention. The editors may present their books to the publisher's sales force at the regular sales conferences.

Some editors, especially those involved with complex and highly illustrated books, or major textbook projects involving supplementary material and new media, get very involved in the product research and development stages.

At the page-proof stage, the book's published price is fixed, as well as the number of copies to be printed and bound. The number printed may be less or more than the number envisaged at the outset.

The editors' involvement with re-pricing, reprinting, pulping or remaindering decisions varies from firm to firm. In some, the sales director is the dominant force.

Skills

No editor can simply sit back and expect marketable ideas and authors to flow in. Building contacts and opportunities takes initiative and quick-footed detective work to identify the sources of books, the best authors and ideas. Editors need to be creative in that they encourage and develop received ideas or initiate ideas themselves and match them to authors. Inevitably these lead up false trails, so editors have to be agile enough to hunt the front-runners, ruthless enough to weed out the wrong projects and to dump unprofitable authors, and tough enough to withstand this highly exposed position within the publishing house.

Profitable publishing depends on a perception of trends in markets and timing (good editors pre-empt competitors – in textbook publishing the lead time can easily be three years); constant vigilance, inquisitiveness and receptivity to new ideas; and responsiveness to changing needs. In specialist fields it involves asking experts the right questions, being able to talk to them intelligently for at least some minutes and being aware of their personal prejudices, professional jealousies and ideological positions. The skill lies in choosing the right advisers/readers – and assessing the assessors.

The consumer book editors, who face great difficulty in ascertaining market needs, base their judgements on a combination of experience of what sells, having a finger on the pulse, and intuition. Backing one's own hunches takes considerable audacity and confidence.

Fundamental to book and author selection is the editor's ability to assess the quality of the proposal and of the author's writing and purpose. This critical faculty (underpinned by skills in speed reading and sampling sections of writing) develops from experience and intuitive discernment. Editors should be able to contribute to structural improvements, and in specialist areas appear to the author not merely as a cipher for expert readers' comments.

The authors, who supply the raw material on which the success of the enterprise is founded, are engaged in long spells of isolation when writing with little else to draw on but experience, knowledge and imagination. In their books rest their dreams and hopes. In their eyes the editor is exclusive to them; to the editor an author is one of many. Authors expect editors to represent their interests in-house, to get things done and so judge editors on their in-house clout. Conversely editors must represent the best interests of the publisher to authors – at times a fine juggling act. Most authors are extremely sensitive about their work and the way it is published. Good editors persuade authors to write, foster author loyalty to the house, and nudge and encourage them in certain directions. Major skills lie in deciding when an author will appreciate intervention and its form, and in conveying constructive opinions honestly without damaging author self-confidence. Authors need encouragement, reassurance and praise – that, and the editor's diplomacy, are vital. Those authors who rely on their books for income (unlike teachers, academics etc.) centre their whole life around their writing. To some, an editor becomes inseparable from their private lives.

Editors need a knowledge of production methods (limitations and costs) and new media opportunities and of contracts; the skill to negotiate with authors, agents and others; and the appreciation of the inter-relationships between costs and revenues, and the risk factors involved. They deploy politicking and manipulative skills (especially during the publishing proposal stage) and their infectious enthusiasm, selling and persuasive skills, used to promote the book's fortunes within the house, get communicated to the outside world.

DESK EDITING

Although a commissioning editor may edit manuscripts in detail, this work (desk editing) is usually done by junior and lower-paid in-house staff (variously known as desk, junior, assistant, house, or sub-editors) or, more often, by freelance copy-editors or firms which may undertake the entire production process up to the delivery to the publisher of the final digital file of the book ready for manufacturing, and for electronic publication, such as in journals.

Those who undertake desk editing inside the publisher supervise the progress of books from manuscripts to bound copies, working closely with the production/design department, and giving information to marketing and sales people. They may copy-edit manuscripts and organize illustrations themselves; they may (or may not) edit manuscripts for overall clarity and pass them to freelance copy-editors for the detailed work. They subsequently send proofs to authors and to freelance proofreaders, collate corrections and generally oversee the book's production from an editorial standpoint. Some academic/STM book and journal publishers employ 'production editors' who are also responsible for the design and production stages. In some highly illustrated book publishers, or packagers, editors work alongside designers to create the book.

Only in firms where job demarcations are drawn not too tightly, and where desk editors work specifically for sympathetic commissioning editors, is there the likelihood of commissioning experience, usually without responsibility. Below the desk editor level there may be editorial assistants: their work ranges from secretarial and administrative support to editorial work under supervision, such as proofreading, collating corrections, finding pictures for the text, applying for the clearance of third party copyright material, and handling reprints. In consumer book publishing, junior editorial staff may write reports on new book proposals.

Some publishers have a managing editor or supervisor who allocates, financially controls and supervises freelances' work, and there are production firms that offer that service to publishers. In some publishers the production department organizes the freelance editing and proofreading. Very few publishers retain a pool of copy-editors into which the manuscripts are fed.

Some educational, academic and STM publishers have introduced development editors who directly support the commissioning editors on major textbook projects. Such an editor carries out survey research in association with the marketing/sales departments in order to ascertain market needs sometimes by using focus groups, organizes the external reviewing of drafts and helps shape the project with the authorial team from conception to completion.

Manuscript editing

The aim of the copy-editor (who may be the only person other than the author who reads the book pre-publication) is to ensure that the text and illustrations are clear, correct and consistent for both the printer and the ultimate readers. The copy-editor is also usually expected to look out for libellous passages.

The copy-editor, who is briefed on the nature and market of the book, first needs to check that all the manuscript items handed over are indeed present and that they have been clearly labelled and numbered by the author (e.g. the typescript or hard-copy – preferably with disks – and illustrations). The author is asked for any outstanding items, otherwise the book will be held up.

The work of copy-editing falls into three related processes.

- At the lowest order of detail, the task is to ensure that the author's text is consistent in such matters as spelling, hyphenation, capitalization, agreement of verbs and subjects, beginning and ending of quotation marks and parentheses, and many other points sometimes included in the firm's house style. The accuracy and relationship of parts of the text to others, such as in-text cross-references to illustrations, captions, chapters and notes, the matching of headings on the contents page to those in the text and of citations to the reference list etc. and the arrangement and preparation of pages with which authors may be unsure (e.g. the preliminary pages) are also this editor's concern. Each new book presents its own problems in the detailed handling of stylistic points, and decisions have to be made in regard to alternative ways of applying the rules, if at all.
- While some publishers restrict copy-editing to this level, others expect editors to a varying extent to engage in the second parallel editorial process, which may be termed substantive editing. This calls for clear perception of the author's intent and sometimes restraint from the copy-editor; but, where appropriate, attention is paid to discordant notes, such as obscure, incoherent, misleading or ambiguous sentences, or

non sequiturs in factual passages; unintentional use of mixed metaphors or of repetition; unusual punctuation in sentence construction; paragraphing; over or under use of headings etc. Furthermore, authors' errors of fact, and inconsistencies, omissions, contradictions and illogicality in their argument or plot may be found. Substantive editing may thus entail the re-writing of sentences, reorganization, or suggesting other ways to present material.

Editors look out for abbreviations and terms unfamiliar to readers. The avoidance of parochialisms or culturally specific UK examples is especially important in books aimed for overseas. The avoidance of offensive – for example, sexist or racist – language or values and of corresponding stereotypes are issues which confront editors, designers and illustrators, particularly those in educational and children's publishing. These staff also try to ensure that the level of language and of text and illustrations is appropriate for the intended age group.

- The third parallel editorial process carried out, whether the second substantive form is done or not, concerns indicating to the designer and/or typesetter, parts of the text that need special typographic treatment. Items so marked or coded include the labelling of the heading hierarchy (e.g. chapter headings, section and sub-section headings) and the areas of text to be indented, displayed or typeset in sizes or faces different from the main text (e.g. long quotations, lists, notes, captions, tables etc.). In the absence of a designer, the editor may do the typographic mark-up as well.

Work methods

A common method involves the editor quickly looking through the hardcopy and disk to gain a measure of the author and the book. Ideally, decisions regarding the handling of stylistic points (e.g. spelling, hyphenation, capitalization, terminology) are taken at the outset. A style sheet is developed to aid consistency and memory – an editor deals with many titles at any one time – and helps proofreading, which may be done by someone else such as a freelance who may be other than the freelance copy-editor.

To a varying extent, house style editing and substantive editing conflict, in that concentration on one may lead to neglect of the other. Good editors go through the copy several times at different speeds focusing attention at various levels, moving back and forth during each examination. Editors may work on hardcopy or on screen (utilizing software tools), or both.

During each examination editors make alterations on matters – especially those of house style – they believe to be right and defensible, but even so authors may disagree. Other changes and self-queries for later checking are marked on the copy, or listed separately. Those that affect the design or production of the book, and which are in turn affected by the design and production methods, are addressed to the design or production department. Others, relating to content, may be addressed to the author.

If the author is contacted by telephone, e-mail or in writing, editors need to be particularly tactful, explaining the kind of editing that has been done – perhaps by mentioning representative samples – raising matters needing assistance, reaching agreement on matters of concern. The edited copy may be returned to the author for checking. Alternatively, a meeting is held. The editor, for instance, by adopting the reader's viewpoint, and suggesting solutions, may persuade the author to make necessary changes.

Illustrations

The author may also need to resolve queries on illustrations. If the author cannot supply illustrations editors sometimes have to undertake picture research or brief a researcher. If the publisher is responsible for obtaining copyright permission, the editor or researcher writes to copyright holders. Each illustration or table is labelled and compared against the accompanying text and caption. Caption and source copy are prepared.

Drawn illustrations are prepared from copies of those previously published if suitably amended, or from author's original line work, roughs or ideas. They are edited for sense and consistency before being passed to the designer or illustrator who is briefed. Correction cycles follow. The desired position of the illustrations is indicated in the text.

Prelims

Preliminary material ('prelims') is drafted. It usually includes pages giving the book title and author, the name of the publishing house, copyright notice, International Standard Book Number (ISBN) – a unique number identifying the book – and may include a contents page, list of illustrations, acknowledgement of copyright material used, foreword etc. The Cataloguing in Publication (CIP) data (supplied by the British Library and Library of Congress), sometimes included in prelims, is applied for.

Cover copy

Printed covers or jackets are needed well in advance of the printed book for promotion and sales purposes. Thus the cover copy (e.g. title, author, blurb and ISBN) is passed to the designer preferably at this stage and the proofs checked later.

Conventional book production proof stages

Most unillustrated books (or those with only a few illustrations which are easily placed) go straight to page proofs. The typesetter rekeys the marked-up text, arranges the page breaks, inserts any illustrations, and returns proofs of pages numbered as they will finally appear. Proofs are normally read by the author and publisher (in-house or by freelances), and checked against the original copy. The corrections and improvements are collated by the editor and inserted by means of standard symbols on one master set (the marked set). Correction marks are colour-coded (e.g. red for typesetter's errors, blue for author's and publisher's) so that costs can be apportioned. (Publishers may charge authors for excessive corrections.) The marked set returns to the typesetter for correction, and unless second proofs of problem pages are requested, the book is passed for press.

Books with many illustrations integrated with the text follow a different path. The typesetter returns unpaged first proofs. While these are being read, the artwork is finalized and photographs collected. The designer checks the text typography and taking account of deletions or additions to the text proof and the planned size of illustrations lays out the pages of the book by means of a paste-up. On to the grid of facing pages, the designer pastes photocopies of the amended text proofs and indicates the position of the sized illustrations (e.g. by empty rectangles or photocopies) and other elements. The editor checks the paste-up, if necessary amending the text to fit the layout, and inserts the picture credit copy and page numbers on the contents page etc.

The typesetter corrects the text and uses the paste-up as a guide to the page make-up. The typesetter, or another firm, reproduces the illustrations to the specified size. (Sometimes high quality illustration proofs, especially of colour, are requested for checking against the originals.)

The page proofs return and are checked by the author and publisher against the first proofs and paste-up. Further proofs may follow.

The impact of new technology

In conventional book production, the edited and marked-up manuscript is sent to a typesetting firm or printer where it is rekeyed on a computer, editorial changes inserted and the typographic design enacted. Typeset proofs return which contain new errors. But now most authors hand publishers disks accompanied by hardcopy. The editorial changes, and codes that will determine the typography, may be inserted on disk, by the editor; by an in-house keyboarder; by a computer bureau or the typesetter.

Publishers receive disks from authors using a variety of hardware and software, software which is sometimes outdated and which often has to be converted and reformatted.

The advent of authors submitting their text on disk, and the widespread application of sophisticated and affordable word-processing, pagination and text output software have led to the transfer of some tasks previously carried out by typesetters to the publishers and their employees (in-house and freelance). Most significantly, the expensive, error-prone and rather slow process whereby external typesetters rekeyed the edited marked-up hardcopy, and then subsequently updated their electronic files at proof stage is dispensed with. But the tasks involved in what is termed the 'electronic pre-press process' and where they are carried out, and by whom, have if anything become more complex, varied and blurred. Furthermore, the publishers still use typesetters to rekey hardcopy manuscripts or to reset new editions of books of which the publisher has lost the electronic files; and the typesetters themselves have re-defined their roles, for example, by extending their typographic and pagination services to include artwork preparation on technical books, and the electronic styling, tagging and structuring of text for print and the encryption of electronic publications – beyond most publishers' in-house capabilities.

The first publishers to adopt in-house electronic pre-press methods were the directory, dictionary, reference and high level professional and STM book and journal publishers needing to create databases and products for eventual electronic delivery, and the highly illustrated information book and low level textbook publishers and packagers wanting to take advantage of in-house desk-top design of complex double page spreads. The consumer book publishers were the slowest to change, not least because their authors drawn from the general population were slower to equip themselves with computers compared to academics who used their institutions' computers (and secretaries); and the technological conservatism of the publishers.

The involvement of editors in the electronic pre-press process varies considerably. The main working methods include the following. The editor works on the hardcopy, and the typesetter transfers the author's disk to its wordprocessing system, inserts the corrections, style codes the document (e.g. levels of headings indicated on the hardcopy by the editor) which enact the typography, incorporates any illustrations, paginates the book and returns page proofs. Or the editor transfers the author's disk into his or her wordprocessing program (such as Microsoft Word), amends the electronic copy and inserts the style codes for the typesetter to enact the typography and to output page proofs. Or the editor, additionally, structurally tags the document, by applying Standard Generalized Markup Language (SGML), or its subset Hypertext Markup Language (HTML) for web presentation. The more recent eXtensible Markup Language (XML) aims to provide flexibility and control in online delivery over the web.

The idea behind these various markup languages is to provide an international and standardized way of defining a document's structure, not its typography, that is independent of any particular make of software or hardware system. They are designed to enable the portability of information between different systems and publishing mediums. However, they are far from 'standard', are difficult to learn and to put into effect.

Thus while some editors prepare the final digital paged file from which books are printed, in the main typesetters handle the complex coding and pagination of the electronic files prior to printing. A few publishers employ their own inhouse 'typesetters' to carry out the task.

A further dimension is the transformation of a printed book into an e-book. Many straightforward and lightly illustrated titles can be converted relatively easily to e-book formats provided that they are held in digital form designed for re-use in a consistently structured way. However, in order to take full advantage of the e-format, complex and highly illustrated titles (such as lower level textbooks) require a web or software designer (often freelance) to prepare the web template or architecture for editorial consideration. For example, this involves attending to the functionality and the visual presentation of the elements – the ways in which the reader can search, locate and use the material (on screen and print it out); navigate between text, illustrations and possibly multimedia elements; link to the publisher's other resources, and link to other sites.

Index

Serious non-fiction books should have objective indexes that anticipate readers' needs and expectations. The authors are often responsible for index preparation and the cost, and either do it themselves or are supplied with a freelance indexer, found by the deskeditor sometimes from the Society of Indexers. If not, the index is done in-house or by a freelance who is briefed. Indexes are prepared from a page proof and have to be edited and typeset at great speed because the publication date is close. The professional indexers have usually passed their Society's course exams, use specialist indexing software, and may wish to retain copyright. Indexers are applying their skills to electronic publications.

Skills

Getting on with authors and senior editors and other in-house staff, and briefing them are crucial skills. Agreeing changes with authors and getting them to return proofs on time takes tact, self-confidence, persuasion, tenacity and negotiation face-to-face, in writing, by e-mail or on the telephone.

Editing manuscripts and proofreading demands a meticulous eye for detail, a retentive memory, sustained concentration, endurance, patience, commonsense detective work and an ability to check one's own and others' work consistently.

Copy-editing and proofreading skills can to some extent be learnt from books, but added to that must be an editor's sound grasp of grammar and spelling, and preparedness to look things up. Editors should be able to place themselves in the reader's mind whatever subject knowledge they hold.

The enhancement of an author's work involves not only a knowledge of current stylistic conventions and language, but also judgement on the desirability and extent of their application, recognizing when it is necessary or unnecessary to make changes. Breaking the 'rules' for effect is not restricted to fiction. Appreciating the intangible quality of the author's voice can be important, especially in children's books.

Although an editor needs an enormous capacity to soak up detail, the ability to examine the text's overall sense is equally important. Visual awareness is also valuable, especially in highly illustrated adult and children's publishing and packaging, and low-level textbook publishing. Knowledge and understanding of production processes and ways of minimizing costs at all stages are essential, as is clear marking of the text: misleading instructions, sloppy work and/or poor handwriting cause errors and expense. Black-belt wordprocessing skills are required.

A publisher's office is hardly conducive to concentration. Editors dealing with many books (all at different stages of production) are pressed by the production office to meet deadlines, and are constantly interrupted by colleagues wanting instant information. Good editors are unflappable, they set priorities, manage time efficiently, switch quickly from one activity to another, and expect crises.

PICTURE RESEARCH

Picture research (the selection, procurement and collection of illustrations of all kinds) usually lies with the editorial department. The number of in-house picture researchers is however very small. They are concentrated in some of the highly illustrated, non-fiction, adult and children's book publishers and packagers (where they may create a picture library), and the large educational houses. Some commission photographers. A publisher or packager may, however, use expert freelance researchers, who may specialize in particular subjects and serve a range of media. Otherwise, picture research for the text or cover or both may be just part of an assistant's work in an editorial or jacket/cover department.

A general working specification for a book is drawn up in the editorial department (e.g. title, author, publication date, print run, book's market and its territorial extent, number of pictures required, ratio of colour to black and white, page size and picture budget). The editor and/or the designer/art director may either brief the picture researcher at the idea stage, before the author has completed the manuscript, or later. The brief can range from being very specific (the author or editor supplying a complete picture list citing most sources), less specific (just listing the subjects), to very vague (requesting pictures to fit the manuscript). It is vital for the researcher to clarify the brief, especially the specificity of pictures.

The researcher may read the outline or manuscript in order to generate a list of ideas for approval by the editor and the author or amend the picture list supplied by the author to something more feasible. An estimate of cost is produced, based on the researcher's experience and the researcher advises whether the time and budget allocated are realistic; and potential sources are listed.

The researcher cannot progress quickly with selection without knowing where to look for an image, and without contacts to telephone, e-mail or write to, or visit personally.

Sources, both home and abroad, include museums, libraries, archives, commercial picture agencies, photographers, public relations departments, professional and tourist organizations, charities, private individuals etc. Some major collections are held on silver disk or are accessible on the web in low resolution, and there are low cost banks of images which can be purchased on disk. Sources come from consulting directories and picture source books, museum and library catalogues, guide books, brochures, magazines, acknowledgement lists in books, foraging around reference libraries etc. Researchers build up personal contacts with picture libraries and agencies, interview photographers, visit photographic exhibitions, and form contacts abroad. They compile their own records, indexes and address books. Their knowledge accumulates with each assignment.

The criteria for selecting sources include the nature of the material required (subject range, type of material – colour or black and white, quality) and the service offered (accessibility, speed and reliability, terms and conditions restricting borrowing or use of material, costs).

With the list of potential sources compiled, the next task is to request and collect the pictures by telephoning, writing letters and visiting. Replies are reviewed, and the incoming material is logged and labelled with sources' names. The researcher responsible for the good care of the material, selects suitable items and quickly returns the rejects to avoid paying holding fees and to reduce the risk of loss. Some sources, unable to supply, may suggest others; otherwise the researcher tries alternatives. The sources of pictures held for further consideration are approached, if necessary, with a request for an extended holding period.

The researcher does the initial selection and rejection of the pictures from a large assortment. Among the criteria for selection are the picture's **editorial content** (e.g. does the picture make the points or convey the impression or mood the author/editor intended?); **composition** (which should give the content clarity and impact); **reproducibility** (tonal range, colour range and definition), bearing in mind the quality of paper and reproduction method to be used; **costs** (reproduction and holding fees, digital use fees, print fees if buying prints, search and loss/damage fees etc.).

Once the researcher has sufficient suitable photographs, the cost is estimated again and a meeting (or several meetings) held with the editor and designer (and sometimes the author) to make the next selection. It might be that the researcher has to find more pictures very quickly before the final selection is made. Photographs must be ready by first text proof stage to enable the designer to start the page layout. The researcher organizes the pictures for handover to the designer, and supplies the picture credit copy and information for the captions (provided by the sources of the photographs) to the editor.

The next task is to write to the sources for copyright permission to reproduce pictures, and to negotiate the fees. The researcher passes the suppliers' invoices for payment and calculates the total picture costs. After checking the page proofs (some sources want copies), the book is printed, and the final responsibility is to return the pictures to the sources when they come back from the printer.

Skills

While a degree level of education is not essential, some picture researchers have a fine arts degree, helpful in that this develops an appreciation of composition. Knowledge of foreign languages eases contact with overseas sources; and ICT skills are essential.

Picture researchers are only as good as their source address books and accurate visual memories. They must keep up-to-date and use imagination in research, not just in visualizing fresh uses for remembered pictures but almost instinctively knowing where to start looking for pictures on any subject, thinking methodically, finding cheap sources, and having a dogged persistence to get into new areas, getting behind closed doors. It is vital to forge good relations with sources – on the telephone, in writing and face-to-face. Researchers need the ability to interpret the message the book is trying to convey and, during selection, to make critical judgements on technical possibilities and costs as well as on aesthetic values. An understanding of the complexities of copyright and permission fees backs up their knowledge of sources; and allied to budget consciousness are the skills of negotiation especially with commercial picture agencies. Researchers must have a neat and tidy mind, and a good filing system, not least to avoid incurring holding fees and to reduce the danger of very expensive originals going astray. As one art director put it, 'It's a fascinating job – creative as well as administrative and business-like.'

DESIGN

Vast numbers of titles, such as fiction, lightly or unillustrated non-fiction, academic and STM and professional books, follow pre-set typographic designs. Thus most in-house designers are employed by medium to large publishers issuing complex illustrated books (e.g. illustrated adult and children's non-fiction or textbooks), and by the more established book packagers. They may work in a design department or in a production department, reporting directly to the production manager. The design manager, responsible for the overall style of all the firm's books, is concerned with the deployment of in-house and external services, budgets, scheduling and administration. In-house designers may be graded, the senior designers co-ordinating the junior designers' work; there may be design assistants; and some in-house designers specialize in particular lists (e.g. children's or craft books) or a series. However, the design of book covers for most kinds of books, other than the most utilitarian, requires specific design attention which may be executed by in-house cover designers, or by art directors, who may commission freelances. The designers responsible for covers are usually quite distinct from the book designers.

Small publishers may ask a good printer to help with the design; and in some large firms issuing relatively straightforward books (such as adult fiction or some high-level academic or professional books), editors or production controllers may design the books while commissioning freelance designers for covers. The use of freelances or agencies to design books and/or covers/or web sites is widespread. They are commonly commissioned by editors or production staff, and by in-house designers.

Designing of promotional material may be the responsibility of in-house book designers, or solely of designers attached to the promotion department; or freelance designers or agencies are commissioned by that department. The execution of artwork is mainly done externally. Only a few large publishers (such as those issuing technical works, atlases and guidebooks) have in-house technical illustrators or cartographers. Some publishers and packagers employ illustrators (and designers) on short-term contracts. Photography is normally commissioned.

The basis of a book designer's job is visual planning. A designer, operating within technical, cost and time constraints, and taking the views of the editor, and the production and sales departments into account, solves the problem of transforming and enhancing the author's raw material, text and illustrations, to make a printed book that appeals to book buyers and users alike, and legibly and aesthetically conveys its purpose – whether for leisure, information or education. The drawing element of the job, if any, usually extends only as far as providing blueprints or rough visuals for others (technical illustrators, artists, typesetters, colour originators or printers) to execute.

Good design standards sell books – whether it is the cover attracting an impulse buyer in a shop or a teacher at an exhibition; the display of a contents page stimulating an academic or professional; the effective use of typography and illustrations conveying mood and excitement or pedagogic aims; or the overall feel bringing pleasure to a giver or collector.

Some publishers, especially in the highly illustrated book (including the high quality book packagers) and art book fields are actively design-led. Their design standards are used as a marketing and sales tool internationally.

Designer's tasks in producing a new title

The point at which a designer is first involved with a new book varies. It may occur before or after the author has completed the manuscript, the designer receiving either an edited or unedited copy. By then the book's overall parameters (e.g. format, extent, illustrations, binding, paper) have been planned by the editor and management.

In some firms editors personally brief designers while in others meetings are organized, attended by the production team and sometimes the sales staff. The outcome is a production specification (part of which determines the budget available for design or illustration services), covering the production methods and proof stages to be used, and the time schedule. It is vital for a designer to be given a clear brief by the editor at the outset. A designer may be able to suggest alternative ideas to save money or to improve sales potential. Assuming the book is not part of a fixed format series or that a pre-existing design cannot be adapted to suit it, the designer's opening tasks are to prepare the type specification and page layout which are supplementary to the book's overall production specification.

Type style specification and page layout grid

The type style specification sets out how the main text, hierarchy of headings and sub-headings, displayed quotations, captions, tables, running heads, page numbers etc. should be typeset in respect of typefaces, sizes, line lengths etc. and of the positioning and spacing of the elements. The page layout is a graphic representation of the printed page – invariably of two facing pages. Layouts are based on a grid – the underlying framework within which text and illustrations are placed on the page. Layout and typographic style considerably affect the readers' perception of a book. The two are interdependent and should, if well designed, allow the author's work to be presented consistently and flexibly, taking into account the aims, character, market, and technical and cost constraints of the book.

Factors affecting their development include the fitting of the author's manuscript into the desired extent; the ability of certain typefaces to cope with mathematics or foreign languages, or to ease reading by early or poor-sighted readers; their suitability for reduction if the book is to be reprinted subsequently in a reduced paperback format; and the typefaces available from a supplier etc.

The designer presents one or more designs in the form of mock-ups to the editorial and production staff for their comments and approval; sometimes typeset or DTP specimen pages are produced.

Typographic mark-up

Once the complete manuscript is edited, the designer may carry out the typographic mark-up, that is the addition of typesetting instructions to the manuscript or disk. Some instructions, such as the indication of the heading hierarchy and use of italic or bold within the text, should have been marked in copy-editing. The designer checks, for instance, the editor's hierarchy of headings to ensure they conform to the agreed type specification, and may want them modified. The typesetter follows the specification or style coding. However, depending on the complexity of the material, the designer may indicate the design treatment of recurring text matter which, though covered by the specification, may still need to be marked by using abbreviations or codes. Complex text (including tables) as well as displayed text, such as that of the prelims, may require specific mark-up.

Drawn illustrations

The illustrations may reach the designer before or, more likely, after the author has handed over the manuscript to the publisher. At a much earlier stage, the designer may have briefed the author or supplied the editor with guidelines to help the author prepare drawn illustrations. Designers are usually responsible for commissioning the technical illustrators or artists who execute the final artwork which may be prepared electronically.

When many complex diagrams need to be drawn the designer prepares an artwork specification to serve as a technical reference for illustratiors.

Chosen freelance illustrators or artists are contacted directly, or are recruited from artist's agents or commercial studios. The designer, who may have developed or sometimes revisualized the author's roughs, briefs the contact about the purpose of each illustration and the style of execution (including the final appearing size), gives a deadline for completion; the cost is estimated in advance.

The finished artwork returns. The designer checks that the brief has been followed and that the technical standard of the artwork is suitable for processing and reproduction by the printer. Correction cycles follow until all approve. The designer ensures that mistakes attributable to the illustrator are not charged to the publisher.

Proofing stages

With unillustrated books that go straight to page proofs, the edited and style coded manuscript (together with the type specification and grid) are sent off to the typesetter. But for a book with illustrations grouped on pages, the designer provides a layout. When illustrations are interspersed with the text, the sized artwork and photographs are sent off with the text, or the designer instructs the typesetter to leave specified spaces for the illustrations to be inserted later. During or after the author and editor have read the proofs, the designer fine-tunes the typography and corrects any bad page breaks or layouts.

With illustrated books that go to first text proofs, the designer controls and plans completely the book's layout by means of a manual layout on screen, often using QuarkXpress. The designer may be involved with the final selection of photographs and advises whether they will reproduce well. The layout of a page can affect the choice, and the integration of text and illustration influences the sizes of photographs which may be cropped (changing the fixed size of diagrammatic artwork is often too difficult and expensive). The designer tunes the ensuing page proofs and any illustration proofs, spotting visual errors which authors, editors and printers may fail to recognize.

Highly illustrated colour books

The design approach to such books (e.g. adults' and children's general books sold on the quality of their pictorial content; and some low-level textbooks and ELT courses) differs and is closer to that of quality magazine and partwork publishing – the designer's role is more central. Fundamentally, the interrelationship of the word extent and illustrations, and the positioning of colour within the book is planned and controlled, page by page, from the outset and subsequently through numerous internal proof stages.

Specimen pages of selected double-page spreads are produced to aid authors'/contributors'/editors' writing. Moreover, such material (supplemented with the cover and the book dummy) may be used to interest book clubs and/or overseas publishers in copublication. The designer normally has a greater say over the format, appearance, art direction and creation of the book, which allows more scope to vary its grid and pace, and to provide surprise elements. Some books (including school/ELT texts) use double-page spreads on topics. The strong headlines, dramatic illustrations and extended captions (often read first) capture the interest of a bookshop browser, mail-order buyer, or pupil.

Books for international copublication have special design needs. To gain economies in coprinting (i.e. the printing of two or more editions simultaneously), the colour illustrations should remain unaltered in position, whereas the translations of the text are changed on the presses. Thus the typographic design allows for greater length of foreign languages, chosen typefaces have the full range of accents, type running around illustrations is avoided, type is not reversed-out within colour illustrations, and illustrations are not culturally specific to the UK.

Cover design

The cover or jacket protects the book, identifies author/title/publisher (the ISBN and bar code facilitating ordering), carries the blurb and often the author biography. But its main purpose is to sell. The design should inform as well as attract, be true to the contents, and be tuned to the market. The sales objective of the image is more significant in consumer book publishing (especially paperbacks) than other areas because of the importance of retail impulse purchase; and covers are used by the sales department to sell books well in advance of publication to wholesalers and retailers. The image must be powerful enough to attract a browser to pick the book up within a few seconds, and be clear enough to be reproduced in catalogues of the publisher, of a book club, and of overseas publishers or agents, and on the web sites of the publisher and booksellers.

Printed covers are usually needed three to six months or more ahead of book publication. The designer is briefed at the manuscript editing stage by the commissioning editor and generates rough visuals for approval by the editorial, marketing and sales departments. The chosen image is developed (and illustrators, photographers, picture researchers commissioned if necessary), the copy typeset, the artwork prepared and proofed. Photoshop software may be used but may be avoided. The author may be consulted. Covers arouse strong passions among all participants, and at worst may be revised up to publication.

Skills

Designers usually have a vocational qualification and technical proficiency. Underpinning design is a thorough knowledge of typography and the ways in which books and covers are put together. Designers need perception, clarity of thought, an ability to take a raw manuscript (perhaps badly presented), to analyse it, and come up with an effective design within financial and technical constraints. They should be able to anticipate the problems of readers. It calls for combination of imagination, a knowledge and understanding of current technical processes and current software, awareness of the work of leading freelances and of trends and fashions in book design. For cover design a creative mind is pre-eminent, combined with a gut feeling of what sells.

Designers must develop the ability to extract a brief (tactfully overcoming some editors' quirks and preconceptions) and be able to explain to authors, editors and sales staff (who rarely think in shape, colour and form) how they arrived at a solution, and why it is the best; and they must be able to give clear and unambiguous briefs and instructions to other designers, illustrators, production staff and printers.

Highly illustrated book work requires designers to get under the skin of a subject, to undertake research if necessary, to ask probing questions of experts and to pay due regard to ethnic or cultural sensitivities. The establishment of the all important rapport with in-house staff and external suppliers takes time and experience to develop. The handling of artists, illustrators and photographers, some of whom can be awkward, calls for a special mixture of tact, pleading or coercion to induce them to produce their best work.

Most designers work on many books simultaneously, all at different stages in production. Thus, like editors, they need to be flexible and self-organizing.

PRODUCTION

The publisher's production department is the link between editors and designers and external suppliers. As the publisher's big spender, it buys the materials and services of the suppliers who manufacture the books. Increasingly it manages the electronic pre-press technologies and the digital archive of the publisher's products for print and electronic publication. Before a description of that work, there follows a brief summary of the main book production processes provided by firms in the printing industry at home and abroad.

Book production processes

Typesetting and textprocessing

Typesetting is carried out mainly by specialist firms or by printers. Some pundits thought that the invention of Desk Top Publishing (DTP) would put such firms out of business but this has not happened. Established firms put aside old equipment and high-priced unionized craft labour, and new firms arose sometimes founded in back bedrooms by former employees, sometimes by computer bureaux. Their core business is textprocessing. They offer a range of services. They re-key manuscripts in the conventional way and enact the typography at very low rates (re-keying is sometimes carried out by out-workers in the UK or in the less developed world); translate authors' disks, re-format and correct the inevitable errors; style-code disks supplied, including SGML and XML in selected cases; transfer onerous editorial corrections from the hardcopy to disk; or merely produce the paginated output from fully coded disks supplied. Some firms offer additional editorial and design services while others concentrate on highly technical material or text database management. The vast number of titles with no or minimal illustrations do not require designers to layout the pages – the typesetters' largely automated pagination systems do it for the publishers. Typesetters can generally re-key a 100 000 word manuscript and submit page proofs to a publisher within six weeks, much faster if supplied with style-coded disks.

The typesetters use various Post Script-based programmes, the successors to the DTP programs, such as QuarkXpress (pronounced quork), PageMaker and Framemaker for the pagination. Only typesetters who have the specialist-trained staff usually operate the very expensive and sophisticated programs such as Quoin and 3B2, designed especially for academic/STM books and journals. LaTex (TeX), pronounced laytek and tec, is a free open source program with many variants designed by mathematicians in Chicago for authors of physics and maths to present their papers and books full of equations in an attractive way. (Some publishers employ maths graduate production editors to operate it.)

After the publisher has approved the proofs, typesetters may be asked to supply the paginated output on to photographic paper called bromide – the camera-ready-copy (CRC) from which the printer makes the printing plates; or if the book contains illustrations which demand a better quality of reproduction, on to film. However, further technical advances in the printing industry in respect of the way printers make their printing plates, may cause the publisher to ask the typesetter to convert the output of its pagination systems into PostScript (PS) files (Adobe's page description language) or Portable Document Format (PDF) files and to supply a voucher proof (or press proof) for the printer. From such files printers may either output them on to film or go straight to plate. The voucher proof, produced by the typesetter, is yet another check for the publisher to ensure that the digital files combining both the typography and illustrations have been converted correctly (or not), and is a reference to guide the printer.

Reproduction of illustrations

Originals of illustrations are converted to digital form by a 'repro-duction (repro) house' or a by a typesetter or a printer, to sizes specified by the designer, or by the designer, or are already in digital form supplied by sources.

Book printing presses cannot reproduce directly the continuous shades or tones of grey appearing in monochrome photographs, pencil drawings etc., thus 'the half-tone process' is used. The image of the original is screened, i.e. broken into hundreds of dots of varying size (larger, closer or adjoining dots in dark areas; smaller, further apart, or no dots at all in light areas) which, when printed in black ink only, create the illusion of continuous shades. An electronic scanner digitizes the image and produces the 'screened' effect.

In order to print full colour photographs or paintings, the press carries four plates, each inked with one of the basic colours: cyan (a blue); pure yellow; magenta (a pinkish red), and black (termed as CYMK). In combination these produce the illusion of full colour. 'Four-colour printing' dictates that the colour originals be separated into the four basic colours and screened. A scanner produces the four screened images for each illustration.

Various kinds of proofs are submitted to the publisher before the final digital file of the illustrations is accepted.

Imposition and platemaking

The printing plates on a press do not print one page at a time. Rather each sheet of paper, printed both sides, carries 8, 16 or 32 pages (or multiples of these), and is subsequently folded several times and cut to make a section (or signature) of the bound book. Since printers have different plate sizes on their presses and different binding machinery, each printer is responsible for its own imposition: the arrangement of the pages that will be printed on each side of the sheet so that once the sheet is printed and folded the pages will be in the right sequence and position.

Printers impose the pages on to each plate in several ways. The publisher may supply the printer with individual pages of CRC or of film for the printer to impose on each printing plate; or supply it with digital files such as PS or PDF files on a disk. From whichever source the printer may make one large piece of film of the imposed pages that will be exposed on to the plate from which one side of each sheet will be printed. But printers increasingly want to cut out the intervening film stage and go directly from Computer to Plate (CTP), again typically using PDF files as their usual origination method.

PDF files can be conveniently put on the web for either downloading or viewing within a browser. The user sees a replica of the final printed page. Electronic journal articles are often presented in PDF format for the ease of librarians and others wanting a common standard, and of the publishers developing from print-designed documents. However, for publishers not starting from such a legacy the web is a different medium needing different design approaches *not based* on print-based linear textual organization and typographic design.

Printing

Most books are printed by offset lithography (abbreviated to litho). Lithographic metal plates have a smooth surface which is so treated that the image areas to be printed attract grease (ink) and repel water; and the non-printing areas attract water and repel ink. A plate is clamped around a cylinder on the press, dampened and inked by rollers. The plate rotates against a cylindrical rubber blanket on to which the inked image is offset (printed) and from which the ink is transferred to the paper.

Many rotary offset presses are sheet-fed and vary in plate size and in capabilities: e.g. print only one colour on one side of a sheet during one pass of the paper; print a single colour on each side of the sheet during one pass (perfector machines); print two or four colours on one side during each pass etc. There are also offset presses that print on to reels, not sheets, of paper termed 'web' fed.

Binding and finishing

After printing, the sheets are folded by the printer or possibly by a binding firm. The folded 8, 16 or 32 page sections are collated in sequence to make up every book.

Some hardbacks and some quality paperbacks, especially those printed on coated papers (including some textbooks) have their sections sewn together. With quality hardbacks, the sewn sections are trimmed on three sides (leaving the sewn spine folds intact), end papers are glued to the first and last sections (unless the text paper is sufficiently strong), any decorative head or tail bands added, strong material glued to the spine to reinforce the hinge with the case, and the spine sometimes rounded. Meanwhile the case is made by gluing the front and back boards (and paper backstrip of the spine) to the 'cloth' which in turn is stamped with title/author/publisher etc. The outer sides of the end papers are pasted, the finished case dropped over the book (spine-side up), and the book squeezed. The jacket (printed on a small colour press, sometimes by another firm) is often laminated with clear plastic film and wraps the finished book. Sometimes the printed cover is glued to the case before binding, called a 'paper cased' edition.

Adhesive binding methods are increasingly used (instead of the more expensive and stronger sewing) for paperbacks and some hardbacks. With 'perfect binding' (used typically for cheap paperbacks) the spine folds of the sections are cut off and the spine edge of the now individual leaves roughened. Glue is applied to hold the leaves together and to stick the printed cover to the book, which is then trimmed on three sides. The cover may have been varnished (on a printing press or special machine) or laminated. Other methods, cheaper than sewing but stronger and more expensive than perfect binding, are 'notch' or 'burst' bindings. With these, the spine folds of the sections are not cut off. Instead they are perforated during sheet folding. The perfect binding machine merely injects the adhesive to hold together the folded sections, applies the cover and trims the book. Further developments in adhesive technology may avoid the costly sewing of books printed on coated papers.

The printer/binder packs quantities of the book by shrink wrapping, parcelling or in cartons and delivers them on pallets to the publisher's specified warehouse.

Manufacturing developments

Publishers want to conserve their cash by ordering just sufficient quantities of books to meet expected demand. If a book is selling well, they need to replenish stock quickly: with fast-moving consumer books within one week. If a specialist book has sold out its first printing after a year or so, they need to be able to reprint it in small quantities economically. Traditional book printing was characterized by much skilled hand work in assembly, imposing the film, and making the plates. There were many stop/start processes. The 'make-ready' on the printing press involved loading the plate and paper, inking the plate and running trial copies to attain quality. On a press which prints 5000 sheets per hour the make-ready consumed a high proportion of the time taken. In the bindery there were free-standing folding and collating machines, lines of women operating sewing machines, guillotines, and men humping paper from one machine to another. But modern printers are capital-intensive. They need to streamline and integrate the process, reduce labour, and have machines turning with the minimum of make-ready time. Advances in the manufacturing of books include greater automation in imposition, CTP, reduction in press machine make-ready time, control of inking by electronic monitoring, and the integration of binding machinery.

Such advances increase the speed and lower the cost of the litho printing and binding of books and journals. Most importantly, from a publisher's viewpoint, they have led to lower unit costs on lower print runs. Publishers are thus more able to reduce the print quantities of first printings (thereby reducing the risk of being stuck with copies destined for the pulp mill); and to reprint those titles which continue to sell in smaller quantities, more frequently.

However, high-speed digital printing is beginning to challenge litho printing, particularly on very short runs. It facilitates the viability of printing a book on a very short run of say 50 or so copies, or of printing on demand just one copy ordered by a customer. In the mid-1990s the first generation of these machines, such as the Rank Xerox DocuTech and IBM Infoprint, printed on single sheets of paper and accepted hardcopy input (which is scanned in), or preferably digital input of the paged document. They were designed primarily for use in the reprographic units of large organizations and could be run by just one person. The second-generation machines developed in the late 1990s were faster and printed many pages at a time on web-fed paper, which is folded and cut to make the printed sections of the document. These machines print only monochrome and reproduce photographs rather poorly. But in due course digital printing is expected to reproduce full colour and photographs.

Digital printing was first used from the late 1990s by some of the high-level academic and STM publishers issuing high priced monochrome titles, such as monographs in standard sizes. After the initial printing (probably litho printed), such publishers may face a small but continuing demand. Thus they may reprint a short run by litho or digital printing (whichever gives the lower unit cost), or a very short run by digital printing to hold in stock if that is thought worthwhile, or digitally print one copy in response to a firm order. Once the title has moved to 'on-demand' status it need never go 'out-of-print'.

The large bookselling chains and distributors may also use digital printing to produce copies for end-users from digital files supplied by publishers. The printing of hardcopies becomes 'distributed' as opposed to being centralized by publishers through their own print suppliers. For instance, the bookseller may customize for a teacher a pack of teaching resources drawn from a variety of publishers for student purchase.

Publishers' production departments

Production is closely related to book design. Production staff may design the books or hire freelance designers, or in-house book designers report to the head of production; or there is a separate design department. The production department gives the accounts department information on anticipated costs and their likely timing, details of work in progress, and materials held in stock.

In a small firm an editor may carry out production duties or use freelances or external companies which provide a production service; but with increasing size a firm will employ production specialists. Within a department, there are commonly three main levels of job.

- A production manager/director is responsible for the purchasing policy on sources of supply; establishing standard book sizes and papers; controlling the flow of work and maintaining quality standards; contributing to the preparation of the publishing programme by planning schedules and cost budgets for forthcoming books; and responding to major technical changes such as managing the electronic pre-press services. This manager contributes to the firm's profitability by buying materials and services at the least possible cost, by conserving the firm's cash by influencing the timing of major items of expenditure and by obtaining the longest possible credit periods from suppliers. The manager also handles the production of certain important books.
- A production controller is responsible for seeing books through the production stages from manuscript to receipt of bound copies. He or she may or may not specialize in part of the list, e.g. illustrated or non-illustrated, technical or non-technical books.
- A production assistant/secretary gives clerical or administrative support to the department by typing, answering the phone, moving proofs around, keeping an eye on the schedules, and telephoning suppliers; and/or by looking after the records, keeping invoices in ledgers and recording production costings etc. Some people start their production careers at this level.

In some publishers, however, the above division of labour has been changed. Production activities are split. One section attends to the electronic pre-press process: essentially concerned with originating the products with external suppliers, or creating them in-house, or both; and with the maintenance of the digital archive and its internal and external connections. Another section purchases the manufacturing of books and journals: essentially from printers and paper suppliers; and sometimes of other non-print items, such as silver disks, audio and videocassettes and their packaging.

Provisional estimates

The production manager (or an automated costing system) supplies the commissioning editor with estimates of the costs of producing a proposed new title, and may suggest alternative production options. The book is envisaged in broad terms (e.g. format, extent, illustrative content, quality desired, binding style). The estimate summarizes the costs of typesetting, of any illustrations, of the cover design, origination, printing of the text and cover and binding (inclusive of paper and materials) and enables the costing of different print runs.

Once the author has signed the contract, production may advise the author, directly or via the editor, on how the manuscript should be keyed on a wordprocessor so that if appropriate the text can be handled electronically. Some publishers issue authors with style sheets or templates.

Preparing the specification

Once the publisher has accepted the manuscript, a cast-off (an estimate of the printed page extent) may be done in the production, design or editorial departments, or by a typesetter. The production controller, who gathers information from the editor or from pre-production meetings, prepares a specification (i.e. a detailed technical description of the book).

The book's desired physical attributes, the amount of money and time available for its production, its destination (home and abroad) and any special market needs (e.g. particular typefaces, a subsequent paperback edition or co-edition) are taken into account, and the choice of production processes and of materials is made.

Requesting quotations: print and paper buying

The same clear and unambiguous specification is sent to one or more suppliers who have the right machinery so that they can tender quotations (i.e. a definite price). Although there are printers that carry out all the processes, they may not do all economically or well. Thus, textprocessing, illustration reproduction, and printing/binding specifications may be sent to specialist firms.

A publisher deals with a core of regular and trusted suppliers whose machinery, staff, strengths and weaknesses are known; but new ones are tried. Sometimes price schedules are negotiated with major print suppliers for standard types of work, which reduces the need for quotations and simplifies estimating. Suppliers may quote discounts on titles processed in batches or during slack periods. Moreover, the long time (e.g. six to eighteen months) books take to produce gives publishers and packagers the option of using overseas suppliers (e.g. in Europe, the Far East or the USA). Most colour book printing now goes abroad. The competitiveness of overseas suppliers vis à vis the UK, is affected greatly by exchange rates, but other factors such as freight and communication costs, longer timescales, and the book's final destination are considered.

Suppliers are assessed on three main criteria: price; quality of work; and service (e.g. ability to keep to dates, or to make up for slippage, and communication). The priority given to each varies by title. For example, a small saving from the cheapest source may be outweighed if that supplier produces inferior work or misses dates.

The quotations are assessed, prices sometimes negotiated downwards and the work awarded. From the quoted prices, another in-house estimate is prepared for management.

Paper is a major cost item and is bought either by the printer, or by the publisher from a paper merchant or directly from a mill. Pulp and paper is a world commodity subject to exchange rates and to price instability. For example, during the 1990s the price of most grades of book papers remained virtually static, apart from a surge in price in 1995 of around 30–40% which was partly accounted for by SE Asian demand, and probable fictitious stories about worldwide shortages. The ensuing actual slump in demand, over capacity at the mills and the appreciation of sterling caused prices to fall back towards the 1988 levels. During periods of price instability or of real or imagined shortages, publishers may peg the price by buying forward, or store paper as an insurance against non-availability for quick reprints, even though that ties up the publisher's cash and incurs storage costs. Some publishers are responsive to environmental concerns, such as purchasing paper derived from sustainable forests and made with minimum pollutants, and others use acid free materials to ensure their books last an eternity, but not in their warehouses.

Scheduling and progressing the book

The controller draws up the time schedule of the internal and external operations that end with the delivery of bound copies to the warehouse a few weeks ahead of the publication date. The schedule, related to those of other books, takes account of any optimum publication date, cashflow demands, the time needed for the tasks and to route material to and from suppliers.

Production staff record progress and chase editors (who chase authors), designers and external suppliers to keep to agreed (or revised) dates. As all the book's material passes between editor and designer, and between publisher and suppliers it is routed via production at every stage, as are editor's and designer's problems with suppliers. Outgoing material is accompanied by documentation and orders, incoming material is logged, and return dates given to editors and designers. If the return dates are not adhered to, the machine time booked at the printers will be missed and the book unduly delayed.

In some of the electronically advanced publishers, the pre-press processes are carried out in-house and the documents progress through the stages and staff entirely in digital form. Document management systems monitor the movement of jobs through the stages, and the work loads and performance of staff, against the targets.

Monitoring costs and quality

Some books, especially if illustrated, change during author writing and production. Deviations from the original estimate and specification (on which the book was judged to be viable) are monitored and costed. There is a constant danger that the estimate of costs made at the outset will be exceeded. Substantial proof corrections quickly erode a title's profitability. Costs incurred to date are recorded and revised estimates of total costs produced, particularly at the page-proof stage. Then the publisher normally fixes the book's retail price and the number to be printed influenced, for example, by the actual advance subscription orders from booksellers. Suppliers' invoices are subsequently checked, queried, or passed for payment.

The controller checks completeness of material at every stage as well as the accuracy of editor's and designer's instructions and the perfection of illustration originals sent to suppliers; and, conversely, the quality of material returned from suppliers. Technical advice is given to editors and designers to help them in their work. Constant contact with suppliers' representatives, and visits to suppliers maintain relationships.

Highly illustrated quality colour books may involve the production manager or controller in approving the first sheets of each section run off the press – whether in the UK or abroad – and taking responsibility for the quality on behalf of the publisher/packager. The printing is compared against the final proof to ensure that corrections have been made, and against the colour proofs.

Advance copies of the bound stock are checked to ensure that the specified materials have been used, and printing and binding are acceptable. Exceptionally if a major error is discovered, an enquiry is held to determine who is to blame and who is to pay. Finally, all the costs of producing the book are compiled.

Other production work

Controllers also cost and organize reprints and new editions; some large publishers employ staff solely for this task. The publisher or packager owning the digital file or film does not always use the original printer in which case the job is moved to the new supplier.

Electronic pre-press technologies are changing fast as are the opportunities for e-publishing in various forms. Production plays a key role in their introduction and in ensuring that the publisher's titles are archived in suitable digital form to facilitate their exploitation.

The printing of editions for other firms (e.g. book clubs, English and foreign language publishers) involves supplying the rights department with estimates of costs. The costs will include printing the bulk order – or if the buyer does the printing, the cost of making duplicate film or digital files – and costs of imprint changes – for example, the name of the co-publisher will have to appear on the title page instead of the original publisher's and the details on the copyright page will change; all of this makes a halt in the printing and costs money. When the publisher or packager prints foreign language editions, the overseas publishers supply the typeset film or file of the translations which is checked by production to ensure it fits the layout of the colour illustrations.

Production staff may also be concerned with the purchasing of the manufacturing of non-print items and their special retail or mail-order packaging requirements.

Skills

Most production staff now have a vocational qualification or equivalent professional background. Fundamental to production is a thorough understanding of current technical processes, of machinery and of materials (their advantages and disadvantages) and, in international buying, of freight systems and methods of payment. (A knowledge of German or French is useful in a department handling international co-editions.) Numeracy, computer literacy skills, the conception of alternative options and the consideration of all components are necessary in costing titles; as are planning and progress chasing skills (e.g. ascertaining and clarifying objectives, setting priorities, assessing strengths and weaknesses of colleagues/suppliers, foreseeing crunch points) to the development of specifications and schedules.

Effective and fluent communication (face-to-face, on the telephone and in writing) with in-house staff and external suppliers is crucial. Production staff must be able to work with editors and designers as a team even though their priorities of tight cost control and the maintenance of dates may conflict with those of editors and designers.

The work is highly administrative, thus requires a good memory and meticulous attention to detail and record keeping. While friendly working relationships are formed with suppliers, production staff must never get too close to suppliers (otherwise the negotiating edge is lost) and sometimes have to be very tough. They must have the integrity to reject bribes offered by some suppliers.

Production staff come under great pressure. As the buffer between publisher and suppliers they receive kicks from all sides. They must buy competitively, conserve the cash, meet the deadlines, and not make mistakes (which in this area are very expensive to correct). Much time is spent troubleshooting and trying to keep everyone happy. They need to resolve problems, to think laterally and find the best solution, to switch quickly from one thing to another, and thrive under the strain; and to have the constitution of an ox to withstand suppliers' hospitality – still generous.

PUBLICITY AND PROMOTION, AND
MAIL-ORDER SALES

The aim of this department is to make the media, book trade, and consumers conscious of the company and the wares it offers; and to stimulate demand. The promotional material produced and the interest generated help the sales staff to sell to the book trade (or to schools or colleges) and the rights staff to their customers. Home and overseas customers use the promotional material as a reference source for ordering. Public relations (PR) includes generating free publicity and furthering a company's good image with authors and the media.

The manager of this department usually reports to the marketing/sales director. Many departments consist of just one or two people who do everything, but in medium to large firms there are usually three levels: manager, publicity or promotion controllers who carry through the publicity/promotion campaigns for individual books, branded series, and assistants.

Staff in large publishing groups may be attached to particular firms or imprints or lists in the group, concerned with adult or children's publishing; or with educational, ELT, academic, or professional book publishing etc. The work may be divided by task. In some publishers, especially consumer, specialists deal solely with public relations (e.g. called 'press officers'), or with the development of promotional and point-of-sale (POS) material and catalogues, or with space advertising or copywriting; or in some academic and professional book publishers with textbooks, mail-order sales or journal promotion. Publishers of all kinds also hire advertising agencies (especially for major projects or authors), freelance publicists, direct mail and web site specialists etc. While in-house designers and production staff are sometimes used, publicity and promotion staff make extensive use of DTP and may commission freelance designers and buy print themselves because these suppliers are not those producing the books.

Publicity and promotion encompass numerous, diverse activities. The publicity manager may first become involved at the publishing proposal stage or immediately post-contract. From discussions with editors and sales staff, each book is evaluated and decisions made on the promotional material (and any advertisements) required, and what publicity and media coverage might be sought. The (usually small) promotion budget set may be proportional to the expected sales revenue. It is impossible to promote all books equally and, especially in consumer book and textbook publishing, the lead titles receive by far the largest budgets. The key judgement on every title lies in deciding how much to spend to generate profitable sales that more than recoup the outlay.

Before a review of specific techniques, a basic strategy used on most new books follows preceded by the effects of the internet.

The impact of the internet

At the start of the century many publishers' web sites were in early stages of development and were beginning to perform a range of functions. For example, those that delivered content online were present in the advanced professional and journal publishers (charged-for content), or on sites linked with textbooks (free or password-protected). Some of these publishers established associated computing conference and updating facilities for professional groups, ranging from school teachers to high level research communities, mainly the latter. However, for most book publishers their sites at the outset performed the direct marketing function of providing information on their titles, in effect an extension of their print-based promotion system, increasingly with an online facility for ordering printed books and as a prelude to ordering e-books.

This core function addresses three audiences, modified as appropriate. It supplies title information to the publisher's own employees on the firm's intranet; to the businesses with which the publishers trade – variously called business to business (B2B) or password protected extranet connections; and it promotes the publisher's presence publicly on the internet (including if relevant corporate information to attract investors), with links from other relevant sites.

The internet marketing function usually includes at the basic level, listing (with or without an image of the book's cover) each title's bibliographic and author information, table of contents, plus possible sample material, such as the introduction. (A few publishers put the entire content of their books on the web for free – early examples were the *Rough Guides* – and claim that it stimulates printed book sales, but most publishers think otherwise.) Such product information can also be conveyed to other businesses in the supply chain, such as to the merchandising editors of the internet booksellers. Some publishers in the consumer field embellish their web pages, for example with author interviews and interactive material, such as activities or games linked to particular books or childrens' characters.

Publishers of consumer books written by brand-name authors face the challenge that their imprint name is a sub-brand to that of their authors in the public's mind. In order to co-ordinate the promotion, such publishers may offer to host their authors' web sites. Arguably, the greatest potential for internet marketing may be for the niche publishers both large and small. They may establish specialist interest, internet communities around their titles to whom they can directly sell their titles. For some of the well-known academic and specialist publishers, direct sales of their books from their web sites grew quickly, along with sales via internet booksellers.

It used to be said that publishers' brand names were in themselves of little consequence to sales in that readers do not select books on the name of the publisher. The general public's recognition of publishers is weak indeed, apart from some exceptions such as Penguin. Their names were and are, however, important to their business connections – to agents, authors and to the book trade intermediaries – and to media relations. Branding is used to good effect on book series, for instance in language learning, travel and computing guides, and in children's publishing especially. Now it can be argued that in the internet world over supplied with information of uncertain provenance, publisher branding might assume greater significance in conveying quality assured products and services.

A basic promotion strategy

Around manuscript delivery, the author completes a questionnaire. It returns via the editor. The author supplies personal information, a biography, a blurb, a short synopsis, the book's main selling points and intended readership or applicability to courses, lists of print and broadcast media (and individuals) that might review or publicize the book etc.

Advance information sheet

The promotion controller prepares the book's advance information (AI) sheet and its electronic equivalent which contains bibliographic information (e.g. title, author, format, extent, illustrative content, hardback/paperback, ISBN, planned price and publication date); synopsis/blurb/contents; main selling points, market profile; author biography etc. It is mailed, say, three to nine months ahead of publication to all the people who help sell the book: the publisher's sales force and overseas agents, booksellers, whole-salers, and library suppliers etc. Wholesalers and library suppliers need the information (at least three months in advance) to enter the title in their catalogues and online databases to secure advance orders.

Cover

The cover is another promotional item used by the publisher's home and export sales departments, some library suppliers, internet booksellers and overseas agents. It is produced preferably well ahead of publication. The cover blurb is written or re-written by the editor, by the controller, or by an in-house or freelance copy-writer.

Catalogues

Catalogue preparation is a major task: it involves a controller in gathering information from all round the firm, updating it, collecting illustrations, copywriting, briefing a designer, sometimes print buying, and carrying through all the production stages, as well as database management.

The maintenance of the publisher's in-house title database includes the titles' current status (e.g. future or actual publication dates, whether it is reprinting or out-of-print), current prices, the coding of a title by product category or subject, and additional information on each title built up over time (such as long and short promotional and contents copy, and reviews received). Further extensions, especially in consumer publishing, relate to contractual matters, such as rights held, rights available for sale or licensed to others, supplied by the contracts and rights department. The advantage of such a database is that it is a central depository of definitive information about the publisher's titles. It allows the publisher to retrieve and manipulate information in forms most suited to the intermediaries and end-users, in print and online.

The twin aims of catalogues are to present the firm and its products attractively so that buyers (the book trade and consumers) select its wares; and to act as an informative, readily understandable and accurate reference so that products can be ordered easily through the supply chain at home and abroad.

Consumer book publishers normally produce catalogues announcing their forthcoming books geared to their six monthly marketing/selling cycles, the autumn/winter catalogue appearing in time for the preceding mid-summer sales conference, the spring/summer catalogue appearing for the preceding Christmas sales conference. Consumer publishers following the tradition of paperback promotion issue monthly catalogues or stocklists about three months ahead of the publication month covered. Catalogues are distributed to all members of the supply chain and to main libraries, to the public (e.g. via booksellers to account customers), and to review editors and the media. The stocklists covering new and backlist books and their prices which accompany catalogues are used by the publisher's reps and the book trade for ordering.

Educational, academic, STM and professional publishers usually arrange their catalogues by subject or by groups of allied subjects. Different subject catalogues may be produced for different levels of the education system and books within a textbook catalogue (which includes selected backlist) may be arranged or classified by the age group, or examination or academic level served. Catalogues are produced annually to cover the following year's publications, or six-monthly or more frequently. Although the catalogues are mailed to selected booksellers, they are aimed primarily at teachers/academics/professionals – those who decide to purchase or adopt the books – and are distributed to schools or academic libraries, institutions, departments (and where appropriate to targeted subject specialists or professionals, and to industry).

Publishers also produce, say annually, complete catalogues containing summary information on all new and backlist titles. As the main reference source of the publisher's output, it is used by the book trade, libraries and others at home and overseas, even though the information may be available on the publisher's web site.

Bibliographies

Giving the main bibliographers accurate information on each new title (and updated prices) at the right time is essential. It promotes the book worldwide cheaply, and facilitates its ordering through the supply chain. There are two main commercial suppliers of bibliographic information to the book trade (terrestrial and internet), and to libraries etc. Information given to long-established Whitaker at least three months ahead of publication lists the title in the week of publication in *The Bookseller*, and on Whitaker's electronic databases. Its main competitor is Book Data founded in 1997, which built its business on supplying bibliographic information enhanced with additional information provided by the commercial publishers. It used to be said that Whitaker had greater and more comprehensive title coverage, while Book Data offered greater depth on a more limited range of titles. However, competition between them has eroded that view. Both companies have established international links, for example Whitaker with the US bibliographer Bowker, and Book Data with the US library supplier Baker and Taylor.

The statutory obligation to send six gratis copies to the copyright libraries, ensures that the title is listed in the weekly additions to the *British National Bibliography* (BNB) and alerts the libraries. The advantage of sending the British Library and the Library of Congress information earlier so that they can prepare the Cataloguing in Publication (CIP) entries is that the book is listed in their bibliographies sooner (especially important for academic and STM titles).

Reviews

Once bound copies are received, a review list is prepared, tailor-made for the title, taking account of the author's ideas and contacts. The review copies are sent out with a review slip which details the title, author, price, binding, ISBN and publication date, and requests a review. Any reviews received are circulated in-house and to the author.

Additional publicity and promotion techniques

Free publicity and public relations

Engineering free publicity in the print and broadcast media is more important in consumer book publishing than in any other, and spreads word-of-mouth knowledge about the book. On some major titles prior to contract, the publisher's innovatory publicity ideas (and promotional spend) may win them the author against competitors. The publicist is in constant contact with press and magazine editors, journalists, radio and television producers. With so many books and authors competing for media space, a book or author (especially fiction and non-fiction writers) has to be carefully positioned in the market place. At the manuscript stage, the publicist targets the market, and formulates a publicity plan. A key part of the task is identifying the appropriate media (e.g. particular newspapers and magazines, programmes) that would be interested and helping them make their decisions. Book publicity departments are in effect extensions of the media and the media become part of the PR machine. The stimulated coverage should occur around publication. Coverage is gained from features, author promotions which authors may be contractually obliged to fulfil (e.g. tours, signing sessions, radio and television appearances), press releases, parties etc. Signing sessions, competitions for booksellers, and joint promotions with booksellers, especially the main chains, are arranged in close conjunction with the sales department. Sales staff are warned about any impending coverage so that they can inform the booksellers who are thus more likely to stock the book which in turn sells more copies. Major TV or film tie-in titles (adults' and children's) receive cross-media promotion involving the link-up between the publisher and the media company for mutual benefit.

Other publicity involves informing the trade press (*The Bookseller* and *Publishing News*) about the firm, distributing bound proof copies to influential people, entering titles for literary prizes, helping to plan and attend exhibitions (including the publisher's own sales conferences), maintaining contact with The Publishers Association, the Book Trust and the British Council (all of which promote books) and sometimes answering queries from the public, teachers, librarians and booksellers.

Serial rights

In consumer book publishing, publicity staff instead of the rights department may sell serial rights to their contacts in the press and magazines. Extracts or serials should appear around book publication and produce income and publicity.

Point-of-sale material

Eye-catching material (e.g. posters, display kits, copy holders, brochures, badges etc.) is designed to focus booksellers' and readers' attention on major books, series or brand imprints; to make shops more enticing; and to capture display space, at home and abroad. Produced mainly for consumer books (but sometimes for major reference books and textbooks), most is declined or thrown away by booksellers. Nevertheless, it shows the publisher's commitment to the book and assists advance selling to the book trade and customers abroad.

A publisher may provide major retailers with spinners or special shelving to display its books, though competitors' titles may creep in.

Media advertising

For most books, the high cost of advertising in the press, magazines, or on television or radio, or by poster would not be recouped by the sales generated. Thus it is used very selectively, and short-lived large-scale consumer advertising is restricted to major consumer books, revision aids and reference books etc. Although its effectiveness is intangible, it encourages the book trade to buy and display the book and pleases authors and agents. Consumer book publishers also advertise to the book trade in *The Bookseller* or *Publishing News* – any advertisement appearing two to four months ahead of book publication so that the sales force has time to back it up.

The non-consumer book publishers advertise very selectively in specialist magazines, and journals (especially their own) – ostensibly to sell books, but also to please authors and attract new ones.

The main tasks involved in advertising are conceiving selling ideas from editorial concepts, relating advertising to the other promotions, copywriting and visualizing with a designer, media planning, negotiating the best rates and positions, and maintaining tight budgetary control.

Direct mail promotion

The preparation and mailing of brochures or leaflets advertising a major title, or allied titles, direct to targeted specialist audiences at their place of work forms a large part of the work of promotion controllers in educational, academic, STM and professional book and journal publishers. Together with mailed subject catalogues (and to some extent reviews) it is the main promotional means by which teachers/academics/professionals and librarians learn about new titles and (for textbooks and journals) about backlist titles (monographs are normally promoted only once). Together with the editor, the promotion controller works out the scope of the market, the best approach, what kind of mailing piece is appropriate including e-mail, the time it should be distributed and to whom, i.e. which mailing list to use, within the allocated budget.

The controller writes the copy, often designs it, and carries through the production stages. While publishers keep their own mailing lists, lists are acquired from associations and conference organizers, other publishers or are selected and rented from specialist mailing houses which may distribute the material. Depending on the export arrangements, material may be mailed direct to libraries, teachers, academics and booksellers in selected countries.

Textbook inspection copy service

Teachers and academics are unlikely to prescribe a book for student use unless they have examined a copy first. Titles (e.g. textbooks and children's books) that are expected to be ordered in bulk for schools or placed on a reading list of books which students should buy (excluding monographs and professional reference titles) are marked on catalogues/leaflets, which contain inspection copy order forms. The teacher, having placed the order, completes a reply card (enclosed with the book) which asks for comments on the suitability of the book; and if the book is adopted, the number of students on the course and the name of the supplier. If adopted, the recipient keeps the book free; if not, pays for it or returns it. The results and response rates are used for market research. In tertiary publishing the information is passed to the sales staff who alert the booksellers through which the books are purchased. Lecturers' reading lists, which may be available on the internet, are the key determinant in student's choice of books, though one-third of students purchase books not on reading lists (according to the PA's 1998 survey). In school textbook publishing the UK schools ordering class sets directly are recorded. Textbook publishers of all levels build databases of adoptions (e.g. institution, course, student numbers) for subsequent follow-up and targeting.

Some publishers send unsolicited free copies of textbooks to influential teachers.

Mail-order sales and direct marketing

Most books are sold via booksellers to end users. Some booksellers, especially the specialist, sell by mail order and may produce catalogues. The book clubs (general interest and specialist) and internet booksellers are the main mail-order channels. But some publishers sell a proportion, or indeed a major proportion of their products directly to end-users.

In the consumer market Reader's Digest is best known for its large scale direct marketing campaigns. There are a few publishers which sell directly into people's workplaces and homes via agents who display their products and distribute brochures soliciting orders through the agent, on which they earn a commission. The publishers of high priced reference/loose leaf/online works sell directly to defined professional markets (e.g. legal, accountancy, finance and business), though some of their products, such as books, pass through booksellers and library suppliers. The academic and STM publishers likewise actively solicit direct orders of high level books from academics/scientists/professionals to supplement the majority of sales via the book trade. The learned journal publishers promote their journals directly to researchers and librarians primarily to secure institutional subscriptions from libraries (fulfilled mainly via subscription agents). However, journal publishers also offer subscriptions at much lower rates for personal use, which are supplied directly. Their aim is to turn personal subscriptions into full priced institutional subscriptions. The school market is ideal for direct marketing and selling of books and new media with its fixed locations, with teachers who do not look outwardly to select products, who are poorly organized and 'non-commercial', who need to examine products before they decide to buy, and who buy multiple copies with repeat purchases, and who pay eventually. Most consumer publishers, on the other hand, rarely solicit direct orders because most are unable to identify readers and addresses, and many of their books are priced for the retail outlets, too low for their distribution systems to supply one paperback book cost effectively by mail order.

The greater a publisher's reliance on bookshop sales, the greater the pressure from booksellers against the publisher's use of direct marketing: some booksellers believe it erodes their business. However, paradoxically, it leads to increased sales (the echo effect) through booksellers or library suppliers – people in organizations who are prompted to buy raise an internal Purchase Request which passes to the library or central purchasing office which orders the goods from a consolidating intermediary.

The direct marketing vehicle may be a space advertisement, an insert in a magazine or book, or a mailed item (a catalogue or leaflet and personalized letter) or an e-mail. Whatever the means, the promotion controller encourages direct purchase (sometimes by special offers) and includes a response facility which eases ordering and payment (e.g. by freepost, telephone, fax and credit card) or which may facilitate, for example, a journal subscription via the library. By assessing the response rates, direct marketing allows the statistical testing of the effectiveness of different offers and creative approaches (such as the design of the envelope, letter and leaflet), their timing and frequency, and of the vehicle.

The main vehicle is usually direct mail – the extension of direct mail promotion described above – giving much space for the message at little extra cost. The mailing list (ideally up-to-date, accurate and appropriate for the product) is of prime importance. List brokers may be used, lists are rented or acquired free, and are tested initially. Lists may be gathered from firms which specialize in constructing lists in educational, academic and professional areas, from associations, journal subscribers, conference delegates etc. and from authors. In time the best lists are the publisher's own, built from successive sales and recorded and coded into the publisher's own database. Sometimes they are rented from, or to, other publishers. The most likely customers are targeted regularly with the most appropriate titles, and varying amounts are spent to acquire and keep different levels of customer.

Direct marketing sells books quickly (most feedback is usually in weeks, not many months) and a response rate of 1 or 2 per cent would be thought a success, though rates of up to 5, 10 or 15 per cent plus are possible. But if poorly executed much money can be lost even though the books are sold at full price or at modest discount.

Telemarketing, by a publisher's own staff or by a retained agency, is sometimes used to follow up a mailshot, for example, to reach teachers and professionals at their place of work. However, it plays a relatively minor part in the marketing mix.

Export promotion

The promotional items (catalogues, leaflets, POS material) are distributed abroad, usually unaltered, but may be prepared especially for overseas agents and booksellers, such as in ELT, academic/STM and professional fields.

Children's publishing

Children's books, reaching a general retail market, libraries and schools, combine the techniques of general and educational publishing. The publicist creates and mails the catalogues etc. (distributed to the book trade, schools and libraries), generates free publicity (e.g. through author promotions), organizes exhibitions, attends conferences and liaises with schools and libraries; and, unusually, may dress up as a large, ungainly creature for a delighted audience.

Skills

Overall, an interest in the firm's books and the ability to identify the editorial reasoning and sales potential is necessary. Creativity is needed in originating ideas for promoting a wide range of titles, as well as an understanding of the relationships between costs and expected sales in maximizing the profit potential of each title, within budget.

Good personal relations inside the company (particularly with editors) and outside the company are vital, as are administrative and planning skills.

The development of promotional material engages copywriting (which can be learnt by literate people who appreciate the different styles demanded for different lists and books), editorial, production and DTP skills. In direct mail promotion or selling a controller acts like a detective (working out where the people are and how to reach them). Public relations' work involves living on one's wits, exchanging favours with the media, establishing a rapport and trust with all kinds of media and authors, knowing when to hype and when to hold back, being able to talk oneself in and out of situations fast, having supreme self-confidence and a high tolerance of rude people and working anti-social hours.

HOME SALES

Although promotion staff stimulate demand, it is the sales staff who realize the income by sustained face-to-face selling to the buyers of the intermediary firms (in textbook publishing they promote and sell books to teachers).

The marketing/sales director, usually supported by a home sales manager, plans and organizes the sales effort. The sales management comments on editors' new book or edition proposals (e.g. sales forecasting and pricing), and is involved with reprinting and re-pricing decisions, and with the disposal of overstocks by remaindering or pulping.

Broadly speaking, publishers derive most of their sales revenue from a small number of customers, and small revenue from a great number. Typically 20% of customers account for 80% of sales. In consumer book publishing, especially, the bookselling chains dominate such as Waterstone's and WH Smith, followed by wholesalers and library suppliers. Since most independent booksellers rely on the trade wholesalers with their own sales forces, they have lost face-to-face contact with many publishers. However, they may deal with selected publishers from which they may receive higher discounts than from wholesalers.

The sales manager sells titles say three or more months ahead of publication to the buyers of such key (or house) accounts (terrestrial and internet), and discusses the publisher's and the large retailers' promotion plans (major titles are discussed further in advance). Although some chains delegate purchasing decisions to branch buyers who are called on by publishers' sales representatives (reps), others buy centrally and relate order quantities to the sizes and character of their branches. Chains adopting strong central buying preclude visits by reps, which has reduced the number of reps. CTN's, drug and department stores, supermarkets etc., serviced exclusively by the wholesale merchandisers or supplied directly by publishers, buy centrally.

A 'special sales' manager may also sell to non-book wholesalers, major non-book retailers, and sometimes to remainder or promotion book imprints, bargain bookshop chains, display marketing companies, book clubs, newspaper book offers etc. Highly illustrated own-brand titles may be sold to supermarket chains. In academic, STM and professional publishing, special sales encompass direct supply deals made with institutions and businesses. Furthermore, some reference and directory publishers sell advertising space in their books and on their web sites to supplement copy sales income. The business model of some directory publishers is virtually entirely based on selling space advertising in their books which are mostly given away through mailings, now paralleled on the internet. Premium sales, where the book is given away with a product or service, may be made.

Publishers sell books to customers on the following terms (definitions of which vary). On firm orders the bookseller agrees to accept the books, to pay for them (preferably on one month's credit, unless otherwise agreed) and not to return them for credit without prior permission from the publisher, usually from the rep or the sales manager. The bookseller takes the risk that the books may not sell and that the publisher may sometimes refuse returns. Powerful booksellers may thus either request a higher discount and/or be more cautious on the quantity ordered.

Under the following terms the bookseller takes less risk. On see safe orders, the bookseller can within a specified period return books (provided that they are in saleable condition) for credit, or in exchange for other books. The bookseller's account is charged at the time of supply, and payment is due at the expiry of credit. Publishers prefer see safe to sale or return, on which the bookseller within a specified period can return books and no charge will be raised. Payment is not usually due until the end of the specified period, or the books are sold. In each instance the bookseller pays for the return carriage, unless otherwise agreed.

Sometimes an individual large order for a new book placed by a branch book buyer or an independent bookseller may in part be firm, the remainder bought see safe. The terms of trade between publishers and their customers and their effect on discounts, credit periods and levels of returns are in a state of flux. As the large retailers have gained in strength, the consumer publishers essentially trade with them in reality on a sale or return basis on longer credit terms.

In medium to large publishers a home sales manager (supported by office staff) runs the sales force. Small publishers may not be able to afford the high cost of employing their own reps. Thus they may have their lists sold by freelance reps who are paid a commission of say 10–12% on net receipts from sales, or by marketing and sales firms, or by the sales force attached to their distributor, or by a larger publisher. But preferably a publisher employs its own full-time reps. Each rep covers a discrete area (a territory), is supplied with a car, sometimes a laptop computer, and receives expenses and a salary. Some publishers, more often consumer book firms, pay reps bonuses for exceeding sales targets. The reps, who usually live in their territories, meet together with the in-house staff (e.g. senior managers, editors and publicity staff) only at the sales conferences (two to four times per year), where they learn about the new books, promotional plans and priorities. Following the manager's instructions (about such things as frequency of visits to customers), the reps manage their areas. They are sent all the promotional material (advance information sheets, jackets/covers etc.), publicity and marketing details, and feedback orders and reports on their activities, and on the response of customers.

Trade reps

The large consumer book publishers may have several sales forces specializing in particular groups of imprints, selling hundreds of titles.

It is important to realize that good trade reps do not just merely walk into shops with a bag of new titles to sell, authorize the return of unsold books and leave. In a rapidly changing world, affecting publishing and retailing, and of changing consumer preferences, the retailers must concentrate their time and effort on marketing and selling the right titles to their customers. The rep's role extends to representing the constituent parts of the publisher – the sales and marketing departments, and the editorial thinking behind projects – to the retailers, and helping them market and sell them to their customers effectively.

Each rep keeps a file on customers, listing their interests, opening hours etc. They visit mainly booksellers (the branches of the chains and significant independents), any wholesalers or library suppliers within their areas, and other outlets which justify the high cost of calling. The reps prepare their own folders with clear plastic sleeves containing neatly placed covers, and other information to show buyers. The folder contains the covers of forthcoming books over, for instance, the following two, three or more months, and the lead titles are usually at the front. They use the folder as a visual aid to sell books on subscription (in advance), and the catalogue for covering the backlist. They rarely carry finished copies, apart from exceptions such as children's illustrated books.

The reps work out their own journeys, taking account of the sales manager's instructions. Retailers are graded by importance: the small number of large bookshops receive the most frequent visits (e.g. weekly/fortnightly/monthly); others receive regular visits (e.g. quarterly); whereas smaller ones are seen only occasionally (e.g. six monthly).

In addition to their daily selling, reps discuss with customers, especially with the major booksellers, the latter's promotional plans and the availability of a publisher's own promotional in-store support (such as POS material and authors' presence).

Reps usually make appointments with buyers and sometimes send them the current stocklist. The following example gives an impression of a rep's visit to a bookshop.

A rep's aim is to obtain advance orders on forthcoming books usually three months ahead of publication from all the main bookshops in time for the stock to be delivered before publication. As most buyers place orders electronically via Teleordering (Whitaker) and not through the reps, the reps want the orders to be sent to their publishers, not via higher discount wholesalers. During a call they will cover the new books to be published in a certain period and take up the new books from that point in a subsequent visit. However, smaller and infrequently visited bookshops may be sold new books post-publication.

The meeting with the buyer takes place in an office or across the counter. The first few minutes are spent discussing trade gossip and the shop. Reps provide the main contact between booksellers and publishers, and should be able to supply the most recent information on all the firm's titles and to determine what information would be useful, and what marketing and promotions the bookseller could use.

The rep usually leads off with a major, strongly promoted title. The prime aim is to put the buyer in a positive buying frame of mind. Two to three minutes are spent in presenting a lead title. Showing the cover, the rep talks about the book and author, covering such aspects as its contents, what part of the market it is aimed at, why it is good, and sometimes the competition, previous books by the author, and the promotion. Although more time is devoted to the main titles, the rep generally has under a minute per title, just one or two sentences, to sell it. If the book is of local interest or is going to receive publicity, this is mentioned. Reps keep records of orders, so that they can remind buyers of orders placed on authors' previous books.

Some publishers provide their reps with lap-top computers which allow them to provide current information on stock availability, order status, sales history etc. and to download information, such as orders and reports, back to their publishers through their home, mobile or hotel telephone that evening.

To avoid diluting the buyer's interest the rep, aware of his or her buying pattern and customers, concentrates on those titles likely to sell in that particular shop (retailers' customer profiles differ greatly). The running order for presenting books varies: e.g. the rep may keep a fairly attractive title near to the end to stimulate a buyer's waning interest. But if the buyer is on edge, the rep may bring forward all the stronger titles, and try the weaker ones at the end. The actual total selling time may take only ten to fifteen minutes, but it may last well over the hour if the rep has many exciting books or if the buyer and rep are friends. Large shops with departmental buyers can take all morning.

There is a common understanding between an experienced rep and a good buyer with regard to the titles and order quantities that can be sold in that particular shop. Weak buyers need help. A good buyer is often aware of the books before the rep calls and can estimate within a few seconds the number of sales. But a buyer may want a larger quantity than the rep had in mind or conversely an order which the rep feels too low. Knowing that the book is selling well elsewhere or sensing that the buyer does not appreciate some aspect, the rep mentions that and suggests a higher quantity. If the rep is trusted, the buyer may increase the order. Part of the persuasion may involve the rep in allowing greater freedom on returns within the firm's overall policy. But selling too many copies which merely return erodes the bookseller's and publisher's margins.

While there are bookshops which expect reps to do their stock checking and re-ordering for them, booksellers' electronic stock control systems should in theory override their intervention.

In practice reps may tactfully remind buyers of titles missing from the shelves, re-shelve mis-placed titles or mention a title that is gaining media attention etc. They may even, on the quiet, set up recommended stock orders directly into booksellers' EPoS systems.

Other aspects of the reps' visits include the following: backed up by attractive POS material, the rep tries to persuade the bookseller to mount special window or instore displays offering incentive terms if necessary. The bookseller may ask the rep to arrange an author signing session in the shop. The rep reports back to the publisher's marketing and sales department to see whether it is feasible. Reps also feed back promotion needs requested by customers or promotion ideas used by other publishers which could be emulated; and occasionally reps make editorial suggestions. They may also debt chase.

Paperback forces

Some of the major paperback houses retain separate sales forces who visit a greater range of retailers more frequently, such as twice weekly or weekly, to meet the demands of the faster stock turnover. They may also cover regional paperback wholesalers.

Paperback reps tend to make more calls per day of shorter duration and may win subscriptions for many titles in a matter of seconds. Booksellers must order a minimum quantity (e.g. 20–30 assorted copies) but the returns policy is far freer. Reps sometimes stock the shelves devoted to their house.

Publishers with extensive, fast-selling and complex backlists may retain 'stock-checking merchandisers' who visit major city centre and airport bookshops. They check the stock, and the store buyer either orders stock up to a previously agreed level or agrees the order with the publisher's rep who calls the next day. Some publishers use 'planagrams' whereby the buyer and rep or merchandiser manage stock within agreed display units, such as spinners, devoted solely to the publisher's books.

Academic and STM reps

The sales forces (smaller than those of consumer book publishers) visit a limited range of bookshops which stock their titles, and may call on specialist mail-order booksellers and library suppliers which supply books to home and export markets.

Additionally they may visit campuses in order to identify courses and the lecturers who take the textbook recommendation decisions. While to a limited extent they encourage academics to order personally, or through their library, monographs and reference books (and sometimes journals and software), their main thrust is to secure textbook adoptions. Using the promotional material and occasionally bound copies, they present the most relevant texts to individual lecturers who, if interested, are followed up by e-mail and are sent inspection copies. The rep, apart from supplying general information on the firm to academics, also undertakes market research such as looking at reading lists to check new and old adoptions or recommendations, and discussing with lecturers trends in subjects generally and particularly in relation to the firm's and competitors' titles. Sometimes they pick up new ideas and potential authors, to be developed by editors.

There is a great disparity among publishers regarding the proportion of the reps' time spent visiting booksellers and campuses. Many firms rely on direct mail promotion and reps devote most time to booksellers, whereas the reps of the American-founded scientific and technical publishers, and some of the large UK textbook publishers emphasize college calling. Owing to the difficulty of combining bookseller and college calling cycles, they may separate the activity. The college reps aim to see say 15 lecturers per day, about 4000 over the year.

When visiting bookshops, a main task is to ensure that adopted texts are stocked in good time, in the right quantities. Many students like to examine the books in a bookshop, their library or their friends' copies before they buy. The busiest time of college-related shops (which derive say 70% of sales from five months of the year) is from the start of the academic year through to Christmas, followed by a secondary peak in the New Year to serve semester course starts. Thus the rep's key period, from mid-summer onwards, is the run-up to October. Although good booksellers forge links with lecturers and solicit reading lists around May, reps alert buyers to adoptions from information gathered from campus visits and from inspection copy reply cards and inform librarians. Reluctant buyers are eventually triggered into building up their stock by the students. Only a small number of booksellers stock monographs and very high priced reference books; such books are supplied by bookshops in response to orders. However academic reps also sell titles more dependent on retail exposure and lacking a safety net. With these a crucial aim is to get bookshops to stock and display the books, otherwise sales are lost. Booksellers are encouraged to distribute the promotional material and to mount special displays. Another activity is setting up and attending exhibitions at academic conferences. Large firms employ full-time staff solely for UK and European conferences.

Educational reps

School textbook publishers and some children's book publishers employ full-time educational reps supplemented with term-time reps (often parents or ex-teachers) managed by the full-timers. The large publishers have separate sales forces covering primary and secondary schools, and possibly the further education sector. Additionally, they may appoint specialist advisers (ex-teachers) in the major subject areas. They provide product training for reps, give talks to teachers and promote to local advisers. A rep of a large company may cover just two counties while one in a small company may have to cover a whole region.

During term time reps usually visit two to three secondary schools per day or up to five primary schools. Large primary schools warrant coverage similar to a secondary school. The number of schools visited per day is related to their proximity.

Educational publishers usually hold two or three sales conferences a year (before the opening of terms), at which the commissioning editors present the new books. The marketing/sales manager directs the priorities. The reps relate what they are told at the centre to their particular areas and schools. Conferences enable the reps to report on sales, and on the response from their schools.

The key period and busiest time for reps is the spring term when teachers select what they will use for the next school year (their financial year usually begins 1 April). The summer term is quieter though there is quite a lot of pick-up work. The winter term becomes progressively more important towards its end.

Educational reps carry heavy cases of books (sometimes several hundred titles), and the promotional material, including advance information on forthcoming titles. A rep sets up the exhibition of books (arranged on the shelves formed by the open cases) usually in the staffroom, or, sometimes less satisfactory, in the library or marking room. The idea is to catch the eye of teachers as they come in for morning coffee or lunchtime breaks or have a free period. The aim is to make sure that the people who influence or determine the choice of teaching material used are aware of what is available; that they know the key aspects of the books displayed. The rep can then decide what inspection copies should be sent and to whom. In small primary schools, headteachers usually choose the materials to be used; in secondary schools and large primary schools departmental heads have the most influence. Thus a rep will try and see them, sometimes by appointment to talk about forthcoming titles, but mainly to show them finished copies. Teachers are asked what they are using and whether they are satisfied. If it is a competitor's book and there is a sign of hesitation, this provides an opening for a rep to discuss the merits of his or her books. Experienced reps know the content not only of their own books but of their competitor's too, and recount the experience of teachers in other schools. If a teacher shows sufficient interest a rep will ask for an inspection copy to be sent. Occasionally copies of key books are left behind. Although priority is given to new books, especially those introducing a comprehensive course of study for National Curriculum core subjects, the promotion of the backlist is vital. In those schools which manage their own budgets, reps encourage direct orders to the publisher, offering incentive discounts on sizeable quantities if necessary.

Market research includes the regular feedback of information such as teachers' suggestions, the response of teachers to their own and competitors' books, information on competitors' books, buying policies, local authority guidelines affecting purchases, and gaps in the market. Sometimes reps suggest ideas for books to the commissioning editors, give advice to teachers who are considering authorship and discover new authors.

Apart from visiting schools, reps ensure that their books are included in reference collections, maintain contact with inspectors and local authority advisers, and sometimes conduct seminars. They are also involved in setting up and staffing local exhibitions, and the major exhibitions linked to national subject conferences held in vacations. Generally speaking, however, reps who work long hours during term time, benefit from the school holidays.

Skills

Common features of all good reps are their energy, self-motivation and discipline which gets them out of bed very early, and makes them work long hours, and withstand the physical ardours of driving and carrying heavy bags. They should have clean driving licences. Being alone, reps need to be well-organized to keep up with the paperwork and very good organizers of their own time.

A good trade rep knows the books and the customers' businesses and their customer profiles, interests and systems, calls repeatedly and regularly with good warning, appears on time, introduces the books well, succinctly and enthusiastically, gains the buyer's confidence and trust, gets the order and is welcomed back. Although reps are given priorities, their skill is to determine which books are best for their area and each outlet, and what size of orders are suitable. They gain the confidence and respect of buyers by recommending books that prove themselves.

On meeting buyers reps need to be alert and make a good first impression. Listening and watching they adjust their selling style and procedure to a buyer's character and mood. They need to be flexible, pitching their style within a range from soft to hard sell, and sense when to talk and when not to. A rep is part amateur psychologist, part actor. Both buyers and sales managers want reps to present their firms honestly, to be diplomatic and have authority. When a buyer asks for special terms or wants to return books, or some other favour, a rep must be able to make decisions which are best for the company but at the same time good for the customer. Their marketing and customer service skills give the publisher a competitive edge.

Educational and college reps must have a lively interest in education and ability to get on well with the kind of people in those professions and understand their attitudes, mindsets and pressures they work under. Overt hard selling is inappropriate. Rather a rep (who needs to be fully conversant with all the important changes in approach and course content in the main subject areas) needs to be able to talk about the problems faced by teachers, the kinds of materials used, and the ways a teacher likes to use them, and then has to be able to suggest and promote a suitable book.

EXPORT SALES

There are various ways of organizing export sales staff within a publishing house. In small firms the sales director may be responsible for home sales and for export arrangements, spending perhaps one or two months abroad annually. In larger firms there are separate export departments headed by an export sales manager (the counterpart of the home sales manager) who may report to the sales/marketing director. An export manager may be supported by office staff. In still larger firms (often the major publishing groups) there may be an export director in charge of staff such as regional sales executives or area export managers who look after all the group's lists in specific areas of the world, or are possibly concerned with particular lists of the group. They are usually responsible for all export sales within their designated areas and for the arrangements made with various kinds of over-seas agents. Their direct selling may also extend to bookshops. A characteristic of all these export specialists is that they are usually expected to spend anything from three to six months abroad annually. Medium and large publishers may employ British export sales representatives who may cover parts or the whole of Europe or other areas of the world. Generally speaking, the larger the company the smaller the geographical area covered by each representative; but compared to the home market their territories are vast (e.g. one or more countries) and their calls to importing book trade customers far less frequent. They are either home-based, travelling abroad for up to six months annually, or resident over-seas. Some of the major publishing groups station UK nationals in small offices in countries outside the fields of operation of their overseas firms. They are mainly concerned with promoting the firm's books, liaising with and supervising arrangements made with local distributors, opening up the market, and when appro-priate employing local representatives. The export-orientated ELT divisions of major publishers typically have their own export sections deploying any of the above methods. Publishers may also employ full-time local nationals in some areas to represent their interests.

The staff numbers of UK export departments are paradoxically far smaller than the home sales side because much of the work of promoting and selling books is carried out abroad. The main export arrangements are as follows.

Main export arrangements and terms of sale

- In countries where there are firms connected through owner-ship with the UK publisher, such firms usually have the exclusive right to publish the UK firm's output. Nevertheless, certain UK titles may be licensed to, or distributed by, other firms.

- Within a territory (e.g. a country) a stockholding agent usually has the exclusive distribution rights for part of, or the whole of, the publisher's output – the market is closed. The agent services the orders originating from customers within the territory and collects the money. Normally, but not always the agent carries out the promotion and sales representation as well. Such agents may be wholesalers/booksellers, importers or branches of other UK publishers. Sometimes, exclusivity is restricted to part of the publisher's output or important named customers within the territory deal directly with the publisher – the market is semi-closed.

- In the open market – countries outside the closed markets of the exclusive stockholding agents (and of the publisher's overseas firms) – the publisher deals directly with the local book trade. However, non-exclusive distribution arrangements may be made with certain local 'preferential' stockists (e.g. wholesalers) which receive more favourable terms from the publisher. The local booksellers can order either directly from the publisher or from the stockist. Some stockists also promote and sales-represent the publisher's books.

- Independent reps or firms ('bag carrying agents') are appointed to promote and sales-represent the books in specified countries – usually but not always in open markets. Carrying many publishers' lists, they are based in the UK or abroad. They receive a commission of from 10–15% on net sales revenue from the territory. On mainland Europe, especially, such reps face a loss of commission on orders sent by booksellers to UK exporting wholesalers instead of via the rep or direct to their publisher.

The agents, wholesalers and booksellers trading in the books receive discounts, usually off the UK published price, and normally higher than home discounts, from the publisher. They then add their costs and profit which results in book prices being higher than those in the UK. Compared to the UK, customers' credit periods are longer (e.g. 90 days from date of invoice) but can extend to six months or more from slowpaying parts of the world. Wherever possible 'firm sales' are made, though some unsold books are returned (especially general paperbacks).

Commonly, the books are supplied 'Ex-warehouse' – the customer bears the cost from the publisher's (or printer's) door; or 'Free on Board' (FOB) – the publisher delivers the books free to the buyer's appointed UK shipping agent (buyers within a country may co-ordinate and nominate a UK export consolidator for economy). However, some books may be supplied 'Cost, Insurance and Freight' (CIF) – the publisher bears all the costs up to their arrival in a port or town. In return for saving the customer cost and (if the goods are sent air freight) time, the discount and credit period may be cut back. Sometimes bulk stocks are supplied 'on consignment': the customer pays only on sales made and has the right to return unsolds.

Other export sales not under the control of the publisher are made by the UK and US export wholesalers/booksellers/library suppliers. The largest are internationally based and promote, sell and distribute books worldwide (such firms are major 'home' customers of academic and STM publishers). And end-users seeking the cheapest source of supply (especially libraries) 'buy round' the publishers' arrangements by ordering books from library suppliers, US exporters, wholesalers etc. which ignore exclusive territorial markets. Furthermore, internet bookselling is breaking down national frontiers for the trading of different kinds of books in different languages.

The information flow and personal selling

Communication with the international network is vital. People abroad must be persuaded to concentrate on promoting and selling the firm's titles rather than those of others. Constant contact takes the form of the supply of information, e-mail, fax, telephone calls and overseas visits.

The export sales manager who initially provides market intelligence and sales forecasts to editors (taking account of any excluded territories), participates in discussions regarding any competing overseas rights sales and selects titles that, it is anticipated, will generate the major part of new book export turnover: they will receive the most emphasis abroad generally, or specifically in particular markets.

The advance information sheets, catalogues, leaflets, jackets/covers, point-of-sale material cascade on to the agents and representatives who use that material to publicize the publisher's titles within their markets. (Some agents prepare their own catalogues from information supplied, while others send out UK originated material.) Agents may generate free media publicity, secure reviews, mail catalogues, sometimes place advertisements, attend exhibitions and operate a textbook inspection copy service.

The UK publisher too may mail promotional material direct to, for example, wholesalers, booksellers, libraries, British Council offices, academics and professionals, send books for review to learned journals, send complimentary copies of textbooks to influential people and operate an inspection copy service from the UK. The promotion efforts of publisher and agent may overlap.

Of equal importance is the quality and regularity of the response from agents and representatives who provide general feedback on their activities and on market conditions, and specific feedback on individual titles (such as requests for more material).

Overwhelmingly, however, export sales are generated by personal selling. The senior export staff give presentations to agents and main customers when visiting the UK, and in their countries. Carrying very heavy bags abroad, their trips may last two, three or more weeks, and encompass half a dozen countries, thirty to forty customers or just one. They primarily sell to agents' sales managers or directors concerned with imports and may brief the agent's reps at a conference. They discuss all aspects of their trading relationship and assess agents' effectiveness. Other sales venues are the book fairs around the world.

The junior export staff, the reps, usually sell to the book trades in open markets. They try to get subscriptions for new books, do not overlook the backlist, respond to complaints and collect debts. When appropriate they supply promotion copy for inclusion in wholesalers' or retailers' catalogues, check orders in order to alleviate expensive distribution mistakes, and sometimes co-ordinate booksellers' ordering. The academic reps may additionally call on lecturers and librarians in order to secure textbook adoptions, facilitate inspection copy orders, and encourage booksellers to carry out joint promotions and exhibitions. The ELT reps promote and sell courses directly to private language schools, state schools and to government agencies.

Skills

The ability to speak preferably two or more languages is invariably needed, but is not a top priority: most customers can speak English to some extent. But linguistic ability enables you to understand and relate that much better to the market and the customers to you. Fluency in one or more of the European languages such as French, German, Spanish and Italian, and semi-fluency in some is ideal. Standard Arabic and Chinese etc. are sometimes particularly desirable for certain firms.

Export sales staff have a commitment to publishing and exporting, and have to enjoy working with books. First and foremost sales people, they have a burning desire to ring up the till, to increase profitable turnover.

Most of the personal skills required for selling to the home market are paralleled in export selling; but exporters face the complexities of understanding many different and diverse markets and need an appreciation of the political, social, economic and cultural factors pertaining to each country, as well as an empathy with, sensitivity to, and enthusiasm for the market to which they are selling or playing a part in. Good exporters are able to sell and adapt to different environments and situations fast.

In that the work involves much time abroad, exporters must like travel, have the self-motivation to work far away from headquarters, take high-level decisions on behalf of their firms, and cope with loneliness. Exporting calls for tough survivors. (Some of the overseas postings made by non-general firms are to less-developed countries with arduous climates.) With a large amount of the publisher's money in the pocket, profligacy is something employers expect you to avoid.

RIGHTS SALES

The author–publisher contract (in consumer book publishing frequently drawn up by an author's agent) delimits the scope of the publisher to license various kinds of rights to other firms. These rights allow other firms to exploit the book in different ways, media, territories and languages. The large publishers maintain separate contracts departments which put into the contractual detail the outcome of the agreements reached with authors, agented authors and with publishers from whom they have bought, and with licensors to whom they have sold rights. There are also contract specialists who offer their services to publishers and agents, such as Roger Palmer Limited Media Contracts.

The selling of rights may be done by editors and sales staff. However, medium to large publishers and packagers employ small numbers of specialists to sell rights actively.

Rights staff may also check and monitor the contracts made between the publisher and others. The reactive work involves responding to people (often authors, sometimes publishers) seeking copyright permission to reproduce material (such as extracts of text, tables, technical illustrations) from the firm's books. They are usually granted a non-exclusive licence to reproduce the material for a particular use, with due acknowledgement, for a specified quantity and in a specified language throughout the world, though the territories may be limited. The applicant is charged a fee, usually equally shared by the originating publisher and author. The Copyright Licensing Agency's Rapid Clearance Service (CLARCS) facilitates the collection of fees from educational and other organizations wishing to copy extracts for class sets.

The majority of books have no significant rights sales income, but some (such as in consumer publishing, especially in adult and children's highly illustrated colour books) earn much or depend on rights deals for viability.

A small department consists of a rights manager and assistant; larger ones have staff who specialize in particular rights or regions of the world. A publisher or packager may use rights selling agents abroad (e.g. in Europe, the USA and Japan) who receive a commission of, say, 10% on sales made.

Rights work involves close contact with the editorial, production, promotion and sales departments, and accounts; selling to customers (mainly editors or directors of other firms) in a regular and personal way; processing a great deal of paperwork (e.g. correspondence, maintaining customer mailing lists, record keeping); negotiating deals and contracts; and foreign travel (at the very least attending major book fairs, Frankfurt, and – for children's books – Bologna). Staff who sell many books of international appeal (especially highly illustrated colour non-fiction) travel widely and frequently.

As in other areas, rights selling is aided by technology. For example, there are specialist rights sales software programs, and the international book fairs are creating their virtual equivalents for the trade of rights.

The rights department may get involved with a title before the author has signed the contract. An editor may ask the rights manager to assess the title's rights sales potential particularly if that affects the author's advance, or the viability of the book depends on rights sales. Around manuscript delivery titles are assessed, and a strategy drawn up regarding the choice of possible customers, how and when they will be approached. There are many kinds of rights and the deals struck are both intricate and varied. The following description of the main rights gives merely an impression. (Sometimes, the author's approval is needed before deals are concluded.)

Book club rights

Book club rights are normally granted to the publisher. A book club editor selects the books for a club's programme. They are sent sample material, often manuscripts, sometimes proofs. The publisher's aim is to secure a firm bulk order from the club early enough, so that the club's edition can be co-printed with that of its own, thereby lowering the per copy cost of production to the benefit of the margin on the trade edition, especially on illustrated colour books. A major club will sell the book to its members at say, 30–50% off the publisher's catalogue price. It therefore seeks a high discount off the publisher's catalogue price, of, say, 75–80%. The author's royalty is included in the price paid by the club, and is usually either 10% of the publisher's net receipts (which equates roughly to 2% of the publisher's catalogue price) or 50% of the manufacturing profits. Some book clubs, however, offer royalty-exclusive deals where the publisher receives a royalty of 5–7½% based on the club price and on copies sold.

A book club may itself reprint the book under its imprint with the publisher's permission, in which case it also pays a royalty on the club price on copies sold of say 10%. The royalty paid to the publisher is likewise shared with the author 50/50 or 60/40. In such royalty-exclusive deals the rights manager negotiates the advance payable and charges the club an offset fee (not shared with the author) for the right to reproduce the publisher's typography etc. There is a trend for clubs wanting to print themselves their own editions.

The quality paperback clubs take run-on paperback copies of the publisher's hardback edition printing and typically price their same size paperback edition for club members at say 50% off the publisher's hardback catalogue price. The publisher makes minor changes to the cover of the book club's edition, such as deleting its own imprint, barcode and price.

Other permutations include a club purchasing a small quantity of a book from a publisher's existing stock, and the licensing by a publisher to a club of a hardback edition of a title which the publisher could sell itself only in paperback.

A book club is usually granted the right to sell its English language edition in the UK (and sometimes other overseas territories in which it operates) but is excluded from North America.

Reprint paperback rights

Owing to the emergence of consumer book publishers with their ability to publish both hardbacks and paperbacks, the selling of reprint paperback rights by originating hardback publishers to separate paperback publishers has undergone a dramatic decline. But a small or medium size publisher while capable of selling a trade paperback itself, may not be able to sell a mass market paperback edition demanding different distribution channels. Thus it could access that market by licensing that edition to a larger publisher.

The key features of such deals are as follows. The seller defines the rights granted, i.e. the exclusive right to publish a particular kind of edition in specified territories is stated and the duration of the licence is delimited (e.g. eight years). The buyer reprints its own edition and pays royalties on copies sold to the originating publisher. These royalties are shared between the author and the publisher, for example, 60/40 or 70/30 respectively. A rising royalty scale and the size of the advance (representing a proportion of future royalties) are negotiated. The advance payable is split (e.g. on signature of contract and on publication). The buyer usually pays the originating publisher an offset fee (not shared with the author) for the right to reproduce the text prior to printing, and sometimes a fee for use of the digital file of the illustrations. The timing of reprint paperback publication is set, so as not to undermine the originator's other sales.

US and North American rights

Authors' agents, on behalf of authors, and book packagers may retain US rights or North American rights (the USA plus Canada). But if held by the publisher and the book is not to be sold via the publisher's North American firm or through a distribution arrangement, the rights may be licensed. The USA is by far the largest and richest English language market.

Selling to US editors is carried out at a distance or personally when they visit the UK en route to Frankfurt or Bologna book fairs, or at such fairs. Sometimes, the rights manager attends the annual US book fair, BookExpo (Reed) or visits New York to see, say, five publishers per day. UK-based scouts of US publishers may be used; and UK editors are also in contact with US publishers. The submission method may be simultaneous (the chosen editors receive the material together) or occasionally auctions are held; editors may be given a synopsis/manuscript/ proofs/bound copies; and depending on the stage reached the rights manager uses the author's previous sales figures, the jacket and blurb, pre-publication quotes, the UK subscription order, reviews and other rights sales made etc. to stimulate interest.

There are essentially two types of deal. In the first the US publisher manufactures its own edition, pays royalties and an advance which are shared by the UK publisher and author – usually the larger part goes to the author say 75–80%. In effect the UK publisher acts as the author's agent. Additionally the US publisher may pay for the use of film or digital file of the illustrations, or an offset fee if it does not edit or Americanize the book. This type of 'royalty exclusive' deal tends to be used on most fiction and on some illustrated books of considerable US interest.

In the second, the UK publisher or packager preferably co-prints the UK edition with the US publisher's edition. The bound copies are sold at a small marked-up price; and the author's royalty of say 10% of the UK publisher's net receipts is sometimes included in the price paid. (However, a US publisher may pay royalties exclusive.) This type of deal can apply to any illustrated consumer book, and to academic books published by UK firms without a strong US presence.

Whichever applies, the US publisher is granted an exclusive licence, sometimes for the full term of copyright. The US publication date is stated, the UK publisher is obliged to supply the material by a set date, and the US publisher, too, to publish by a certain date. Attempts are made to forestall premature release of an ensuing US paperback or remainder, which could jeopardize export sales of a UK paperback. The price paid or the royalty rates, and advance, are negotiated as well as the territories. The US publisher is granted exclusively the USA (with Canada open to negotiation), is excluded from the UK publisher's territories (e.g. the Commonwealth and mainland Europe), and has the non-exclusive right to publish in other countries. The US publisher may be granted other rights (e.g. book club, reprint paperback, serial) and pays a proportionate sum from such sales to the UK publisher (then shared with the author like the royalties). With some co-edition deals the US publisher may be territorially limited to North America, and the subsidiary rights granted too may be fewer.

The *Literary Market Place* is a useful guide to US publishers and book clubs, and the *International Literary Market Place* (both published by Bowker) lists foreign language publishers; as do the Frankfurt and Bologna Book Fair catalogues.

Translation rights

In the case of adult consumer books, these rights (for some or all foreign languages) are often retained by agents and by book packagers. North European language editions may increase export sales of the English language edition owing to the book's increased exposure. But if they are held by the publisher, the titles are promoted abroad by catalogue rights guide, e-mail, fax and telephone, and personally at major book fairs. Publishers within a language market area are selected and sent material simultaneously. Academic/STM titles take some time to be reviewed.

In many cases the foreign publisher translates and produces the book (and may be charged for the film or digital file of the illustrations), pays royalties and an advance (usually lower than English rights), or occasionally a lump sum to reproduce a set quantity; is granted an exclusive language licence for a particular edition, and other rights, for a set period throughout the world. Sometimes, on a consumer book, a Spanish or French publisher is excluded from Latin America or Québec, respectively. The author receives say 50% of the royalties if academic, or up to 80% if popular trade.

The alternative deal used for many highly illustrated colour books and children's picture books, is for the foreign language publishers to supply typeset film or digital file of their translations to fit around the four-colour illustrations. Several language editions are preferably co-printed together by the publisher or packager in order to gain economies of scale. The printing press usually has five cylinders carrying the printing plates. Four cylinders carry the plates which print the four-colour illustrations (made up of yellow, magenta, cyan and black), and the fifth cylinder carries the plate of the text printed in black outside the areas of the illustrations. The press operator changes the fifth plate for each language edition printing. The ordered quantities, carrying each publisher's imprint, are often supplied royalty inclusive, possibly exclusive.

The co-edition deals made with English and foreign language publishers are central to the work of rights staff of highly illustrated adult and children's publishers and packagers. They usually initiate deals well in advance of publication with English language publishers and book clubs first, using the future book's contents, and mock-ups of the jacket and 'blads' of selected double-page spreads etc. The co-printing of foreign language editions follows because these publishers translate from the final English proof or the bound copy. The English and foreign language co-printing of children's books of few words can coincide. Negotiations with customers on the price paid per copy for the books, the timing of the deals and their combined printing are critical. The complexity of these deals, involving close contact with the UK publisher's or packager's own production/design departments, and those overseas, makes it more difficult for authors' agents to enter this form of rights selling.

Serial and extract rights

First serial rights (the most valuable because they appear before the book's publication and offer a national newspaper or magazine a scoop) are often but not always retained by authors' agents, sometimes by packagers. The second and subsequent serial rights (usually granted to a publisher) appear after book publication and may be sold to a succession of regional or evening newspapers, or magazines, at rates equal to or above that paid for original articles of comparable length (of which the author shares 50–80%), or for zero. Ideas for extracts, which may come from the editor, are marked on the manuscript or proof and are sent to chosen journalists, with first serial rights twelve to six months ahead of book publication. The author's share of first serial rights (often as much as 90%) may be offset against the advance, so as well as providing valuable publicity for the book the sale of such serial rights is particularly valuable financially.

Other rights

Examples include condensation (i.e. a right sold mainly to Reader's Digest), film and television, radio (straight reading from text and dramatization), promotional reprint rights and English language paperback licensing rights to export territories. Audio or talking book rights can be licensed exclusively in two forms: abridged and unabridged. Some of the main trade publishers operate their audio divisions which often abridge their own books (on to say two to four C90 cassettes or silver disk equivalent, at c. 9000–10 000 words per hour) or license titles from agents or other trade publishers which do not have their own talking book lists. There are also independent and specialist talking book publishers. The unabridged talking books tend to be produced by specialist publishers supplying public libraries, which may also publish large print books – another right available for licensing. Digital publishing may in due course supersede such rights.

The licensing of electronic media rights is in its infancy. Some publishers may sub-license whole works, preferably not the family silver, and try to protect themselves by granting short term, non-exclusive or narrow exclusive licences, in particular languages, limited to specific formats or platforms, with performance guarantees and advances. Alternatively they may enter into joint ventures in which costs and income are shared in agreed proportions.

Skills

Rights staff preferably know French and/or German, and if concerned with co-editions especially, Italian and Spanish as well. But negotiations are in English (except with the French). However senior, the work involves typing and much administration.

The essential prerequisite of selling is knowing the books and the customers. Editorial insight of the firm's new titles and lateral thinking aids the assessment of rights prospects and their worth, the drawing out of salient points and the realization of sales revenue. With highly saleable titles, skilled judgement is needed on the kind of approach and its timing to selected customers.

The perception of customers' needs entails an understanding of the way they run different kinds of businesses (e.g. product range, markets and financial structure) in different cultural, political and economic contexts; and of their personal interests.

Dealing with relatively small numbers of senior people regularly and personally demands the development of good and close relations. Sales skills encompass the enthusiastic promotion of titles in writing, on the telephone and in person, even when there is scant information available on a new title. Where customers are in competition or when time is short in co-printing, they have to be pressured and manoeuvred to clinch deals quickly.

Negotiation skills allied to experience, numeracy and fast thinking help a rights person to tell if a customer is offering too low an advance or too little in a co-printing deal. The full implications and catches in customer contracts must be spotted and adverse clauses removed or modified.

Where physical or digital elements are supplied, the knowledge of production processes and of terminology are required. As so much of the job involves remembering and recording which books are on offer and who is looking at what, a meticulous, methodical mind which registers fine detail is essential – the consequences of selling the same book twice in the same territory are horrendous.

Long working days precede and follow the major fairs, such as Frankfurt, at which customers are seen on half-hourly appointments during the day, and informally into the nights, over a week. The job calls for immense stamina and a strong voice box.

DISTRIBUTION, ACCOUNTS AND PERSONNEL STAFF

Distribution

The distribution of the books, journals and other new media products is inherent to the publisher's role of getting its products into the customers' hands at the right time and in the right quantities. The key aspects of distribution (sometimes called logistics) are customer care, accuracy in order fulfilment, speed and reliability in despatch, the physical protection of the product and economies in despatch. Failings in these areas lead to lost sales, diminished retail display, increased cost to the publisher and loss of confidence by bookseller and reader; improvements give the publisher a competitive marketing edge.

Book distribution is an enormous challenge and exhibits most unusual characteristics. Many other kinds of goods produced by manufacturers (often on continuous production lines) are supplied directly to wholesalers and then on to the retailers. But publishers hire printers to manufacture the books which are delivered to the publisher or its distributor; and for their size carry an enormous range of new and backlist products stored for a long time. In the main, publishers supply retailers – individual shops or their centralized warehouses – directly. Despite the growth of the trade wholesalers, book wholesaling in the UK is still relatively weak and is concentrated on consumer books.

Publishers' customers extend beyond the book trade – to schools and to individuals needing single copies (e.g. review, inspection, mail-order sales). Publishers receive massive numbers of small orders, the profits from which may not cover the distribution and credit cost. Yet book retailers demand faster and more reliable distribution in order to compete against other kinds of products. UK publishers export vigorously and distribute to most countries from the UK via a myriad of arrangements and carriers. In material handling terms, book distribution presents extremes, ranging from one or more titles of varying size or other media products up to a container load. Publishers face the return of unsold books from the book trade (typically in the range of 10–20% of sales), which are credited accordingly; and if the books are damaged or of low value they destroy them. KPMG in 1998 estimated that the average cost of publishers' distribution was amongst the highest in industry and represented 13% of sales, while that of a consumer good manufacturer was 6%.

The foundation stone on which all book trade electronic transactions and information systems are based was the introduction in 1967 of the Standard Book Number (SBN). By 1970 it had become internationally accepted. The ISBN incorporates the language of origin, the publisher, and the unique identifier of each book or edition (the last digit is a check to ensure the preceding digits are correct). ISBNs are also used by publishers to identify other kinds of products such as audio books, silver disks and e-books. The digital identifier for journals is the International Standard Serial Number (ISSN). In 1979, Teleordering was launched by Whitaker. This enabled booksellers to transmit orders electronically overnight into publishers' computers. Teleordering was the book trade's first proprietary electronic trading system deploying an early form of Electronic Data Interchange. EDI facilitates the exchange of data between computer systems, saving trading partners' time, errors and cost by avoiding the use and handling of paper and making it unnecessary to re-key information.

By the mid-1980s standards were developed to convert the ISBN into the European Article Numbering (EAN) bar code. This appears on the back cover of books. By the early 1990s most main UK bookshops had installed electronic point of sale (EPoS) systems which read the bar codes. The collection of EPoS data from the UK general retail market by BookTrack from the late 1990s aided publishers' management of stock and ongoing promotion during the rise and decay of a title's actual sales.

In the drive towards electronic ordering, invoicing, information gathering and transmission, Book Industry Communication (BIC) was founded in 1991 by the Publishers Association, The Booksellers Association, The Library Association and British Library.

BIC aims to help develop and to promote standards for e-communication and e-commerce, and to aid supply chain efficiency, in the UK and internationally. Its membership embraces publishers, distributors, retailers, wholesalers, library suppliers, bibliographic providers, system suppliers and shipping organizations etc. The adoption of 'standards' is critically important to the trading of physical and digital products, and there are many agencies in the UK, Europe and in America working on standards for the description and trading of different categories of products. However, for the publishing industry and the intermediaries, BIC focuses on three main areas.

The first is the development of standardized product information – a classification system whereby publishers describe consistently the bibliographical details of their products – and the technical and procedural standards whereby they communicate electronically that information and its updating to others, such as to the bibliographic providers, to wholesalers and retailers etc. The second relates to the supply chain such as: bar codes; B2B e-commerce transacted through EDI (e.g. orders, acknowledgements, delivery notes, invoices, credit notes, and price and product availability updates); and the standardizing of book returns authorization procedures in order to reduce costs. The third concerns digital publishing.

As publishers move into licensing and selling their products online either via intermediaries or directly to end-users from their digital warehouses, there is a need for common standards to facilitate electronic copyright management in order to trigger payment systems. For instance, an intermediary may want to print on-demand a publisher's title or to customize a product including chapters from a range of book sources, or a researcher may want to follow-up an electronic journal reference in an article from another publisher's journal server. The classic digital identifiers – the ISBN and ISSN – are the basis for electronic rights management systems at the macrolevel. But the Association of American Publishers sponsored the concept of a microlevel identifier – the Digital Object Identifier (DOI) which is now promoted by the DOI Foundation. The ideas behind the DOI are that it is a simple or dumb number which can be attached by the publisher to an object, such as a journal abstract, author's name and address, or book chapter, or piece of text or an illustration – whatever the publisher considers could be re-usable or tradable. The publisher maintains a continually updated directory, which acts as a routing system where the dumb number is associated with the publisher's internet address. The publisher's database stores the most accurate information about the DOIs such as the copyright ownership, terms and conditions of sale and prices. The journal publishers were among the first publishers to deploy DOIs, though their take-up in other areas has been slow.

The major publishing groups run their own distribution and generally place the facility in the country away from headquarters while the very small publishers do it from home. Small and medium publishers may also carry out their own distribution. They, however, increasingly use independent distributors, or larger publishers, or wholesalers – all of which are eager to increase their turnover. Such third-party distributors may offer to publishers the complete service of bulk storage, invoicing, customer service and cash collection, and delivery for which they charge around 12% of sales: less for larger publishers and more for smaller publishers. Some publishers, especially the smaller ones, use a third-party distributor for storage and despatch. Whatever, the independent third-party distributors occasionally go bust which can be a disaster for the publisher if unable to retrieve its cash and books from the receiver. The trend is towards fewer and larger distributors. Size gives to the distributor the turnover to invest in expensive electronic, book handling and warehouse systems, the ability to bulk up order values, greater leverage in debt collection, and the securing of lower rates with carriers. With the development of faster and more reliable transportation systems, including air-freight, there is a movement away from overseas stockholding agents to direct supply from the UK, giving a greater opportunity to price books more competitively in many markets.

The 'trade side' of distribution is concerned with processing received orders, raising invoices and documentation. Not all publishers can accept teleorders, and many orders are received in writing or by fax, telephone, e-mail. Thus there are order editors who clarify ambiguities in orders. The orders are loaded on to computer, so that the invoice, documentation, labelling and physical distribution begin. There are many standardized codes which tell a customer a book is unavailable for various reasons. UK booksellers are identified by the Standard Address Number (SAN) which is a unique identifier of the delivery address. New books or reprints not yet in stock are recorded on a 'dues listing' and despatched when available unless otherwise instructed. Export orders need additional documentation to comply with the receiving country's import regulations and taxes, such as VAT. On orders to mainland Europe some publishers invoice in Euros or local currencies and offer banking arrangements. Mistakes in export orders incur severe penalties. (Pro-forma invoices may be sent to unsafe customers before the books are dispatched.) Most publishers supply books to UK booksellers carriage free, whereas mainland European publishers charge carriage to their booksellers.

The customer services department resolves queries from sometimes irate booksellers regarding problems of distribution and of accounts. The textbook inspection copy service and mail-order or subscription sales are usually handled by separate departments.

The warehouse includes the bulk store of books and journals (and of any raw paper reserves) into which suppliers' deliveries are made and a 'picking' area where titles and back-up stock are positioned for easy location (new books and fast-selling titles in prime sites). The invoices may include the location of titles in the order in which they are 'picked' (gathered ready for despatch). The collated orders move to the packaging and despatch area. Despatch involves knowing the most economic, quickest and reliable method (e.g. road carrier, shipping, air freight, post) and negotiating bulk deals with carriers. If the publisher bears the cost, the incentive is to lower costs to increase profitability; when the customers pays (e.g. on FOB export orders) the incentive is to assist them to save money, a marketing service. In order to treat mainland Europe as an extension of the home market and to compete against US publishers, some UK publishers are using pan-European delivery networks operated by the same carriers as used in the UK. In so doing, the publisher controls the level of service door-to-door, avoids dealing with dozens of carriers (which can be appointed by retailers) and attains economies.

While the computer monitors stock levels, there are staff who physically check the stock and check the returns (the bar codes can aid the task), liaising with the sales office where appropriate.

The application of computers to order-processing, distribution and despatch provides key information for management, such as reports on dues, sales by title, area, by representative (and comparative monthly reports), type of customer, discount structure, return levels, stock and re-order levels, method of despatch, carriage charge analysis, debtors etc.

Finance and accounts

All firms of any size need accounts staff to handle the payroll, tax, pension scheme etc. and to deal with the firm's financial activities with its suppliers (e.g. printers, freelancers and authors) and customers. The credit control staff assess and set new customers' credit limits, monitor their performance, debt chase and liaise closely with the sales department especially when UK and overseas customers are placed on the stop list. A bookseller placed on a stop list and denied any further deliveries is most likely to tell a customer that the book requested by the customer is out-of-print rather than admit to debts. The quick recovery of debts is a vital factor in aiding the firm's cashflow and improving its profitability. The costing section of an accounts department is concerned with monitoring book costings at the publishing proposal stage, subsequently comparing actual costs against estimates, and preparing book profit and loss statements.

The royalty section is particular to publishing (and larger author agencies) and the staff have a rarity value. They have copies of the author–publisher contracts, and the contracts covering rights sales (the buyers are pressed for settlement so that the income can be apportioned). Different royalties due to the author from the publisher's edition are calculated by applying the contractual details to the title's sales record. Sums owed by the author (e.g. for excessive proof corrections, or for books purchased) are deducted from royalties and the royalty statement prepared. If authors have the royalty paid in advance, it is similarly set against the royalty income. On some titles, the income from sales never reaches or surpasses the advance paid, in which case the unearned advance owed by the author to the publisher is written off. While some publishers, especially in the consumer book field, hold a reserve of royalties to set against future returns of books from retailers, an author may be paid royalties on copies which are later returned. Such sums owing are carried over to the following royalty statement, but at the end of the book's life are usually written off. A royalty manager, conversant with current double taxation relief, overseas tax regulations and VAT and able to explain their ramifications, patiently, tactfully, clearly and promptly inspires authors and agents with confidence, and is invaluable to the publisher.

The finance director and senior accountants are responsible for producing the annual statutory accounts, and for strategic financial management. They monitor the cashflow, analyse and interpret the firm's financial performance (assisted by many indices) against budgets and past figures, for top-level management decisions which affect the evaluation of new projects. The large groups usually centralize this service, and their senior staff examine take-over targets.

Personnel

Personnel (or Human Resources) departments which deal with staff recruitment policy, discipline, development and training tend to be restricted to large publishers. In smaller firms these tasks form part of the work of an office manager, or of the managing director's office etc.

Chapter 5

The business of publishing

From a financial viewpoint, the senior management strives to increase the rate at which capital is earned and turned over and to improve the profit margin for expansion and for the owners; for example, its members try to:

- maximize the income and minimize the production costs;
- contain royalty rates while keeping competitive, in consumer book publishing monitor the amount of money and level of risk tied up in authors' advances in relation to actual sales;
- control prudently the stock levels (just sufficient to service sales) by selling a high proportion of a print number on publication or soon after, and storing only adequate stock of backlist titles that sell;
- re-price regularly the backlist titles (usually upwards) in line with current prices;
- control tightly the firm's overheads (e.g. staff and office costs) while maintaining effective management: if profits fall, overheads have to be reduced and output increased;
- take all available credit from suppliers (e.g. authors and printers);
- keep discounts as low as possible (while customers will demand increases) and costs of returns but, at the same time, maintain display space in customers' outlets;
- collect debts quickly from customers;
- obtain the best terms from capital providers (e.g. banks);
- invest in fixed assets (e.g. warehouses, computers) only if a favourable return can be shown in comparison with sub-contracting or leasing;

- sell off under-used or under-performing assets (e.g. buildings, lists/imprints);
- buy complementary businesses at home and abroad;
- forecast regularly the cashflow (the flow of money payments to, from, or within the firm) over time; even a profitable publisher can exceed its borrowing requirement before profits are earned and go bust.

One key aspect is the compilation, say at least six months ahead, of a financial plan showing a profit target for the forthcoming year (or longer). It is built up partly from the historic costs of running the business and from forecasts (e.g. the estimated costs of producing the new titles – authors' advances, royalties and production costs, and their timing; and the revenue from estimated sales made through various channels at home and abroad, over time; similarly for backlist titles – their costs and sales revenue over time). Furthermore the departmental managers prepare budgets for carrying out their activities.

Actual performance is compared regularly with the plan at, say, monthly intervals, and with the performance of the previous year's; and the plan itself is updated. Some long-term publishers (e.g. textbook or reference) compile rolling plans for up to five years ahead.

PROFIT AND LOSS STATEMENT: PUBLISHER'S COST PROFILE

The annual profit and loss statement of a publisher reveals the cost profile of the business as a whole, and each publisher's differs. Furthermore such statements of different kinds of publisher (adult general, children's, educational, academic etc.) differ in aggregate, reflecting the different nature of their businesses – the following figures give an impression.

The total net sales revenue (NSR) is the sum of money the publisher receives from home and export sales after the discounts have been deducted from the published prices. Taking the NSR as 100% and subtracting from that the production costs of the books (say around 30%, plus or minus 5%) plus the write-off of stock unsold (say 2–10%) and the cost of royalties (10–15%), leaves the publisher with a gross profit of say 45–55%. (While a consumer book publisher may suffer from the write-off of unrecoverable authors' advances, it may benefit from greater rights sales income.) From the gross trading profit, the publisher's costs are deducted: e.g. editorial 8–10%; production and design 2–3%; publicity and sales staff 6%; promotion expenditure 5%; sales commission 1–3%; order processing and distribution 10–13%; general and administrative expenses 4–7%. These overheads and expenses roughly total 39–47% which when deducted from the gross trading profit leaves the publisher with a net profit (before interest charges on borrowing and tax are deducted) of say 9–12%. After interest and tax, a dividend may be paid to shareholders and the remaining profit re-invested in the business. During recessions net profitability declines and even during buoyant periods some publishers make a loss, while others reap net profits much higher than that above.

The publisher's overheads and expenses are very important, not just because they must be tightly controlled from one year to another (monitored in response to changing work practices and salary increases etc.) and kept in line with those of competing publishers in the field, but because they should be apportioned to and recovered from each new book – at least in theory. Successful publishing is founded on contracting good books that sell and each new book is a business in its own right contributing or not to the business as a whole. The decision to take on a new book, its costing and pricing prior to contract were touched on in Chapter 4. The decision to publish is the crux of the whole enterprise. If bad mistakes are made here, all efforts of management to control overheads will come to nothing. The sum total of profits of all the new book proposals must equal, preferably exceed, the publisher's overall profit target. Thus new books which are planned at the outset, but fail in reality, to achieve the target must be counterbalanced by equal profits from other books which exceed their target.

Two general ways of pricing books are the gross profit and the unit cost mark-up methods.

COSTING A BOOK: GROSS PROFIT (OR GROSS MARGIN) METHOD

In essence, this method mirrors the profit and loss statement. Put crudely, the management may say to their editors, 'We want to see each publishing proposal attaining a gross profit of (e.g. 55–60+%)'. That percentage represents the sum of money the publisher would have left after the production costs and author's royalties have been deducted from the NSR, provided all the copies were sold. That money would then, in theory, be sufficient to recover the overheads and expenses (expressed in overall percentages) and to provide a net profit as follows.

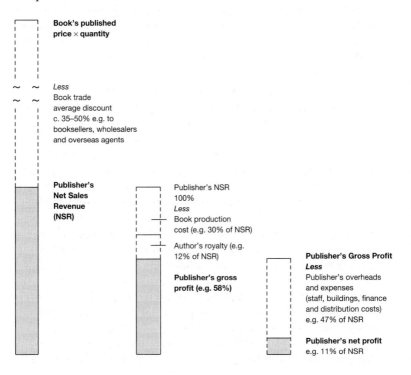

Who gets what in the book business

Note: The publisher's *Net Sales Revenue* (NSR) is the sum of money the publisher receives after the trade discounts have been deducted, and its *gross profit* is what is left after the costs of production and royalty have been deducted. The publisher's *net profit* should be the sum finally left after all the costs of running the business have been deducted.

At the outset of the calculation the editor considers the book's desired physical attributes, the costs of production, and the possible prices and sales potential in unison. Here they are separated.

The income

Factors affecting the book's possible published price include its perceived value to end-users; their ability to pay low or high prices (e.g. high earning professionals); competitors' books (especially if the book can be compared against similar books in shops, rather than stand alone by advertized mail order); its uniqueness; whether the book will be bought primarily by end-users or by libraries or businesses; and whether there are established price ceilings in the market which, if breached, could reduce sales (e.g. to an impulse buyer, gift buyer, student or school etc.).

The raising of a published price would usually lead to a fall in the quantity demanded, whereas lowering the price would usually (but not always) lead to a rise in the quantity demanded. Products which are thought to be 'price inelastic' (i.e. changing the price has only a limited effect on the level of demand) tend to be highly specialist and professional titles (e.g. those which convey need to know information for well-off users) while many consumer books, especially paperbacks, bought on impulse, and many textbooks, tend to be 'price elastic' (i.e. changing the price has a greater effect on the level of demand). The price elasticities of various kinds of book differ. (It can be difficult for an editor to persuade an academic or professional book author that lowering the price would not open the gates to a flood of eager readers.) There are also common price points in the market which arise at a particular time for given categories of books, such as general hardbacks, trade and mass-market paperback and for the different kinds of books within those formats. Similarly in textbooks: for example, tertiary humanities and social sciences paperback texts are priced at price points lower than those for management and STM titles. Periodically brave publishers break such prevailing price points, by lifting the price or lowering it to undercut competitors.

If a book were greatly overpriced, few copies would be sold and a low revenue results; if the price fell within a market price band, changing the price would have a greater effect on demand; but if the price were fixed even lower, the level of demand fails to respond as the market for the book reaches saturation, the total revenue falls again. Thus if one objective is to maximize the firm's income, a published price and a sales forecast which when multiplied together produce the maximum revenue, are aimed for.

The sales forecast is related to a time period. Publishers print stock sufficient for a limited period only (say six to eighteen months, or for mass market paperbacks under three months).

The net sales revenue is calculated by multiplying the sales forecasts for the home market and the export market by the published price less the discounts. While each book is sold at many discounts, an average discount derived from all the transactions by the firm is applied for home sales and the higher average for export sales. The average on some books (e.g. those sold particularly to high discount customers in the home market) would be adjusted upwards. The revenue from any co-edition deals made at very high discounts to other firms (e.g. UK book clubs or US publishers) which order in advance bulk quantities of bound copies from the publisher, are included, as would be the inter-company sales to overseas firms that are part of an international group, such as in the academic/STM fields. The ways in which trans-national publishers trade within the constituent parts of the group vary and depend upon which territory – or nation – it is advantageous to declare profits for taxation and shareholder benefit. For instance by transfer pricing they may sell internally a UK-originated book to their sister US firm at a very high discount thereby increasing the profit in the US, or possibly vice versa. If an un-agented UK author's royalty is based on UK net receipts, i.e. the sum of money remitted to the UK from the US sister company, then the author may receive substantially less money per copy than if the author's royalty is based on local net receipts, i.e. net receipts from US sales by that company.

The costs

The costs of producing a book usually come under two headings. The 'fixed or plant costs' are incurred before the printing presses roll and do not change whatever the quantity of books ordered. They may include: sums paid to external readers; translators; contributors; legal fees; permission fees for the use of third-party copyright material (text and illustrations); payments to freelances (e.g. editors, illustrators, designers); cover design; indexing (if not done by author); and major payments to print suppliers for typesetting, origination of illustrations, proofing, corrections, imposition, plates etc.

The 'variable costs' occur after the presses start to roll and depend on the quantity of books ordered. They include the costs of printing and binding, and the paper consumed. The quantity ordered would be the sales estimate plus an allowance for copies wasted or given away for review etc.

Roughly speaking, the fixed costs account for a third to a half of the total production costs on consumer books and textbooks, and more than half on short-run professional titles and scientific research.

The cost of producing each copy, 'the unit cost' (the print quantity divided into the total cost), diminishes with increasing print quantities. The unit cost falls rapidly on short printings of between, say, 500 to 2500 copies and then more slowly. The rapid decline in unit cost results not from the variable cost but from the fixed costs being spread over larger quantities. Although the per copy cost of producing the book becomes progressively lower with increasing quantities, the total cost increases in a near linear relationship.

The costs of author's royalties are calculated by applying the different royalty rates to the sales forecasts for home and export markets etc.

Combining the income and costs

The editor strives to balance the income and costs so that the desired gross profit is attained. If too low, the production costs could be reduced (e.g. shorter book, fewer illustrations, cheaper paper etc.) or the author's proposed royalties cut. Conversely the price and sales estimate could be increased. But while the publisher worries about costs and margins, the end-user is concerned with price and perceived value, and does not care about the costs, the number printed or the author's effort. For an editor publishing a book with a limited market, there is the fatal temptation to imagine a non-existent larger market and to increase the print-run in order to lower unit cost.

The book's peak profitability may occur at a slightly lower sales figure than the number which yields the maximum revenue, owing to the increased costs of producing that quantity. The publisher could choose a lower published price which increased sales but the revenue from that may not recover the increased costs. The publisher could have made a profit if only it had not printed too many copies in excess of actual demand.

When the publisher takes the final decision on fixing the price and print quantity (and it has only one chance of getting it right), the fixed costs have already been incurred and cannot be changed.

On account of the uncertainties of estimating demand a prudent publisher favours a higher price and a lower quantity rather than a lower price and a higher quantity. If the actual demand for the book is less than expected, a price on the high side may still return a profit, whereas too low a price could lead to substantial loss. The great dangers are underestimating costs, overestimating demand and printing too many copies, and underpricing. This leads not only to a loss on the individual book, but can wipe out the profit on others. Successful books can always be reprinted, but at a price and quantity which again are chosen to avoid loss.

Other factors entering the pre-publication decisions concern the amount of investment at risk (e.g. very high authors' advances, or a large investment in a major reference book or textbook), and its duration. The calculation of 'worst case scenarios' or of the project's break-even point (e.g. the minimum quantity that must be sold to cover the production costs, author's advance or royalty, plus a proportion of overhead) can show the level of risk. On some proposals, if break-even is considered attainable, that may inspire sufficient confidence to go ahead. Some publishers calculate a project's cashflow and the interest incurred over time. From the outset to after publication, the publisher usually endures a net loss before the income surpasses the outlay. The estimated income is derived from the sales forecasts broken down over time (e.g. monthly, quarterly, yearly).

Possible rights sales income, other than that from co-printing deals, usually does not enter into the early costings and thus can be regarded as extra profit. However, it may be included, especially when needed to justify paying the author a large advance.

The costing exercise may apply to more than one edition (e.g. hardback and paperback editions on which most of the fixed costs have been carried on the back of the hardback edition) or to more than one printing (e.g. the first printing of a school textbook may attain no profit, but the hoped-for second and subsequent printings should move into profitability).

Some publishers stop their calculations at the gross profit line while others continue and deduct direct overheads expressed as overall percentages (e.g. editorial/design/production; and promotion and sales) to reach the net profit. The way in which overheads are apportioned, either as actual sums or percentages, varies.

The problems with the gross profit method as outlined above are that titles are allocated overheads in proportion to expected revenue (which may not accord with reality); it focuses attention on a desired percentage rather than money (e.g. a title may attain only a 25% gross profit yet deliver much more cash than one with a 55% gross profit); it encourages a minimum objective (there is nothing wrong in achieving a 100% profit); and it assumes a steady state.

Costing example: *Inside Book Publishing*, 3rd edn

Since 1998, the many publishers, which have published *Inside Book Publishing*, have recorded broadly similar results. The publication of each new edition generates an initial sale of around 1500 plus copies over the first 1–2 years, after which sales plateau at 600–700 copies annually for several years. Although it is classified as a professional reference title, the colleges teaching publishing have adopted it as a set book for student purchase which underpins its shelf-life: most sales are made in the autumn. With such a track record on the backlist, the risk factor of publishing a third edition is that much reduced.

The estimate for the third edition is reproduced below and is adapted from the Routledge Taylor & Francis computerized costing system. It uses the gross profit method. The commissioning editors must show the management that each book proposal is expected to attain the gross profit target set for them. They do not need to apportion the internal costs incurred in publishing the book, which are the overall responsibilities of the management. Since Routledge publishes hundreds of titles in standard sizes, the system instantly gives editors production costs and the calculations are automated. They can try out different combinations of published prices and sales predictions, production parameters and royalty rates.

The overall publishing strategy is for a book of 256pp (8×32pp sections) printed in Demy 8vo size (called 'C' format by the trade publishers). It is published as a quality sewn-bound paperback at £14.99, with a very short run and simultaneously published hardback edition at £45 for libraries. The total print run is 2000 copies, of which 1900 are bound in paperback, and 100 in hardback. But 200 paperback copies are to be given away as free copies for promotion as well as 10 hardbacks.

Notes on the book costing estimate below

(a) *Plant costs* are defined here as the work of copy-editing and proofreading carried out by freelances and of the cover designer (the text design follows a standard style at zero cost). The 'composition and origination' covers the cost of typesetting, proofing and corrections. The plant costs total £2400.

(b) *Manufacturing* relates to the cost of text printing 2000 copies and the cost of text paper which total £1607. Thus the total for 2000 unbound sets of sheets is £4007.

(c) *Finished copies* combines the sheet cost with the costs of printing the cover and of binding the hardback and paperback editions. The overall total for 100 hardbacks is £511 (unit cost £5.11), and for 1900 paperbacks is £5131 (unit cost £2.70). On the paperback edition, the mark-up factor is 5.55 times (£14.99/£2.70). (The run-on cost per thousand paperback copies, i.e. the cost of printing, paper and binding (PPB) is £645 (£0.64 unit), which can give rise to the fatal attraction to the editor of printing more copies.)

(d) *Royalties* are expressed as a percentage of publisher's net receipts (NR), as is common among the non-consumer book publishers, which also try to avoid paying significant advances. (If this were a consumer title written by an established author represented by a powerful agent, the royalty rates based on published price and the advances to be paid, including write-off provisions, would weigh heavily in the book costing.)

(e) *Quantities and published price.* Sales estimates for each edition are set according to the Taylor & Francis territorial division of the world: UK; Rest of World (RoW); and USA/Canada. The published prices on either side of the Atlantic are close to $/£ parity. Sales to North America are conducted through their own company.

(f) *Gross profit calculation.* The publisher's net receipts (i.e. income or NSR) are arrived at by multiplying the estimated sales quantities for each territory by the published prices, less the average trade discounts pertaining to the class of book in each territory. The total net sales revenue is £18 617 provided all copies were sold. The estimated identifiable direct costs of production (£5642) and of royalty (£1689) are £7331 which when deducted from the NSR leaves a gross profit (GP) of £11 286, or 60.6% when expressed as a percentage of net receipts.

While the publisher would be left with £11 286, the major costs in publishing this book are off the page, namely the staff overhead and other costs of running the business.

When the book reprints the gross margin increases since the plant costs have been recovered from the first printing and should not recur. A 1000 copy reprint of the paperback edition of this book would yield a margin of £6,500, or 69%. (The hardback sales to libraries would have been saturated and paperback exports would have diminished.)

But what if this were a different kind of book? Keeping the production specification and author royalty constant, the proposed new book is entitled *Publishing: key concepts*. Classified as a student reference book, the paperback published price is set at £9.99. However, in order to attain a gross profit of above 60%, the publisher would have to sell more than 4,000 copies in paperback. That book would deliver a higher gross profit in cash of £17 612, but the risk factor of selling such a large quantity in a highly specialist area would be greater. At the other extreme, the proposed book *Publishing History* (a monograph) is forecast to sell 470 copies in hardback priced at £55, mainly for the academic libraries (half overseas) and probably to the heads of houses named in the book. The monograph would deliver the same amount of gross profit in cash as *Inside Book Publishing*, provided the author's royalty rate were cut. The monograph would be unlikely to reprint, but would be available by on-demand printing or in digital form thereafter as part of the Routledge eternal backlist.

INSIDE BOOK PUBLISHING EDITION 3

New book   ISBN: HB: 0415230055 PB: 0415230063

Year of Publication: Fiscal Year 2000
Trimmed Page Size: D8: Demy 8vo Sewn
Extent: 256pp
Hardback Edition: HD Unjacketed (Blocked)
Cover: 3 colours
Design Category: Short run PB
Setting Category: Script

Illustrations:	None
Line Drawings:	5
Text Design Category:	B-Standard

A) PLANT COSTS

Cover Design:	£350
Desk Editorial:	£865
	£1,215
Composition & Origination:	£1,185
Total:	£2,400

B) MANUFACTURING

Text Printing:	£905
Text Paperstock:	£702
	£1,607
Total for 2,000 sheets:	£4,007

C) FINISHED COPIES

Quantities:	Hardback:	100
	Paperback:	1,900
	Total:	2,000
Edition Costs:		
Sheets:	Hardback:	£183
	Paperback:	£3,824
	Total:	£4,007
Jacket/Cover:	Hardback:	£8
	Paperback:	£780
	Total:	£788
Binding:	Hardback:	£320
	Paperback:	£527
	Total:	£847
Overall Totals:		£5,642

D) ROYALTIES % NR

HB:	UK Sales:	10%
	RoW Sales:	10%
	US/Can Sales:	10%

PB: UK Sales: 10%
          RoW Sales: 10%
          US/Can Sales: 10%

E) QUANTITIES AND PUBLISHED PRICE

	HBK	PBK
UK Sales:	30	1,300
RoW Sales:	20	200
USA Sales:	40	200
Frees:	10	200
Total Qty:	100	1,900

Published Price:

	HBK	PBK
UK:	£45.00	£14.99
US:	£45.45	£15.14
	$74.99	$24.98

Exchange Rate $/£ = 1.65

F) GROSS PROFIT CALCULATION

NET RECEIPTS

	UK/RoW		USA/Canada		Overall	
	HBK	PBK	HBK	PBK	HBK	PBK
UK Sales (37.00 disc):	£851	£12,277				
RoW Sales (40.00 disc):	£540	£1,799				
USA Sales (35.00 disc):			£1,182	£1,968		
SALES REVENUE:	£1,391	£14,076	£1,182	£1,968	£2,573	£16,044

Grand Total: £18,617

COSTS

	UK/RoW		USA/Canada		Overall	
	HBK	PBK	HBK	PBK	HBK	PBK
Total Production:	£307	£4,591	£204	£540	£511	£5,131
Home Royalty:	£85	£1,228				
Export Royalty:	£54	£180				
US Royalty:			£53	£89		
TOTAL COSTS:	£446	£5,999	£257	£629		

Grand Total: £7,331

	UK/Row		USA/Canada		Overall	
	HBK	PBK	HBK	PBK	HBK	PBK
Gross Profit:	£945	£8,077	£925	£1,339	£1,870	£9,416
Total Gross Profit: £11,286:						
GP as % net receipts:	67.9	57.4	78.3	68.0	72.7	58.7
Total GP as % net receipts: 60.6%						
Prod. cost as % net rec:	22.1	32.6	17.3	27.4	19.9	32.0
Royalty as % net rec:	10.0	10.0	4.5	4.5	7.5	9.3

COSTING A BOOK: UNIT COST MARK-UP METHOD

This traditional and simple method is severely criticized but can be used as a ready-reckoner. Essentially, the unit, or per copy, print production cost (derived from dividing the quantity of books to be ordered into the total cost of printing those books, i.e. the fixed production costs plus the variable cost of that quantity) is multiplied by a factor (e.g. 5, 6, 8) to arrive at the published price. The accounts department calculate for editors the factors pertaining to different kinds of books (e.g. consumer or academic) with different royalty rates and discounts. Provided the copies sell out the factor accommodates the firm's costs and profit. But if the published price is thought too high, the editor is tempted to increase the print run to lower unit cost in order to arrive, by multiplication, at a reasonable price. Conversely, the publisher may print the number it believes it can sell but fix the price too high to absorb that number. Unless careful the publisher ends up with unsold copies or loss-makers. The method, based on a predetermined level of activity, disregards the fact that costs do not act alike as output increases or decreases, encourages rigid pricing and conceals assumptions. Worse, it focuses attention on unit cost and away from the market and price elasticities.

The method can be used in reverse. The gross retail value (price multiplied by sales estimate) is divided by the factor to arrive at the desired unit cost. The book's specification could then be adjusted to match.

The use of a mark-up factor often occurs when consumer book publishers buy books from packagers (e.g. a mark-up factor of between 4 and 5 is applied to the packager's all in, royalty-inclusive, price per copy to arrive at a published price; or if the publisher is translating and resetting, five or six). The packager seeks the lowest mark-up factor attainable.

SUCCESSES, NON-CONTRIBUTORS AND FAILURES

If a book is reprinted and the publisher has recovered all its development and marketing costs from the first printing, its margin (provided the copies sell out) dramatically increases (because such costs do not recur). But substantially revised new editions incur renewed fixed costs and relaunch overheads. Publishing is a high margin business and can be immensely profitable. But for numerous publishers, those profits are a mirage – they make just too many mistakes.

Some authors either fail to deliver manuscripts or submit unacceptable material. The consumer book publishers which pay significant sums on signature of contract, can find them difficult to recover; in some rare cases they are victims of fraudulent authors. If a proposed book is not published, its estimated contribution to overheads needs to be recouped from elsewhere. It is relatively easier for a consumer book publisher to fill its list more quickly (e.g. by buying from packagers or from US firms) than a school text-book publisher. All the decisions regarding the quality of a book, its market, price and sales potential are based on advance subjective judgements. Among the new books there inevitably lurk those that fail to recover their production costs or the author's advance, let alone make a contribution to overheads. Generally speaking, publishers make very little net profit from their new book publishing programme over the first year. Their profits stem from the surviving titles that reprint.

A vigorous and profitable publisher is in a strong position to publish books which, it is estimated at the outset, will not show a profit; indeed there may be good publishing reasons for doing so. A book could be published for prestige purposes. A fiction publisher may believe in a novelist's long-term ultimate success, or want the author's next more desirable book. A textbook publisher may want to enter a new area and undercut competitors. A university press may be obliged to publish a great scholarly work (sometimes supported by a subvention). Some publishers keep titles in print even though the storage costs exceed their revenue. For example a fiction publisher may keep in print an author's body of work, and a university press may keep scholarly titles in print for years.

Chapter 6

Getting into publishing and career pathways

YOUR CAREER CAMPAIGN

Although so many junior jobs advertised state that previous publishing experience is necessary, entry to publishing is paradoxically mainly at the bottom. You should therefore snatch any kind of work in any area of publishing, whatever the size of firm. Publishers usually recruit only to fill vacancies which, at the entry level, often occur at no more than a month's notice. Once in, you will be learning, gaining personal impressions of various jobs by talking to people, and, what is more, be in a position to hear about future jobs. From that bridgehead, it is usually easier to obtain a second job than the first, by moving sideways or upwards within or outside the firm. Do not fear that your first job, or jobs, will necessarily determine your subsequent career. Two to three job changes in the first five years are not uncommon. But at the outset, it is preferable to think firstly of the kinds of books you would be interested in publishing and hence the type of publishing company, and secondly the kind of work for which you feel you might have a particular aptitude.

To increase your chances, the ability to drive is useful and typing/wordprocessing and computer literacy is necessary for all jobs.

During vacations, try proofreading for an academic etc., offer your services to short-staffed booksellers. (If you are a bookseller and want to cross to publishing, two to three years of bookselling is ample.) A temporary job with a publisher during the summer may lead to the elusive first full-time appointment.

Market research

You must carry out research on publishing in general and on an individual publisher or a group of target publishers in particular, and especially you should research the books these firms publish.

Read the trade press; examine the most recent trade directories; read book reviews; and visit libraries and bookshops to look at their books on the shelves and to seek advice on books from librarians and booksellers. For specialist areas visit the appropriate library or bookshop. When visiting bookshops during quiet periods try to talk to the book buyer who deals directly with publishers' reps.

The most useful compendium of publishers' books is the spring and autumn special issues of *The Bookseller: Buyer's Guide*. These bumper issues may be available behind the counter of a library or bookshop. Notable absences are the book packagers and the educational publishers. To trace the latter you could attend one of the annual subject-related or regional conferences at which publishers exhibit. The annual London International Book Fair (Reed) held in March provides a great opportunity to view the wares of publishers and packagers, and the venue to meet their staff – arrive early – and to attend the career clinic. (The Book Fair Catalogue is an invaluable guide.) The annual BETT show held in London in January is the showcase for the educational digital media publishers.

When you have narrowed down the field or have secured an interview, you must read the publisher's catalogue and visit their web site before any further approach is made.

If possible visit the publisher's showroom to examine the books and collect catalogues. While a kind bookseller or possibly a librarian of a large library may show you catalogues, a better course of action would be to obtain the appropriate catalogues from a publisher's publicity department or from the person who has placed the advertisement.

Making contacts

Contacts in publishing (and to a less extent with authors, literary agents, printers, booksellers, review and trade press journalists) can provide insight into particular firms, offering you advice, spreading knowledge of your abilities, and alerting you to impending vacancies. Sometimes these contacts are influential enough to secure you a preliminary discussion or interview, though rarely a job itself. Therefore, first tap your family and personal connections; if you draw a blank there, take the initiative. You can network and learn by joining the Society of Young Publishers (SYP), London and Oxford. It holds monthly meetings – at which senior publishers pronounce – and publishes the journal, *Inprint*. Membership is not restricted to people employed in publishing. Women in Publishing (WiP) holds regular meetings and training sessions in London and Oxford. Membership is open to women of any age in publishing. You may be able to attend meetings of the Independent Publishers Guild (IPG) in London and around the country (mainly small publishers and packagers), the Society of Picture Researchers and Editors (SPREd), the Galley Club, the Publishers Publicity Circle, the Rights Circle, the Children's Book Circle and the Business Publishers Group (see Appendix, *Directories* and *The Bookseller* for addresses). Most of the publishing luncheon and dining clubs are private. However, The Paternosters has no barriers to entry and its members meet for lunch monthly in London to enjoy their company and to listen to distinguished speakers (contact David Hicks, 4 The Retreat, Kings Langley, Herts WD4 8LT). The London publishers (and agents) often enjoy drinking after work – try frequenting bars close to their offices.

The relevance of a degree

The number of people in publishing with degrees has increased markedly. The last area in which change has been slower is in home sales of consumer book publishers. Most new editors have degrees and in academic editing a degree may be thought to be most relevant but even in those areas a degree is not essential for successful publishing. But many publishers faced with so many hopefuls use a degree qualification as a simple device for sorting out applicants. Those without degrees can still enter, for instance via the assistant or sales routes, or with relevant work experience (such as in print production).

People with degrees in science, mathematics and other specialities, such as law or medicine, are at a premium for publishers in those areas. A teaching background and/or experience in English language teaching is particularly useful for educational/ELT publishers, and African studies (or Voluntary Service Overseas) for international educational publishers. Qualification in cartography is useful for map and guide publishers. Language degrees are desirable for rights and export sales departments of all kinds of publishers. The level of degree is less important. Those with doctorates seeking their first junior job may face the difficulty that they are that much older than competing younger applicants. See the graduate careers website: *www.prospects.csu.ac.uk*.

Macmillan is the only publisher which has consistently maintained a graduate trainee scheme over the last thirty years. Four or five graduates are selected each year and are given an accelerated, diverse and international experience to shape them for management positions.

Pre-entry training

Traditionally, the only departments in which formal vocationally orientated qualifications are very desirable are graphic design and production. Many publishers believe new entrants can learn other publishing skills on the job from their colleagues and seniors. The pre-entry publishing courses used to be restricted mainly to a small number of printing, art and design and technical colleges and polytechnics, and usually concentrated on copy-editing and production skills. However, by the end of the 1980s the established institutions broadened their course content to include the business and marketing aspects of publishing; and they incorporated greater academic rigour, sometimes enabling students to study publishing along with other disciplines. The expansion of higher education in the early 1990s and the establishment of the new universities has increased the number and range of courses available at under-graduate, post-graduate and diploma levels (see Appendix), with student places around several hundred per year. Their links with publishers, various work experience schemes for students, and the rise of their former students into management positions, have undermined the traditionalist view that pre-entry vocational training is a waste of time.

Attaining a qualification does not guarantee a job in book publishing but it substantially increases the chances – the established institutions score impressive success rates. Some publishers, recognizing the quality of output of the main institutions, advertise job openings directly to their students (and former students) on institutions' notice boards and web sites. However, some of their students are attracted to competing media sectors or to financial services, which offer superior starting salaries than those of book publishers (often around £12–13,000; 1999), and formal career training and development packages.

Secretarial and assistant entry

The number of secretarial posts has declined significantly in response to pressures to reduce staff costs and with the advent of PCs and e-mail. Most staff, including managers, do their own wordprocessing and spread sheets. The remaining secretarial posts tend to be attached to the most senior levels of management, or are shared within a department. When publishers recruit secretaries they are doing just that and are not making any promises about promotion. Publishers want their secretaries to have a good level of education and literacy, with accurate spelling and punctuation. Most want A level qualifications, such as English, and some favour degrees. The employment of the newly graduated with competent skills is a particular feature in London and Oxford. However, some London-based publishers still prefer to take people who start with them after A levels and build up to senior level rather than graduate secretaries who may be over-qualified and pushing for quick promotion. Skills in foreign languages are a bonus, especially in the fields of rights and export sales.

Naturally every employer wants speed and accuracy in the main skill of wordprocessing, and general ICT skills. However, many employers are happy with reasonable levels of speed and accuracy if they see a candidate whom they like. The minimum acceptable words-per-minute speeds are usually in the region of 40 to 50 for accurate typing; and 90 to 100 for shorthand (fading away). The graduates who lack the basic skills and who try to get into London publishers via secretarial bureaux are doomed to disappointment.

The salaries offered by publishers in London do not compare favourably with those of most other types of business. But the publishing industry, especially consumer book publishers, offers probably the greatest chance for a secretary to progress to other activities.

Publishers outside London recruit locally from people who are unlikely to have a degree. The chances for such people to advance into other activities (especially in the educational, academic and STM publishers and in particular departments, such as editorial, where the holding of a degree is much emphasized) are much less.

They tend to remain on the secretarial ladder, though a few may cross-over.

While the posts that are heavily skewed towards generic secretarial duties have declined, publishers retain assistant posts across every department. The assistants are usually graduates with adequate wordprocessing and ICT skills. Their tasks are focused on carrying out the lower level tasks in editorial, production, marketing and sales, and aiding their seniors with their publishing tasks without bearing responsibility for them. They have the advantage of being in close contact with senior staff and if they keep eyes and ears open they are in a position to gain insight into the workings of the company at a high level, knowledge which may come in useful later. They gain that elusive background qualification 'publishing experience'. But as in other jobs which depend on a transition between one function and another, there is the risk of getting stuck on the photo-copying machine.

Lastly there is always a demand from publishers for temporary staff to fill jobs vacated by people on holiday or ill. (Thursday is a good day to find work through a bureau.) In London this is a good way of getting the feel of different publishers and can lead to a permanent job.

Responding to advertisements

Advertisements for publishing jobs appear in print and on the web in the trade press (*The Bookseller* and *Publishing News*), in the national press (e.g. mainly the *Guardian*, especially on Mondays and Saturdays, the *Daily Telegraph*, the *Independent* on Wednesdays, *The Times* on Wednesdays, the *Observer*, and the 'Books' section of the *Sunday Times*); in job-related journals (e.g. *Campaign*); and occasionally in specialist journals (e.g. *Times Educational Supplement*, *New Scientist*). Secretarial vacancies in London appear in the trade and national press, and in free magazines. Publishers outside London may advertise locally. The very high cost of press advertising has prompted some publishers to advertise low level jobs on free web sites, such as that of the SYP. Some publishers use recruitment agencies for jobs needing previous publishing experience.

When an advertisement catches your eye, do not be put off if you fall short of the employer's stated ideal or feel you are on the borderline (and have a compensatory strength), or are just outside the stated age bands.

PREPARING YOUR CV AND COVERING LETTER

To secure an interview you must attract the publisher's attention by submitting an effective and immaculately tailored curriculum vitae and covering letter, without spelling mistakes, inconsistent punctuation or ungrammatical sentences. Many new entrants applying for their first publishing jobs, as well as those applying for subsequent jobs, fail on these points at this initial hurdle.

The CV is an organized summary of the key facts (not opinions) about yourself. While emphasizing your assets not your liabilities, the CV must be truthful. Each element should prove to the publisher that you have the qualities and skills for the job: omit those that do not. When typed it should take up one or two A4 pages.

For those with short work experience, the chronological CV laid out in a form style is usually the best approach. The information is listed in chronological order under headings.

Under personal details give your full name, contact address(es) with daytime telephone numbers, date of birth and age, marital status and nationality. If your home is far from a London publisher preferably quote a southeast address or stress your willingness to move.

The education and training section lists schools etc., with dates, courses taken, grades achieved, special projects, scholarships, prizes. Spotlight any occupational training courses which are relevant or supplemental to the job.

Work experience (e.g. full or part-time, voluntary, overseas, vacation) may be listed in chronological or, if quite extensive or if your last job was directly relevant, usually in reverse chronological order (i.e. the most recent first), with no unexplained gaps. Provide employers' names, job titles with duties and responsibilities, promotions, special awards, and accomplishments (e.g. ideas that reduced costs, increased profitability, streamlined administration) – one or two short sentences for each job.

If you have worked freelance or run your own business, the work should be described as if you were an employee yet stressing your responsibilities and achievements.

If you have a weak education you may wish to put work experience before education and quote other sources of learning and training. Relevant work outside publishing should be emphasized (e.g. secretarial, office, library, bookshop work, preparing a firm's literature or magazine, proofreading, print buying, compiling mailing lists, public and customer relations, face-to-face selling, accounting, budgeting, computing, teaching, work overseas).

The reverse chronological format for CVs is convenient for publishers who can readily see your career path and progression and relevant experience for a particular job. However, the functional (sometimes referred to as skill or portfolio) format may be favoured, for example, by those with little job experience or with erratic career or job changes, or gaps in employment history – all too evident on a linear chronology. The functional format presents upfront your skills, achievements and relevant experience grouped so that the publisher can see how your skills relate to the job. Your employment history section may then follow.

Whatever the CV format, the skills emphasized may be those pertaining particularly to specific jobs (as outlined in this book) and those which are more generic, such as wordprocessing/computer literacy, web site development, driving, languages, numeracy, administration, communication (e.g. presentations, telesales). Try to link skills, particularly those that relate to the job, to work experience, vocational training, membership of societies, professional and trade bodies etc.

Activities and interests may be incorporated under the above headings or listed separately. If you are about to leave full-time education your skills and keen interests (e.g. photography, sport) assume great importance because with little work experience they mark you out. List leadership or administrative positions, and achievements.

The CV ends with the names and telephone numbers of your two or three referees (e.g. your teacher/tutor, or last employer) who can convey your character, stability and competence to perform the job. Brief them beforehand. One should act as a character reference. You can state, if necessary, that they should not be contacted without prior consultation.

CV and letter presentation

Use factual, concise simple language (without abbreviations or jargon) and active verbs. Have someone who is literate or familiar with staff selection to check and edit it.

Use a wordprocessor with letter quality printing or laser

printer (use no more than two conventional typefaces, such as a serif face as Times New Roman, and two sizes). If necessary, use a professional typist or bureau.

Use white A4 bond paper (avoid colour printing and coloured paper). Set good margins with adequate spaces top and bottom. Leave one line space between sections. Try not to break a section at the bottom of the first page (a heading should be followed by at least two lines of text, or carried over). Number the two sheets. Insert your name at the top of page two.

Although it is preferable to send the publisher the unblemished first copy on bond paper, a top quality photocopy is acceptable (i.e. black crisp type, white background, no spots, clean edges on good paper). The hardcopy you supply must be perfect enough for the publisher to photocopy or scan for circulation – avoid unnecessary folding.

The covering letter must accompany the CV. Its purpose is to show the publisher the benefits of employing you, to whet the publisher's appetite to learn more about you – to read your CV and to call you to interview. The letter should be no longer than one page of A4 say 3–5 short paragraphs, typed on white A4 paper (the same as the CV). If you are applying for your first job in publishing you will not have space, nor would it be desirable, to expound at length on your love of books and reading, or on your envisaged contribution to English literature. Do not include gimmicks, such as poetry or illustrations.

The letter should be headed with your name and contact details and addressed by *surname* to the head of the department to which you are applying, or to the personnel department (or, if replying to an advertisement, to the person stated). Spell the manager's, and the firm's, name correctly. (Check with the receptionist or personal assistant.)

Start with a brief and simple statement of your reasons for writing (e.g. that you are applying for position X, advertised in journal Y, on Z date, or are seeking work, or mention a mutual contact referral) and that you enclose your CV.

Orientate the letter to the job, firm, your suitability and enthusiasm, for example:

- State briefly your current position (e.g. about to leave college with expected qualifications; or currently employed by X firm in Y capacity; or free to start work immediately).

- Show your research of the publisher by referring to recent or future books or promotions or recent acquisitions etc. If you have yet to enter publishing indicate with evidence your commitment to a publishing career and your career objective.
- Stress your motives and suitability: relevant experience, skills and enthusiasm. Select the prime ones (you can cross-refer to your CV). Link your attributes to those specified in the advertisement and/or those included in your CV. Convey your enthusiasm by anchoring it to some credential, or a relevant fact. Try to focus your qualities to the needs of the publisher.
- Give positive reasons for making the career step and for your keen interest in the job/activity.
- Politely request an interview; say that you look forward to meeting them and are eager to learn more about the position. You may suggest your availability or indicate your flexibility.
- Sign off 'Yours sincerely' (if Dear Mr/s). If your signature is illegible, print your name underneath. Indicate the enclosure.

Use relatively short paragraphs rather than a few long ones; plain English, concise and precise language, and the active voice.

Avoid cliches and unappealing abruptness. To judge tone, try reading the letter aloud the next day, or ask someone else to read and proof read it. Remember you are trying to persuade a stranger to interview you. Overfamiliarity, casualness and flippancy are out of place but something more than a cold business letter is called for.

Do not challenge the publisher to employ you or regard the publisher as a career counsellor with whom to share fantasies, or someone to be entertained. Do not heap phoney praise on the publisher, indulge yourself in subjective self-praise, confess to past failures, highlight events which may be seen negatively (e.g. 'I am currently unemployed', 'I gave up work seven years ago to start a family'). Never imply that you see the job only as a stepping stone to further your interests somewhere else.

Completing an application form

Some publishers supply application forms. Make copies of the form if not supplied electronically. Follow the instructions and read it right through twice before starting. You can still select and emphasize your assets. Take particular care with your full answers to the major open-ended questions or 'other information'. Use the photocopies for drafting and layout. If necessary, attach an extra sheet. You must add a substantive covering letter.

What to do now

Keep the copies of your application(s) close to the telephone(s) you have quoted ready for a call from a publisher. Conversely you may telephone them within seven days to reiterate your keen interest and to enquire about their progress, but avoid being a menace. If you have been short-listed, the publisher will contact you to arrange the interview. However, some publishers conduct surprise telephone screening interviews. If you are not fully prepared with a good script, re-schedule. You may receive a rejection – like the majority – or worse, hear nothing. Difficult as it is, do not let depression and frustration colour future applications. No application is wasted: elements can be re-used and modified. Some publishers hold strong but rejected applicants on file.

DIRECT APPROACH TO PUBLISHERS

Many publishing jobs are not advertised, so writing speculatively to publishers can work; but be prepared to write at least thirty applications. Many publishers have high staff turnover at the junior level or need to cover maternity leave and these continually create new opportunities.

Sending duplicated applications is useless. If you are about to leave full-time education, your CV is likely to be thin on work experience, and the scope for slanting it specifically to a firm limited. However, your covering letter must relate to an individual firm, and be addressed to and relate specifically to a particular manager's department (i.e. write directly to a named manager, reveal your knowledge of the firm and your commitment to publishing, point to your suitability, enthusiasm and realistic contribution to the activity). To ease your workload, target your top five or ten chosen publishers and departments. A stamped-addressed envelope may encourage a reply.

Because so many humanities graduates apply mainly to the London consumer book publishers and to editorial departments, you increase your chances if you apply to other departments.

Furthermore, there are many opportunities in specialist areas of consumer book publishing, and in the out-of-London educational/ ELT, academic, STM and professional book and journal publishers. It is well worth writing to less well-known small publishers issuing, say around twenty titles per year, and to packagers. There are thousands of intermittent small publishers producing less than five titles per year, which are unlikely to employ staff, though a few may be prepared to offer unpaid work on a project.

Some publishers do not reply to speculative approaches, others hold impressive candidates on file, to be approached later if a job arises. Some will call you for a preliminary discussion which may lead to an interview, or are prepared to offer advice, possibly recommending you for interview in another house. If you hear nothing or receive a letter of rejection, yet are still very keen on that publisher, telephone the manager and persuade him or her to give you a short chat. People whose commitment to publishing is so strong and who persist usually get in.

BEFORE THE INTERVIEW

If you are called to interview, acknowledge quickly. If you decide not to go, say so, and give others the opportunity. Publishers often shortlist between six and a dozen, with possibly a few marginal reserves.

Prepare thoroughly beforehand. **First**, research the publisher, its books or promotions. 'Why do you find them interesting?' This greatly improves your chances.

Second, think of answers to probable questions. As a publisher, what would you be looking for? From your research, you should be able to deal with questions that relate to your interest in the job and test your knowledge of the publisher. Also you should be prepared to discuss what you think are the most important skills needed. You may be asked what you feel would be the most mundane or frustrating parts of the job and how you would cope with them.

The thinking you put into your CV and letter is apposite to questions such as, 'Why do you want to go into publishing?' (don't just say 'I love reading and books') or, 'How is your previous experience applicable?'. 'Why do you think you are suitable?', 'What are your major strengths?' or, 'What makes you think you will be good at it?', and, 'What are your interests or hobbies?'. 'What books do you read?' is asked especially by consumer book publishers. Cite books which correspond to their interests and be prepared to analyse briefly why you think they work.

When asked about your experience be prepared for questions which probe facts, explore your feelings, judgement and motivation. You may well be asked to explain why you left a job. Do not blame the previous employer or specific individuals. Acceptable reasons include: 'I left for a better opportunity' or 'for more challenging work', or 'to broaden my experience'. Redundancy, even if no fault of your own and a common affliction of many in publishing can be related to 'unique' circumstances pertaining to a particular firm. Beware of quoting shortcomings that may be applicable to the job applied for.

You will need to show that you have thought of medium-term career goals, while stressing your preparedness to commit yourself to the job for an effective time-span.

Many new entrants apply, for example to the marketing and sales departments, with the ambition of becoming editors. You may confess that legitimate target to a manager of another department but you must show strong commitment to the job applied for, otherwise you will be rejected.

Book publishing is an ideas business from start to finish. 'What ideas do you have?' may be asked of any applicant in any department. Do not sit dumbfounded. There may be no 'correct' answer – the question is more of a test of initiative and of commonsense.

Third, jot down your own questions. The best ones relate to clarifying features of the job and showing your knowledge of and keen interest in the publisher. Questions relating to the job include its main aspects, what factors promoted its creation, limits of authority, responsibility and independence, whom you would be working with most closely, terms and conditions, future prospects etc. Those relating to the publisher (such as on new developments) could arise from your research. However, you should ask only a few questions – you are the one being interviewed. You could ask questions to which in part you can guess the answer and which will elicit a positive response.

Be careful not to ask questions that are out of your depth, or cheeky or ask the publisher to give you unreasonable special treatment, or that damn you (e.g. 'Well, what books do you actually publish?'). Your questions, or lack of them, may be more revealing than your answers to the publisher's.

Fourth, optional as a reserve fallback, take samples of printed material on which you have worked (e.g. a college magazine, book, promotional material, sales aids etc.). A powerful visual-aid can focus the interview on your best work. By recounting quickly the brief, the decisions and initiatives taken, the problems overcome, the people involved, you can reveal your analytical, decision-making and organizational abilities, your ideas and effectiveness in dealing with people and your success.

Before the interview, you will need to judge your standard of dress. The style and atmosphere of publishers differs markedly, and some departments, such as accounts, may be more formal than others. Many managers are greatly influenced by the candidate's first impression which, if bad, destroys you. On the whole it is best to appear businesslike and well dressed and groomed.

You must not be late so allow plenty of time, and make sure you know the exact location of the interview. Some publishers are very difficult to find. If you are unavoidably delayed telephone and apologize. On arrival announce yourself to the receptionist and if time allows examine the publisher's material in the showroom. Do not smoke. If you are still waiting, remind the receptionist one minute before the appointment.

THE INTERVIEW

If you are a new entrant, your anxiety may rise outside the inter-viewer's closed door. While some interviewers will greet you at the door, your first test may be to enter the room confidently (an important skill for most jobs).

You should greet and shake the interviewer's or, if a panel, the Chair's hand, positively. Remember the panel's job titles in order to direct your responses, and do not slouch or smoke. Bring out your letter and CV, with the firm's catalogue displayed (resist irritating hand movements).

Throughout the interview try to amplify and slant relevant assets which reveal your suitability and enthusiasm, anchor your skills to evidence, and ground accomplishments on citing exam-ples, perhaps of a statistical nature. Reveal your research of the publisher, but do not over-praise or lecture.

Maintain eye contact with an interviewer at all times and listen to the questions (politely clarify if necessary). Do not mumble yes/no answers. Answer questions fully, but judge the length and depth of your reply by watching the interviewer's verbal and non-verbal cues, and interest level. Be prepared for the interviewer's follow-up questions. When stating views make sure your reasoning is sensible and fairly firm, not vague, arrogant or inflexible. Avoid taking extreme positions, especially negative ones.

The danger of talking too much, apart from boring the interviewer, is to go beyond the question and introduce irrelevant facts or opinions either of which inadvertently reveal weaknesses applicable or not to the job. Indeed an interviewer may keep quiet and let you hang yourself. Interviewers tend to form negative impressions more readily, and on less information, than they form favourable impressions; their judgements are apt to be coloured by one or two striking attributes of candidates; and they tend to reject on negatives rather than select on positives (while ignoring irrelevant weaknesses).

The more nervous you become, the faster you may talk. Strive for measured animation. Undue modesty will conceal you, while boasting is damaging. If you have been dishonest in your CV or overstated the case you will be unable to substantiate your claims.

A quality that most interviewers want to see, which can illuminate all others, is enthusiasm. It means having a positive outlook that shines through whatever subject is being discussed.

Finally, the most intangible and important part of the whole exercise is whether the interviewer likes you and thinks you will fit in because most publishers are relatively small businesses (or profit centres within a large corporation) and publishing is a personal business. Moreover, some managers set great store on their quality of life expressed by the work they do and the people they have around them.

There are publishers, and/or individual managers, who are anti-union and are careful not to employ activists whom they see as wreckers. On the other hand a candidate's leanings or beliefs may be very desirable to individual managers or particular firms. Some publishers' interests are focused on propagating particular views in society, for example in political, gender, race, religious and health areas. They attract and often overtly seek staff in all departments who are sympathetic to their values.

Having asked your questions, by the end of the interview you should have a clear idea of what the job entails, what will happen next, who will make the next move, and the timescale. Publishers typically use either one or two interview stages.

Not all publishers pay travelling expenses, especially if you live in London and apply to a firm there, or if you are travelling from a great distance. Preferably check with the assistant rather than in the interview.

When the publisher is pretty sure it wants you, your references will be checked. If you receive a letter of rejection it may be advantageous immediately to write a courteous thank you note expressing your acute disappointment and re-affirming your keen interest in the job and firm (you may want to apply for another job in the same firm or you may come across one of the interviewers in another).

If you are the chosen candidate reply quickly if you decide either to decline or accept the offer. There is usually little or no room for negotiation in junior jobs. A question you may be asked at interview or subsequently is 'What salary are you expecting?'. It is preferable to turn the question back on to the publisher to make the first offer by asking, for instance 'What are you planning on paying the best candidate?'. Publishers rarely state salaries on advertisements and there is great variation in salary ranges between different publishers. Network contacts and publishing recruitment consultants are arguably the best sources for prevailing rates.

Publishers differ markedly in style of management and atmosphere. The first months at work are a crucial period for quickly assimilating the politics of the organization and learning how to work within it, how to get things done, how to win and retain the regard of new colleagues. Tactics such as throwing your heart into the new job and being seen to arrive early and leave late will establish an enduring reputation.

POST-ENTRY TRAINING

Most people in publishing learn on the job by watching, listening, doing, learning from the successes and mistakes made by themselves, colleagues, and other publishers, and applying that experience to each new project: knowledge is passed on or re-invented.

Not many publishers give sufficient emphasis to training, of their junior staff in their early twenties, or for that matter of senior staff who while having specialist knowledge of their field may often lack a broad overview of the business and general management knowledge; let alone an MBA. Publishers may then complain that they face shortages of talent when recruiting for senior posts. If you are fortunate enough to work in a firm that trains, take all the opportunities offered. But if not, the initiative is yours to seek out relevant meetings such as those of the SYP and WiP, and to make the time to attend courses. There are numerous courses offered part-time by both the main teaching institutions, by professional organizations such as SFEP, Society of Indexers, and ALPSP for journals, and by private sector operators (see Appendix).

The Publishing Training Centre at Book House, London is the premier training body offering the greatest range of short vocational courses for the industry, and runs an internet bookshop for books on publishing.

It is vital to find out tactfully what people do in other departments, to understand their priorities and systems, and to try to work out the publisher's costs and income (its successes and failures), that is if you imagine running that business or another. Successful managers often acquire an overview of the business at an early age, while most colleagues are just content to attend to the next task on their desk. Equally important is the constant building of external contacts. Track talented individuals who may start up new firms or revitalize moribund ones. While hard work establishes your reputation, it is enterprise that puts you in the right place at the right time for the next job.

TERMS AND CONDITIONS

Within book publishing there is a great variation in salaries and no trade-wide statistics are available. However, the National Union of Journalists, which represents some book publishing staff, regularly publishes a survey of the rates of pay of firms with which it negotiates as part of its campaign against low pay, and for graded pay structures etc. Traditionally, the many junior jobs in publishing, particularly the editorial, have low starting salaries (sometimes lower than that paid to qualified secretaries), in part a consequence of large numbers chasing few jobs. (Some people argue that the incidence of low pay and the high proportion of female employment at junior levels are not unconnected.)

The law of supply and demand may also affect salary variation across different types of publishing. For example, publishers wanting staff with a humanities background have a large choice and tend to pay lower salaries than legal and medical publishers which may find it very difficult to find staff with the relevant academic qualifications or experience and are thus prepared to pay a considerable premium for them. Moreover, some people like to work in areas which they see as having intrinsic interest and accept lower salaries than if they worked in other fields of publishing. This has applied particularly to those in the literary and prestigious end of publishing. Generally speaking, some main publishers pay middle management salaries which compare favourably to those of the universities – another low pay area.

On the marketing and sales side, salaries have been approaching those of general commerce; but at the top end, the salaries of most marketing/sales directors of publishing companies do not equate with those earned by the heads of large fast-moving consumer goods industries, simply because publishers, even the largest, are smaller enterprises. At the very top, a few of the chief executives earn nearly fifteen times that of the lowest paid staff.

Four weeks' holiday has tended to become the norm, though sometimes a minimum of three weeks is quoted for new staff, and some companies may offer five or six weeks after many years' service. Whether anyone has time to take all the holiday allowance is another matter.

The terms of a firm's pension scheme (sometimes covering free life insurance), to which employees in some firms contribute say 5–7% of their salaries, become increasingly important to older candidates. A growing number of enlightened publishers give their staff permanent health insurance which could be a far more valuable benefit than life insurance. Some give health insurance free or at reduced rates. Minor benefits include subsidized canteens, or luncheon vouchers, and invariably the provision of buying the firm's books for personal use at cheap prices. (Publishers usually give trade terms to staff of other firms who want to buy their books.)

Though successive governments have drastically reduced the tax advantages of company cars their provision by some publishers to middle management, irrespective of whether they are used for business, is still a benefit and, combined with the salary, can be inducement to people to change jobs.

Compared with many other private sector firms, some publishers score quite highly on maternity leave. Paternity leave and pay may be given sympathetic consideration by some.

Men and women in publishing

There is a very high proportion of women in pre-entry courses and in publishing, particularly London consumer book publishing; but the recruitment of women as home sales representatives has lagged behind recruitment in other departments. The significance of the assistant secretarial route into publishing has been an important factor. For some time, however, women have dominated the work of publicity and of rights selling at both junior and senior levels. About 70% of the workforce is female.

Turning to senior management, the directorships on company boards, the picture is the reverse across all kinds of publishing: on the whole men predominate. But in comparison to most other industries in the UK, the elevation of women to company (mainly subsidiary) boards is better, albeit at a slow rate.

CAREER PATHWAYS

In-house editors

Most staff in editorial departments have degrees. In some areas of publishing, such as educational, academic, STM and professional book publishing, the degree subjects (and/or professional qualifications) preferably relate to the specialisms of the lists of books published: however editors deal with many kinds of books outside the narrow confines of the discipline they studied.

Consumer book publishers, too, favour the recruitment of graduates to junior positions. While publishers may argue that a degree in the humanities (especially English literature) is appropriate, others are not too concerned with the subject and think many English graduates make poor desk editors. Editing has become almost the preserve of graduates, some of whom have additionally studied pre-entry publishing courses.

Like other jobs in book publishing, editorial posts are predominantly filled by people already in the industry and most people work their way up from or near the bottom. Editorial departments receive more hopeful applicants than any other. The hundreds of humanities graduates who apply to famous consumer book publishers (such as to the Editorial Director of Faber & Faber) with nothing more than a good degree are, like unsolicited manuscripts, nearly always rejected.

The few advertised posts for junior positions usually say that previous publishing experience is required and many quote the necessity of wordprocessing. Generally speaking, when publishers advertise secretarial posts in editorial departments they want adequate technical attainments. However, there are 'assistant' posts of a quasi-clerical nature in which the skill of typing is a main requirement – such posts are likely to be open to both men and women. The faster the clerical and administrative tasks can be completed, the greater the opportunity of being given more rewarding work, such as proofreading, editing manuscripts or picture research.

The way into editing via secretarial, or assistant work, is common. But, owing to the intense competition for editorial posts, people enter other departments to acquire publishing experience and some cross over to editing. Another, albeit rare, way of entry is to become a researcher employed short-term by reference or highly illustrated book publishers or packagers.

Most editors learn on the job. Smaller publishers occasionally take on people with little or no experience and train them, and some large publishers send editors on training courses, especially in the specialist areas of publishing where editors are in short supply.

Experience which increases a job applicant's attractiveness includes editing school or college magazines, short-term work in a bookshop preferably linked to the area of publishing, knowledge of printing learnt on a course or possibly from amateur experience, or participation in one of the university or college courses on publishing and/or production – a strong asset.

Editing skills and experience may be gained from areas outside conventional bookwork, such as on learned journals (directly relevant to academic/STM/professional book publishers), on illustrated magazines or partworks (directly relevant to highly illustrated book publishers and packagers), on house journals, catalogues and other published material produced by private, public and voluntary sector organizations and on directories and financial and business publications.

Once inside an editorial department the able normally progress from editing under supervision to desk editing or equivalent, in the same firm or another; or, if progress is blocked, move sideways. To some extent editing skills are transferable to different kinds of publishing, but after a few years staff tend to specialize. Some become specialists in producing highly illustrated books (sometimes moving between publishers and packagers) or children's books; or in broad subject areas of educational, academic, STM and professional books and journals, and so forth.

While some editors leave publishing or are forced out, others cross to other departments or continue desk editing, decide to go freelance, progress to supervising the editing of books in-house or by freelances, or try to get commissioning jobs. The supervisory post of controlling the editing of books is usually a distinct career path – it very rarely leads to commissioning or to the more senior position of editorial director which needs commissioning experience.

The jump to commissioning is big and difficult. There are many junior editors and few commissioning editors. The very skills that make desk editors good – essentially a nit-picking mind which slogs away at the detail – are not in themselves sufficient for the wide-ranging entrepreneurial and risk-taking tasks of commissioning editors who should grasp quickly the general and specific needs of markets and possess the initiative and imagination to chase after and develop authors and books. Junior editors are always overloaded with work (can sometimes feel isolated or become more introverted), are under constant pressure to meet deadlines (especially in learned journals and in packagers), often work beyond office hours and only a few firms give them time to make contacts outside the office. They may, however, help themselves by taking an active interest in the business side, learning from their seniors' successes and failures and, where appropriate, broadening out discussions with authors and establishing a close relationship. Junior editors, especially in consumer book publishing, can develop their editorial judgement by writing reports for seniors on new proposals and monitoring the outcome (some read secretly for editors in other firms). Most editors attain their first commissioning job between their mid-twenties and mid-thirties. While some in their previous jobs may have commissioned books under supervision others have little direct experience. Commissioning editors are overwhelmingly recruited from within publishing, and mainly from junior editors. In learned journal publishing there is some interchange of staff, at both junior and senior levels, between journals and book divisions, and vice-versa. In rare cases people who have wide-ranging contacts or knowledge (such as review journalists or academics) are brought in from the outside and trained in-house. There is also a little cross-movement in consumer book publishing between literary agency, book clubs' editorial or vice-versa. Slightly more significant though is the inward flow of staff from other departments who may cross over at the junior editing level or straight in at the commissioning level from departments such as publicity and promotion (and rights, in consumer book publishing). Moving from a sales job is difficult in consumer book publishing except possibly at the senior level, but easier in educational, ELT, academic and STM publishing where representatives visiting institutions (especially in the ELT and tertiary sectors) build up market knowledge and contacts.

Editors usually stay in their respective areas of publishing: their contacts and market knowledge should become more valuable. When a good editor leaves, the publisher suffers considerable loss of momentum. Management, at least initially, typically want editors to stay for five years, but some editors want to move faster. They may move from smaller firms to larger or from larger to smaller, preferably attaining a more senior job in the process. The acid test of the author–editor relationship is when authors, provided they receive similar terms and treatment, change publisher along with their editors. Editors' reputations spread quite quickly. Those perceived to be successful are courted by other firms. However, editors' overall track records can be unfathomable. Some editors change jobs, possibly wisely, before the full implications of their decisions are reflected in sales records. Consumer book editors, especially if buying in titles from other firms, can build a sound record within a couple of years, whereas textbook editors, especially in educational publishing, take much longer. The timescales of publishing, from commissioning authors through to post-publication, can be a frustration or a salvation.

Higher still, are the even smaller number of editorial director-ships or similar. The editors who attain such positions are drawn more and more into management and administration and further and further away from directly publishing books and contact with authors.

Some senior editors who dislike big public companies stay with the independents or become consultants (e.g. commissioning projects for one or more non-competing companies), or agents, or freelance editors; or they may establish their own list of books which is marketed and sold by a large company; or they establish with colleagues their own publishing or packaging company. Others manage the publishing operations of large corporations, charities, museums, associations and professional bodies which may encompass retailing and mail-order sales, and copublishing arrangements with the commercial publishers or teach publishing. A few try their hand at writing while many in their middle age simply disappear.

Freelance editors

Freelance editors are widely used for copy-editing (including on-screen) or proofreading by book publishers and packagers and other organizations, and usually work from home. Some offer publishers a complete project management service encompassing the entire electronic pre-press operation, i.e. from author's disk to digital file ready for typesetting or printing.

Editors go freelance either from force of circumstances – redundancy or single parenthood – or from preference. They have a much greater variety of editing work and like the freedom of working at home without the rigours and costs of commuting to work. Outside the general hubbub of a publishing house, and with fewer interruptions, they may be able to work faster and plan their day to their own rhythm. But forced to maintain a flow of work and pressured to meet deadlines the freelance's day often extends far into the night, to weekends and public holidays.

Before leaving permanent employment, an intending freelance should arrange a house mortgage if necessary (freelances are commonly viewed as a dubious loan risk), establish an electronically equipped office and obtain firm offers of work from, say, two or three sources, to cover the following four to six months. Publishers' editors normally look for someone with a minimum of two years' experience in an editorial office or with proof of training. The best ways of obtaining work are through personal recommendation, professional contacts (e.g. mainly through the Society of Freelance Editors and Proofreaders (SFEP) which maintains a freelance register circulated to publishers, the NUJ, the IPG, the SYP and

WiP), or by personal approach to specific in-house editors. Advertising can prove fruitful and so can contacting agencies that organize freelances. A letter to a publisher or agency should have attached a list of previous relevant work, whether as an employee or as a freelance.

A freelance, at the outset, should appoint a qualified accountant (preferably one recommended by other freelances), essential for dealing with the Inland Revenue over tax-deductible expenses. The first meeting with an accountant should be free.

In-house editors sometimes test prospective freelances. If given a test, it is vital for the freelance to obtain a brief of the kind or level of work expected.

It is useful for freelances to live reasonably close to the publisher, but many operate via the postal service. Many work for only two or three publishers on a regular basis.

Before starting work freelances should ensure that they are adequately briefed, that they receive any house style or style sheet, and that the material is as complete as possible. An in-house editor, having agreed a realistic deadline, may then state a fixed fee for the job. But it is preferable from the freelance's viewpoint to insist on an hourly rate, and to charge as much as the employer is prepared to pay. The highest hourly rates are paid for project management and/or substantive/re-write manuscript editing, followed by on-screen editing and then 'ordinary' manuscript editing. Proofreading pays the least. Freelances with specialist knowledge, such as of medicine or law, may receive higher rates than others. The National Union of Journalists recommends hourly rates. Rates higher than normal may be agreed for emergency work that involves evening, weekend or overnight work.

When dealing with an unfamiliar publisher, freelances check initially whether or not additional expenses are paid; and establish the period (e.g. 30 days) within which payment is due. A publisher may, however, want a credit period of 60 days or longer. Freelances should send in invoices at the end of each one-off job, or monthly if regularly employed, even if engaged on a job overrunning a calendar month. Payments overdue should be chased promptly. Freelances should not allow publishers to run up debts – personal contact with the publisher's bought ledger clerk can work wonders.

Indexers

Indexers are mainly freelance and learn their skills either in-house as editors, or as authors, or from studying a course, such as the correspondence course tested by the Society of Indexers.

Picture researchers

Picture researchers acquire a feeling for the job and make contacts by subscribing to the newsletter of the Society of Picture Researchers and Editors and by attending its regular meetings in London. Relevant background experience includes work in a picture agency, art gallery museum, or library, or as a photographic assistant.

Because so few publishers and packagers are prepared to train, most researchers are self-trained while doing other work – for instance in picture agencies or in a publisher or packager working as a secretary or assistant who obtains pictures from lists supplied. Thus a willingness to learn alone and from others is needed. Although there is no formal pre-entry training, employers should be encouraged to send researchers to one of the short courses.

Those who gain basic training from collecting pictures from lists supplied, may move up within their firms, achieving a greater say in picture selection; or move to others; or go freelance (the job lends itself to working from home). Freelances (most of whom live within commuting distance of London) may carry out assignments for their former employers as well as others. They either approach managing editors or art directors speculatively or more significantly get work through personal recommendation of publishers, packagers and authors. Freelances who work hard can do quite well – many publishers and packagers pay their expenses in addition to an hourly rate equivalent to or well exceeding the rate paid to freelance editors for copy-editing. Though freelances may specialize in subject areas and in books they may also be in demand from partwork and magazine publishers, film, television, video and multimedia companies.

Designers

Design, like production, is an area in publishing where pre-entry specialist training is virtually essential. People entering usually have a sound school education up to A level and usually hold a degree or diploma in design. Those without design qualifications may be considered if they have relevant work experience in advertising, commercial studios or at a printers. Some start their careers in publishers' production/design departments as assistants and develop an interest in design. They may study at evening courses, or attend a part-time course.

The design managers of publishers and packagers face a continuous stream of students seeking junior design positions; and aspiring illustrators show their portfolios to design managers, to senior cover designers and, in the case of children's illustration, to the editors concerned with picture books. Managers too actively seek new talent by using their contacts in colleges and by attending exhibitions.

Other factors being equal, the most impressive designers are those who have at college equipped themselves for the commercial world by taking short-term work, preferably concerned with books and new media, and those who have been sufficiently self-motivated and open-minded to carry out their own research beyond the confines of their courses, and those who keep abreast of new technologies, especially in textprocessing, page mark-up, and the electronic creation and manipulation of text and illustration.

Design managers do not have time to go through a lot of irrelevant material. Your main presentation portfolio must not have too much in it, it should be well assembled, sharp, precise and to the point – for example show two, not ten, examples of your best illustrative work. If you have, say, three examples available of one type of design you should have developed the self-critical faculty of choosing the best.

It may be that at art college you have insufficiently covered work at which you will ultimately excel. Many candidates from college applying for junior book designer jobs bring along portfolios crammed with graphics. Design managers are more interested in typography. They want see at least several designs of books in the form of layouts, grid, type mark-up, prelims and cover design.

Managers are looking for the way in which you solve design problems and the amount of thinking and research you have done. Therefore think through designs beforehand and include the original brief and development phases leading up to a finished design. You may be tempted to show and stress work which in your view has the best finish. More important is the work which shows the best solution – not necessarily the best execution.

You may fear that your main presentation portfolio of selected and relevant material will not do you full justice, so prepare back-up sections easily accessible and containing supporting examples and additional material covering secondary areas.

Finally, do not include in your portfolio other people's work or work on which you have had much help.

At interview, although the presentation of the portfolio forms a key part, your personality may be of equal or more importance. Managers may be looking for a strength yet to be achieved – the way in which you view your work may differ from the way an experienced manager views it. They may try to discover whether you have a particular bent towards illustration or graphic inter-pretation or typography; whether you have a more analytical or more creative mind; whether you will get on with editors and whether you will fit in with a design team.

College designers joining publishers for the first time can receive several shocks: there are many staff in editorial, production, marketing and sales, who are designers *manqué*. Only by doing the more boring tasks repeatedly can speed and reliability be increased. The hard discipline of the commercial world is absent from college. Praise received from college lecturers may not be mirrored by design managers. The timescale of book production in which the design phases are separated by months can be frustrating. It takes some time to build a portfolio strong enough to advance your career.

Book designers' skills are generally transferable to different types of publishing. Although some designers move readily across the areas of publishing, many become specialists in one particular type, such as in educational publishing or in the highly illustrated book area (which may overlap with partwork publishing), or in covers.

Generally speaking the more senior designers become, the more they are tied to administration. Most aspire to become art director, design manager etc., but not a managing director: being profes-sional designers foremost, they rarely care to be totally withdrawn from creativity. However, a few opt to team up with an established editor and form a book packaging company, thereby combining close creative involvement with books and the leadership of a firm.

Other designers give up in-house work and develop their freelance assignments, leaving gaps for new entrants and juniors to fill.

Production Staff

Traditionally production work did not require a degree level of education. A good secondary school education with GCSE (or equivalent) mathematics was sufficient. It is still possible to build a production career up from the production assistant/secretarial/administrative support level provided such candidates are bright enough to pick up work quickly, are willing to learn and to work alone.

They may be recent school leavers or graduates, and may have or have not worked in another publishing department. (A visit to a book printer stated on a CV reveals an interest in the job.) It is quite possible for a production department to home-grow a production controller from a particularly bright, interested assistant. After a couple of years it is possible to pick up the terminology and gain a fairly broad knowledge of the workings of a publisher, but it is very difficult to learn the job without the basic technical knowledge. Unless they can persuade the publisher to send them on courses, or they themselves attend evening classes, they tend always to be at a severe disadvantage. Nevertheless there are former production secretaries who have worked their way to the top.

However, production is increasingly technically complex, especially in the fast changing electronic pre-press processes which lead to printed and/or digital publishing opportunities, and that creates periodic staff shortages as publishers try to grapple with these issues. Thus the prime candidates are those who have completed a vocational sub-degree, diploma, degree or post-graduate course encompassing production and new media techniques.

The job of production controller requires usually a minimum of 2–3 years' production experience. When a controller resigns and there is not an assistant with sufficient experience to be promoted, a crisis arises. The publisher must recruit someone with the necessary experience immediately, from another publisher preferably with a similar list, or possibly, at the junior level, from the printing industry.

The job of production manager usually requires a minimum of 3–5 years' production experience, preferably, though not necessarily, with managerial experience. Bearing in mind that new technologies continually affect the ways books are produced and that production managers play a crucial role in their introduction, it is important for candidates to be fully aware of new developments. Without up-to-date knowledge it is impossible to manage a department which is highly technical at one end, and highly administrative at the other.

Production is a fairly distinct career area in which competition is not excessive and gives much responsibility at a young age. It is one of the few departments in publishing where there is a structured way in: the technical knowledge can be acquired by studying a course. A relevant qualification does not unfortunately guarantee a job: it just substantially increases the chances.

The promotional possibilities within a department tend to be less flexible than in an editorial department because the staffing levels and grades relate directly to the number of books produced. Unless a company is expanding, recruitment and promotion depend on staff leaving. Generally, managers favour their own staff provided they have ability, on account of their accumulated knowledge. Because the publishing industry is so small, managers meet at functions and events, know each other and can quite easily check candidates' references. Other potential sources for them are to pump printers' reps and to form links with colleges. Needless to say success in production depends very much on doing a job well and building a good reputation, spread by word-of-mouth, acquiring sought-after knowledge and establishing contacts with suppliers worldwide.

Unlike many other departments, production skills and abilities can be applied across publishing. Production staff can cross the frontiers of different types of publisher, especially those who have experience of digital publishing in which there is a skill shortage. However, some specialize in certain lists which need particular production expertise, namely complex scientific texts and journals and highly illustrated colour books.

Production is a career in itself. While there is some interchange with design, only a few succeed during the first few years of their careers to move into other departments. At the top end some production staff gain board status, some acquire an additional administrative role; some have set up their own firms which provide a production service for publishers (which may encompass editorial services, electronic pre-press management, print and paper buying); and some cross over to printers or become UK agents of foreign printers.

Publicity and marketing staff

Most new entrants have a degree, and the subject studied can sometimes have relevance in specialist publishing, such as in educational and ELT (where a teaching qualification/or experience would be an advantage), or in STM and law. Those who have studied publishing courses have additional advantages from their industry overview gained as well as specific technical knowledge of production techniques. Bearing in mind that book promotion involves pushing out a lot of promotional material and letters, competent word-processing is an absolute must for all, preferably with DTP knowledge. (Experience of student journalism, web sites, or of preparing catalogues or bibliographies, would be a plus on a CV.)

The people working in these areas tend to be fairly young. Many managers attain the posts in their late twenties or thirties, the publicity/promotion executives in their early to mid-twenties, while below them are the juniors, the controllers and assistants. Apart from the specialists – the copywriters, advertising controllers, direct mail specialists (especially those who have worked in mailing houses serving publishers) and print and web designers (who may have work experience outside book publishing), publicity/promotion managers and controllers are recruited predominantly from within book publishing.

The following minimum educational attainments are usually preferred: in consumer book publishing good education up to A level – a degree is not absolutely essential; in educational publishing a degree is highly desirable (in ELT, qualifications or teaching experience in ELT would be an advantage); in academic and professional publishing a degree (or equivalent further educational or professional qualifications) is all but essential, and so is a well-developed intellect. An understanding of why people want to read such books illuminates the way to market them. (In scientific, technical and medical publishing, a science degree is very desirable to a publisher.)

Publicity/promotion managers prefer people who have at least one or two years' experience of working in a publicity or promotion department relevant to their type of publishing and thus are familiar with the appropriate techniques, requiring little training. Many of these people gain their foothold by entering departments as assistants; or they may have crossed at this level from other departments, such as editorial or marketing/sales. Sometimes, depending on the economic climate and company policy, companies of all sizes will take people without experience but young and quick enough to pick up the required techniques. The degree of responsibility encompassed by the low level job titles varies, ranging from considerable responsibility for the tasks to working under direction. Another route found in some of the large educational companies (particularly those in the tertiary sector) is to have spent one or two years as a sales representative.

As editorial jobs are so few and far between, people often start in publicity and promotion in the hope of becoming editors. But once embarked in publicity and promotion they find it to their liking: it becomes their career by accident. However, in the early part of one's career, i.e. in the twenties, this area offers flexibility. Indeed, some companies (particularly some of the large non-consumer book companies) regard it (albeit often informally) both as a way in and as a career job, i.e. they would appoint, for example, graduates committed to publishing who would be expected to improve their positions in the industry. Those working in publicity and promotion come into contact with a large number of titles, with people from other industries (the design world, printers, the media and internet), and with senior internal people from editorial and sales, and sometimes from production, rights and distribution. The abilities and learnt skills overlap those of editorial and sales. Thus a few publicity and promotion controllers and assistants succeed in moving across (mainly within their companies) to editorial (desk editing or if lucky commissioning); or to sales jobs (straight repping or, if they already have such experience, to the sales management). In consumer book publishing there is also some interchange with rights departments through the overlap in dealing with serial rights. Some publicity and promotion people might view the jobs of desk editing and repping as restrictive, boring or unglamorous in comparison with the variety of their own activities, and look askance at such moves as being sideways or downwards.

However, experience of being a representative is likely to be significant in the long term to anyone aspiring to be a marketing/sales director with full board status. Most of the marketing directors of large and medium-sized companies today were originally sales people who have spent some time selling on the road, home or export (preferably both). Unless publicity and promotion people have such experience they tend to face a career block below the most senior level. But the aspiration of many people is to be a head of a publicity or promotion department, publicizing a list they like, involved with the myriad activities involved in this area; or possibly to start up or join a PR/promotion agency.

Independent PR/promotion

Most agencies are located in or close to London and Oxford. Such agencies, which are staffed mainly by ex-publishing people, provide services ranging from particular to all aspects of PR and promotion. Only a few are large enough to employ assistants. Their services are offered on a one-off or retainer basis to their clients who are drawn mainly from the consumer book publishers, and sometimes from educational and academic houses. Some agencies also have clients from outside the publishing industry, and some carry out publicity for author clients. Small publishers may use agencies because they lack staff, expertise or contacts. Medium and large houses may use them in a supportive role to their in-house departments, e.g. to cover for a staff shortage due to illness, to overcome the publishing peak in the autumn, or to provide individual attention to a particular book or author which at the time cannot be given in-house.

Home sales

Trade reps

The minimum age of reps in medium or large companies is early to mid-twenties. If younger than 23 they need to look older and responsible enough to be taken seriously by buyers. Small companies may employ younger people. A clean driving licence is essential, though a very minor offence might not hinder a strong candidate. GCSE (or equivalent) qualifications may be sufficient, although some companies want A levels and sometimes degrees, but previous selling experience and a bright personality outweigh educational attainment. Strength is necessary to lug the heavy bag from car park to shop.

Publishers ideally want to maintain continuity of contact and trust with their customers. Career reps with many years' experience (provided they do not rest on their laurels) are valuable to their companies. Sales managers of the main companies like to hold on to younger reps as long as they can. They expect them to stay for, say, five years. Although some reps move around territories, it is not advisable for them to change jobs too often. This tends to work against employment opportunities for graduates in some consumer book companies. Over-educated for the job in the medium term, and ambitious, they may be unhappy to stay for what a sales manager considers a reasonable period.

Sales managers of publishers (and of repping companies and wholesalers) look for people with previous selling experience, preferably in the book trade. Small companies with a few own reps are more likely to take on inexperienced and younger reps. Although they do not pay so much as larger companies, they provide the opportunity to learn. It can be tough going. Reps of a small company have difficulty in getting into the large chains, have fewer books to sell and few of those are likely to set book buyers on fire; nor are there substantial backlists for back-up. But a short spell of under a year should provide just enough calling experience to lift someone off the bottom. Selling experience need not be confined to books.

Bookshop (or wholesale) experience especially of an appropriate type, can provide a way in. Work experience with the large chains is relevant to consumer publishing, and academic bookselling to academic publishing, carrying in its train the advantage of understanding the companies' books and their markets. By talking to visiting reps they may hear of forthcoming vacancies. But after two years' experience it becomes increasingly difficult to move; five years would be too long. For those who do manage to cross over to publishing, repping provides the most likely avenue. Another way in is to enter a publisher's sales office in a junior position, or as a secretary, in the hope that a rep vacancy arises. Lastly, very occasionally medium and larger publishers offer specific trainee rep jobs.

A new rep joining a company usually begins in-house to learn about the company and its systems. The forthcoming books and the backlist have to be learnt before a rep goes on the road. A rep without selling experience often spends an initial period under a senior rep, or goes out with the sales manager. Once alone, the new rep will take at least one season to gain the confidence of booksellers and it takes several years to learn negotiating skills and the niceties of dealing with customers, and to discover what is happening in the trade at large.

The usual movement of reps is from one company to another, for example, from small to large. There is some movement between different types of consumer book publishing but it is very rare for a trade rep to transfer to educational repping. Reps face a number of special hurdles in career advancement not least of which are fears that retail chains will curtail their visits or that wholesalers will erode their business. Moreover, there are many reps and few opportunities for sales management.

The sales managers, if they are good, tend to stick because their continuity of service is often valued by companies though not necessarily, especially when the sales forces are re-organized. A rep's very success may disincline a sales manager to bring him or her off the road. The majority of reps are isolated geographically from the managements of their companies and thus, out on a limb, their presence goes unnoticed. A rep whose territory surrounds the sales office and who operates out of it does not suffer this particular disadvantage. In order to be noticed a rep really needs to secure a position in a sales office, such as assistant to the manager or as an office manager or in a post selling to the main accounts. For many, such a step would involve moving, probably to London, usually the loss of the car, and possibly lower earnings. Another route is to cross over to export sales, important if aiming to be a sales director. Lastly, there is the transition from rep to sales manager. A good rep unfortunately does not necessarily make a good sales manager. The skills required to organize other people's time, to prompt and direct them, differ greatly from those of the self-organizing lone rep.

In consumer book publishing, reps rarely move to other departments. In theory, starting a career as a rep should be a good foundation in that it swiftly reveals the commercial realities of the market place and shows the type of book that sells. The job also matures people quickly. But in practice moving from being a rep to an in-house department, such as editorial, is very difficult. Reps, cut off from other departmental directors, do not have experience of the internal work of companies and are up against those who have. In this respect junior jobs in marketing (publicity and promotion) are potentially more flexible because even at that level they bring people into contact with senior management. There is another snag. The qualities of aspiring editors do not meet the needs of sales managers who look for people with the skills to sell successfully rather than those whose strengths lie in creative work.

People considering the job of a trade rep should weigh up the compensations and limitations before applying. The car, the expenses, staying in hotels should be weighed against loneliness. The initial excitement of seeing new places, or spending a sunny afternoon in an old cathedral city, should be set against the cold and wet early Monday mornings in a drab industrial town. The job involves much repetition, physical strain and long hours. But it gives great freedom. There is no fixed pattern to the day and nobody sits directly on one's tail.

Educational reps

Educational publishers recruit their reps occasionally from recent graduates (who might have started off in the promotion department), from ex-teachers (who have the advantages of relevant background and an understanding of what teachers look for in books) or their part time reps from parents etc. (ELT publishers favour TEFL experience and/or qualifications.) Young reps come out of teaching from about their mid-twenties. They may have found their teaching career blocked or perhaps cannot face a lifetime locked in a classroom. (Some reps with teaching experience eventually return to teaching.) The on-job training usually begins with a spell in the sales office or promotion department to gain a feel of the company and the list, followed by a period spent with an experienced rep. It takes about a year to become fully familiar with a long backlist spreading across many subjects at different levels, and to know the competitors' weaknesses. Their promotion path is likely to be to regional management, to central sales and promotion management, occasionally to editorial positions.

College reps

The academic and STM publishers who employ reps calling mainly on colleges take on young graduates. This job provides a marvellous introduction and background to academic/STM publishing. It is personally valuable in that people learn to be self-sufficient and to motivate themselves, and it can provide the base for a marketing/sales or an editing career. The UK subsidiaries of the US-founded college textbook companies have a tradition of promoting some of their reps to in-house positions. However, candidates who have spent several years as reps are attractive to other publishers both for marketing/sales and editing positions. It is possible for these reps to secure junior or full list-building posts, especially if their jobs have included a strong market research element.

Export staff

New publishing recruits to export sales are usually graduates. However, those without degrees but with foreign languages and/or work or study experience overseas stand a good chance of employment. New recruits in export sales come from a wide variety of backgrounds, and are not by any means all fresh graduates; nor for that matter do they necessarily have a background in sales or promotion departments of publishers. The experience of living, working, studying or keen interest in overseas countries can clinch a job. That experience would not necessarily have been linked to publishing but would be a further advantage if it were. Examples are work in an overseas bookshop or Voluntary Service Overseas, or English language teaching – the latter two being particularly attractive to educational and ELT publishers.

Routes into export sales commonly start at the bottom. First steps are to become an export sales assistant carrying out office work which may later encompass periods of sales representation overseas, or to become a home or overseas-based sales representative. In the latter case those without any publishing experience start in the sales office to learn the list and systems, and spend time selling books to the home book trade; or additionally, if in educational/academic publishing, promoting books to and in institutions, being sent on export selling courses and accompanying senior staff abroad. Training periods before going solo can last anything from, say, a couple of months to a year. Those already in publishing who have experience of a sales office, or home sales representation, or promotion, and decide to enter export sales may well be able to progress more quickly. While there are publishers who are quite prepared to despatch staff in their early twenties, others prefer the greater maturity and authority of those in their mid-twenties or over.

To reach an export management position, the most important experience to be acquired is selling abroad as a representative or similar. Unless they carry the lists of others, smaller firms cannot afford the great expense of employing staff to travel overseas to the same extent as large firms. Furthermore the major internationally-based publishers periodically offer overseas postings: for instance of short duration covering temporary staff shortages in overseas firms or offices; or medium-term contracts of, say, two to three years, to set up offices. The large firms either train new publishing entrants or take staff from other large publishers or smaller firms that have been unable to give their staff much overseas opportunity. Those posted abroad for several years may not be guaranteed a job on return. However, they are usually in a strong position, if in-house jobs are available, to move to another area of the world, to progress upwards in the marketing/sales side of the firm, or possibly cross over to commissioning as in ELT publishing; or to gain senior jobs in other firms.

The people attracted to export selling tend to be well-qualified and very ambitious and often want to progress at a faster rate than a publisher can manage. Those who work in export-orientated firms may feel superior to the home sales side. Customers want continuity of contact with one person over many years but UK publishers frequently re-organize. Moreover, once junior staff have gained valuable overseas market knowledge and contacts they may look for advancement inside or outside the company, wishing to take on more responsibility, or areas of the world that generate more turnover, or other publishers' lists that offer better export prospects. Some set up their own repping business operating out of the UK or abroad, others seek export management positions, or marketing/sales directorships, in publishing or other industries.

Export selling reveals so many different aspects of the publishing business, adds the international aspect and accelerates maturity at a young age. Other factors being equal, those with export experience applying for senior marketing/sales positions have a great advantage over candidates who lack it. Finally, it should be noted that some of the chief executives and senior managers of large international publishers sought overseas experience earlier in their careers.

Rights staff

The selling of rights is a small and specialist career area. Many rights people start as assistants in a rights department, but assistants in other departments – for instance those who have handled contracts – may have an advantage and transfer to a rights department.

Assistants with imagination who take an overall view and show initiative usually soon have more responsible work (such as handling permissions, drafting selling letters, progressing deals etc.) thrust at them. While some assistants are never given the opportunity to advance, or do not have the inclination or the aptitude (perhaps revealing a lack of eye for detail), others say, after a couple of years progress in their own firms or others. The quickest way of building worldwide contacts is by attending international book fairs. It takes several years to get to know faces and form close reliable contacts. Therefore rights assistants need to encourage their firms to send them abroad as soon as possible.

Rights staff tend to specialize in particular rights and may use that expertise to move around publishers. Some attain rights management positions in their late twenties to thirties (though they bring the routine/repetitive work up with them). There is also occasional staff interchange between publishers and agencies and vice-versa (e.g. in the selling of translation rights). The prime example of a specialism is in co-edition books, with some move-ment both ways between highly illustrated book publishers and packagers. (A few export sales staff move into this area.)

Factors which can adversely affect career development are the fluctuating trading conditions which periodically reduce co-edition publishing, and the international consolidation of publishers – all of which impinge on the scope of rights sales.

A good way of enlarging one's contact network and of dis-cussing issues of mutual concern is to join the Rights Circle which holds occasional lunchtime meetings in London.

Distribution, accounts and computing

Traditionally, distribution was regarded by many publishers as the dogsbody end of the business, received little top management attention, and was perceived as a second-rate career area in relation to the publishing side. Such attitudes have rapidly changed in response to escalating costs, pressures from customers for a faster and more reliable service, and the realization that poor distribution loses market share.

People who have taken courses in material handling, work study and logistics management, or who have direct experience of consumer goods distribution are particularly attractive. However, a career in book distribution can be founded within publishing from junior positions. The opportunities are considerable because few graduates apply to this important area, and the specialist knowledge and leadership skills acquired can lead to very senior management positions on the service side. It is a relatively distinct career within publishing but allows cross-movement to independent book distributors, retail chain and wholesale (home and export) and book club distribution facilities.

Cross-movement to other publishing departments is difficult owing to the separation of distribution from headquarters. However, junior work on the trade side of order-processing is a quick way of learning a publisher's business and customers: possible side moves would be into home or export sales offices.

The royalties section, similarly, is a specialist career area, but can sometimes be used as a springboard to other areas. Accountants, part-qualified or qualified, can apply their expertise to any industry and sometimes end up running publishers.

The computer specialists who run publishers' data-processing departments are not tied to publishing. But a growing area demanding specialist programming, system acquisition and design management, is that of electronic textprocessing and graphics manipulation for both book production and related electronic media on the internet. Publishers test the current systems to their limits and are only just beginning to exploit them. They will increasingly need in-house specialists. Such people (together with web editors and designers) are at a premium. From their technical base, they could within publishing broaden to the creative side of developing new products, or apply their expertise gained within the publishing industry to other industries which are publishers in their own right (e.g. large internet corporations or portals requiring content and financial service industries) and to multimedia firms or consultancies. Their job changes tend to be fast – their years are inverse of dog years: one web year equates to seven years in the rest of publishing.

Chief executives and managing directors

The top management has traditionally been drawn from former specialist directors – especially editors, followed by people of a sales and marketing background. However, the highest level of major publishers may not necessarily come from within publishing.

CAREER PATHWAYS: AN OVERVIEW

It was mentioned earlier that the first job or jobs within the first few years may not necessarily determine a career path. Many new entrants have little idea of the work of the departments they join and may find they develop a forte and liking for the work. It is possible to move across to other departments and areas of publishing, but over time it becomes progressively more difficult: there are usually candidates who have acquired specialist knowledge of the activity and market knowledge of that particular area of publishing.

In small firms with few staff and less departmentalism it may be easier to move around the firm and learn different jobs, sometimes simultaneously. But such knowledge may not be considered by a larger firm to be specialist enough. In contrast, junior staff in large firms while often finding it more difficult to cross the more pronounced departmental boundaries, may gain in-depth expertise afforded by the greater resources of the publisher. People move from small to large firms (which usually pay much higher salaries at the top) and vice-versa: for example, middle-ranking staff of large firms may attain more senior jobs in smaller firms. The promotion of staff (with little direct management experience) to departmental management positions is common.

Unlike huge industrial concerns and the civil service, not even the largest publisher has a big enough staff pyramid to be able to fill staff vacancies from within at the time they occur: internal staff may be thought not to be ready. Publishers are not rash enough to advertise career pathways which cannot be fulfilled but in some large firms there are visible grade progressions within departments.

Although some staff progress upwards in publishers, a few rapidly, it is very rare to spend a whole lifetime with one firm. Rather most people move from one publisher to another, sideways or hopefully in an upward direction. The possibility of getting stuck in any job at any level is ever present.

In moving around companies, most people tend to stay with the type of work in which they have acquired expertise. If moving between activities is far from easy, moving across the major types of publishing is even more difficult. Generally speaking people stay within consumer, or in educational, or in academic, STM and professional book publishing etc. Their expertise is applied to the publishing of books and associated products for certain markets and their contacts inside and outside publishing are orientated accordingly.

Some people in their early thirties with much experience want to change direction, for instance, to move from academic to consumer book publishing, or vice-versa. But they are up against people already in that area so their chances of getting a job at the same level of seniority and salary are much more remote. As you increase your expertise of an area the more valuable that expertise becomes and the more difficult it is to throw it aside and turn to something else. There are always exceptions. People do move between departments and types of publishing at all stages of their careers up to and including managing directors but they are in a minority.

Corporate re-organizations and take-overs inevitably affect careers. Employees unfortunately cannot choose their new owners. After a take-over, the acquisitor's staff often enhance their position in the larger organization, whereas the former management of the bought company is realigned: the managers may stay, leave or be downgraded. The more junior staff may leave as the new owners rationalize the departments, for example, by cutting out competing editorial units, sometimes centralizing production and design and rights sales staff, amalgamating the sales forces, centralizing accounting and distribution services, and relocating offices (even across the Atlantic). Many staff who leave with their redundancy payments re-appear in other publishers or go freelance, though some abandon publishing.

Many people in their thirties reach a plateau below management level and fear that their rapidly approaching fortieth birthday is their last chance to make a change. With increasing age the possibilities of movement diminish. However, many senior jobs are filled by people roughly between the ages of thirty-seven to forty-five. After that, unless an individual is particularly well known or brilliant or specialized, changing companies becomes progressively more difficult. By the age of fifty, with the same provisos, it becomes very difficult indeed – there may be no alternative but stay put if possible until retirement age.

Another factor that may constrain intercompany movement is the housing market and your accessibility to a range of firms. House prices in the southeast region are higher and increase at a proportionately faster rate than in the rest of the country; they rise particularly steeply towards the centre of London. If you take a job in a company away from the centre which may offer to pay relocation expenses (and there may be great opportunities in such companies, partly on account of their location) consider the possible career step after that. If you move home too far out, you may be taking a one-way rather than a return ticket.

Staff of commercial publishers are very attractive to the many public, private and voluntary sector organizations operating their own publishing. Moreover, the contacts made and skills learnt in publishing can be applied to other commercial enterprises, not necessarily concerned with publishing.

In publishing, commercial and non-commercial, staff have been traditionally recruited from within the industry; and publishing staff tend to be retained unless they leave voluntarily or are forced out. It has been a relatively closed world. However, with the advent of electronic media markets and the convergence of technologies and accompanying media industries, publishing is opening out. There are now opportunities for people who have distinct skills not only in publishing but also in sound, video and software programing who have the flexibility to apply their skills creatively with others in the evolving electronic publishing mediums. Such people are at a premium, internationally. Publishing businesses have changed dramatically over the last decades and will continue to do so at accelerating speed.

Appendix: Training for publishers

Compiled by Penny Mountain

Association of Learned and Professional Society Publishers
South House, The Street, Clapham, Worthing, West Sussex BN13 3UU. (01903) 871686.
www.alpsp.org.uk

ALPSP runs a growing training programme on a wide range of topics: Introduction to Journals Marketing; Best Practice in Leaflet Production; Introduction to Design for the Non-Designer; Financial Management of Journals; Journal Typesetting; Journal Production; Introduction to Copyright; Electronic Publishing Strategy.

The Association also organizes a programme of topical seminars on aspects of journal and book publishing. These have included: Selling Academic Books; Streamlining the Publishing Process; Relations with Referees and Editorial Boards; Joined-up Publishing – the significance of linking; Licensing – an introduction; Do Electronic Journal Intermediaries Have a Role?; Who should own Copyright in Journal Articles?; Trading Electronic Publications; Digital IS Different; The Future of Learned and Professional Societies; Publishing Partnerships; Competing for Authors.

Arts Institute at Bournemouth
Fern Barrow, Wallisdown, Poole, Dorset BH12 5HH. (01202) 533011.
www.arts-inst-bournemouth.ac.uk

From 2001, HND in Desktop Publishing (subject to validation).

University of Brighton
Lewes Road, Brighton, East Sussex BN2 4AT. (01273) 600900.
www.brighton.ac.uk
MA in Fine Art with Printmaking, Sequential Design or Illustration specialism.

Chapterhouse

1 Southernhay West, Exeter EX1 1JG. (01392) 499488.
www.chapterhousepublishing.co.uk

Specialist in publishing training offering Proofreading and Copy-editing both as correspondence and seminar courses. Small group seminars and tailored courses also available.

City University

Department of Journalism, Northampton Square, London EC1V 0HB. 020-7477 0100.
www.city.ac.uk/journalism

MA in Publishing Studies: one year full time (part-time may be available to selected candidates); includes eight taught units. Students must also complete a placement period in a publishing company and write a dissertation.

Falmouth College of Arts

Woodlane, Falmouth TR11 4RA. (01326) 211077.
www.falmouth.ac.uk

BA hons degrees in Graphic Design, Visual Culture and Illustration. Postgraduate diploma in Creative Enterprise.

Glasgow College of Building and Printing

60 North Hanover Street, Glasgow G1 2BP. (0141) 332 9969
www.gcbp.ac.uk

HNC/D in Digital Media for Printing and Publishing; HND in Imagery for Medical Illustration; HNC/D in Graphic Design (formerly Design for Print); part-time HNC in Electronic Publishing for Print Media; HNC in Print Media Origination Systems; HND in Information and Media Technology; HNC/D in Print Media Management; HNC/D in Visual Information – design and illustration.

Leeds Metropolitan University

Calverley Street, Leeds LS1 3HE. (0113) 2833113.
www.lmu.ac.uk

Three-year full-time and four-year sandwich BSc degrees in Publishing Technology and Print Management.

Leeds University
Leeds LS2 9JT. (0113) 2332332.
www.leeds.ac.uk

Postgraduate MA in Bibliography, Publishing and Textual Studies.

London College of Printing
School of Printing and Publishing, Elephant and Castle, London SE1 6SB. (020) 7514 6700.
www.lcp.linst.ac.uk

BA hons in Publishing (part-time and full-time); full-time postgraduate certificate, diploma and MA in Publishing; part-time MA in Media Technology Administration for publishing and media managers.

A range of short evening classes and one- and two-day seminars on general publishing topics: An Introduction to Publishing; Editorial Management; Effective Marketing; Copy-editing. A range of DTP, multimedia and web publishing courses.

London School of Publishing
David Game House, 69 Notting Hill Gate, London W11 3JS
Tel: (020) 7221 3399
www.publishing-school.co.uk

NUJ approved evening courses, once per week over 10 weeks, including book editorial and proofreading, picture research and electronic publishing.

Loughborough University
Department of Information Science, Loughborough LE11 3TU. (01509) 223052.
www.lboro.ac.uk

BA and BA hons in Publishing (with English).

Marketability
12 Sandy Lane, Teddington, Middlesex TW11 0DR. (020) 8977 2741 or (020) 8892 7857.

One-day marketing workshops at London and Oxford venues with the emphasis on practicality and immediate relevance: Copywriting; Direct Mail That Really Works; Quick and Easy Market Research; Impressive Marketing Plans on a Small Budget; Design and Print Buying. Further courses in development. In-company training and consultancy also available.

Middlesex University
White Hart Lane, London N17 8HR. (020) 8362 5898.
www.mdx.ac.uk

BA hons in Writing and Publishing Studies (with one other subject);
BA hons in Writing; MSc and PgDip in Interactive Multimedia; MA
in Design for Interactive Media.

Napier University, Edinburgh
Department of Print Media, Publishing & Communication,
Craig House Campus, Craig House Road, Edinburgh EH10 5LG.
(0131) 455 6150.
www.napier.ac.uk

BA and BA hons in Publishing. MSc in: Publishing; Electronic
Publishing; Publishing Production.

National Extension College
18 Brooklands Avenue, Cambridge CB2 2HN. (01223) 450200.
www.nec.ac.uk

Correspondence courses: Editing; Desktop Publishing; Design.

Nottingham Trent University
Burton Street, Nottingham NG1 4BU. (0115) 9418418.
www.ntu.ac.uk

BA hons in Graphic Communication Management.

Oxford Brookes University
Oxford International Centre for Publishing Studies, Gipsy Lane,
Oxford OX3 0BP.
(01865) 484951.
www.brookes.ac.uk/schools/apm

At undergraduate level, three-year courses full-time (also available part-time): BA hons Publishing; BA joint hons Publishing, combined with another subject in the modular programme. At postgraduate level, one-year courses (also available part-time): MA/PgDip in Publishing, MA/PgDiP in Electronic Media; MBA Publishing; MA/PgDip Education – educational publishing. Also short courses and evening classes in: Copy-editing; Editing On-screen; Photoshop; QuarkXpress; Website Design; Copyright; Publishing Finance.

Oxford Publicity Partnership
12 Hid's Copse Road, Cumnor Hill, Oxford OX2 9JJ. (01865) 865466.
www.oppuk.co.uk

One- and two-day courses, mainly for people in marketing departments but also for those interested in publishing: Press and PR; Introduction to Marketing; Copywriting; Printed Publicity for Direct Mail. Courses also available in-house.

Password Training
23 New Mount Street, Manchester M4 4DE. (0161) 953 4071.
www.passwordtraining.org

Tailor-made courses and consultancy covering Internet publishing, book publishing, and marketing.

Pira International
Randall Road, Leatherhead, Surrey KT22 7RU. (01372) 802105.
www.pira.co.uk

One-, two- and three-day courses, held in Leatherhead, focusing on printing and production skills: Basics of Printing and Finishing; Introduction to Digital Printing; Introduction to Colour Printing; Computer to Plate; Colour Origination; Systematic Approach to Colour Reproduction; Paper Grades and Properties; Professional Print Buying; Printing Inks – their properties and uses; Dealing with Pictures in a Digital Environment.

Also conferences for the publishing and printing industries. Topics have included Content and Digital Asset Management for Publishers and Printers; Digital Printing; Digital Workflow; Marketing and Branding on the Internet; Exploiting Content on the Web; Proofing.

University of Plymouth
Faculty of Arts and Education, Earl Richards Road North, Exeter EX6 2AS. (01395) 475004.

Postgraduate diploma and MA in Publishing.

Publishers' Training Consultancy
Mobile 07970 807 499 and 07788 663 863.

IT, management and business related training, some in partnership with Oxford Brookes University. Plus consultancy service to small publishers for specific problems such as marketing, financial management, employing staff.

Publishing Training Centre
Book House, 45 East Hill, London SW18 2QZ. (020) 8874 2718.
www.train4publishing.co.uk

A wide range of intensive one- to four-day courses on every aspect of publishing, from introductory to senior management level: foundation training; editorial; rights and contracts; production; computers in publishing; electronic publishing; journals publishing; marketing; publishing finance; management. Plus distance learning courses on Effective Copywriting, Basic Editing, Basic Proofreading, Picture Research and Basic Typography.

Reading University
Whiteknights, PO Box 217, Reading, Berkshire RG6 6AH. (0118) 9875123.
www.rdg.ac.uk

Four-year honours degree, postgraduate diploma and PhD or MPhil in Typography and Graphic Communication.

Robert Gordon University, Aberdeen
School of Information & Media, Faculty of Management, Garthdee Road, Aberdeen AB10 7QE. (01224) 263900.

BA hons and full-time, part-time or distance learning postgraduate certificate, diploma and MSc in Publishing Studies.

Scottish Publishers Association
137 Dundee Street, Edinburgh EH11 1BG. (0131) 228 6866.
www.scottishbooks.org

The official publishing industry training centre in Scotland offers courses aimed at people working in, or wanting to pursue a career in, publishing: Copy-editing Skills; Proofreading; Print Production; Copyright and Contracts; Book Marketing; An Introduction to Publishing.

Society of Freelance Editors and Proofreaders
Mermaid House, 1 Mermaid Court, London SE1 1HR. (020) 7403 5141.
www.sfep.org.uk

A useful range of reasonably priced one-day workshops on practical aspects of publishing for freelances and inhouse staff: Introduction to Proofreading; Brush up Your Proofreading; Proofreading Problems; Brush up Your Grammar; Introduction to Copy-editing; Brush up Your Copy-editing; Efficient Copy-editing; On-screen Editing 1 and 2; Editing Mathematics; Editing Medical Texts; Production for Editors; Going Freelance and Staying There; Working for a Client; Negotiating Effectively; Project Management. New one-day workshops are: Copy-editing and Proofreading Music; Internet for Editors.

Society of Indexers
Globe Centre, Penistone Road, Sheffield S6 3AE. (0114) 2813060.
www.socind.demon.co.uk

Open learning indexing course comprising five units. Self-administered test, formal test papers and tutorial support are available.

University of Stirling
Centre for Publishing Studies, Stirling FK9 4LA. (01786) 467044.
www.stir.ac.uk

Postgraduate PhD, MPhil or diploma in Publishing Studies.

Swansea Institute of Higher Education
Mount Pleasant, Swansea SA1 6ED. (01792) 48100.
www.sihe.ac.uk

BA hons degrees in Media, Graphic Design and General Illustration.

Thames Valley University
St Mary's Road, Ealing, London W5 5RF. (020) 8579 5000.
www.tvu.ac.uk

Postgraduate diploma and MA in Information Management (Publishing). The university offers degrees in Information Systems with various options according to demand.

Training Matters
15 Pitts Road, Headington Quarry, Oxford OX3 8BA. (01865) 766964.

In-house training in publishing-specific and management skills:

Appraisal Skills; Management Skills; Time and Self Management; Introduction to Publishing; Team-building and Team Management Skills; Project Management; Coaching and Feedback Skills for Managers; Influencing Skills; Recruitment Practice; Personal Effectiveness; Author Management; Freelance Management; The Principles of Outsourcing. An approved provider for the Paul Hamlyn Small Publisher Scheme.

The company also offers career management, advice on job search including CV writing and interview techniques.

University College London
Gower Street, London WC1E 6BT. (020) 7679 7204.
http://zeus.slais.ucl.ac.uk

MA in Electronic Communication and Publishing aimed at arts and humanities graduates as well as those who already have knowledge of a specific area within the traditional publishing industry. The programme offers a solid grounding in electronic media and communications.

West Herts College, Watford
Hempstead Road, Watford, Herts WD1 3EZ. (01923) 812661.
www.westherts.ac.uk

Four-year sandwich or three-year full time BSc hons degrees in Publishing, Printing and Packaging. Postgraduate diplomas in Publishing; Journalism, Radio and Advertising; Copywriting. HNDs in Typographic Design (also ND) and in Printing, Publishing and Packaging. Plus distance learning in these areas and short courses in DTP and book, journal and magazine production.

Wolverhampton University
Wolverhampton WV1 1SB. (01902) 321000.
www.wlv.ac.uk

BA hons in: Digital Media (Design for Print specialism) with one or two other subjects; Multimedia Communications (Publishing on the Web module); Illustrations. HND Network (Design for Screen; Design for Print, Graphic Communication).

* * *

A number of editorial correspondence courses are advertised regularly in *The Bookseller* and the *Guardian*. *The Bookseller* publishes a special feature on Training and Recruitment every year, usually in November; this includes a Noticeboard of forthcoming training courses.

SCHOLARSHIPS AND GRANTS

Book Trade Benevolent Society (BTBS) – the book trade charity
Dillon Lodge, The Retreat, Kings Langley, Herts WD4 8LT. Freephone helpline 0808 100 2304 or (01923) 263128. www.booktradecharity.demon.co.uk

BTBS provides confidential and practical support to anyone who has a problem – financial, personal or work-related and who has worked in the book trade (publishing and bookselling) for more than one year as an employee or freelance. In appropriate circumstances, BTBS offers financial help on a regular or one-off basis, for example, to help with domestic difficulties, or to enable redundant or unemployed people to undertake retraining courses. Computers are also available on long term loan to enable freelances to establish themselves.

The Paul Hamlyn Foundation
18 Queen Anne's Gate, London SW1H 9AA. (020) 7227 3500. www.phf.org.uk

The Paul Hamlyn Foundation was established in 1987. Its support for publishing and bookselling concentrates on training and education, aiming to make skills available to those working in the industry who might not otherwise be offered training opportunities. There are a number of initiatives:

- Training grants for small independent publishers employing 20 people or fewer, to a maximum of £500 per employee and £2500 per company in any one financial year, for agreed in-house or off-site training by a recognized institution.
- Skills training grants for freelances in book and journal publishing, for up to £500 in any one financial year to cover a maximum of two courses run by a recognized institution.
- Small booksellers can benefit from a similar scheme, administered by the Booksellers Association. The Training Grants for Booksellers scheme is open to small, independent booksellers, community, school, antiquarian, second-hand and rare

bookshops employing eight people or fewer and whose main activity is retail bookselling. The maximum sum available to any one firm is £750 per financial year.

The Tony Godwin Memorial Trust
c/o Laurence Pollinger Limited, LaurencePollinger@compuserve. com.

www.tgmt.org.uk

Tony Godwin was an outstanding publisher in the 1960s and 1970s, and his contribution to the publishing industry is recognized in the form of a memorial trust and an award that bears his name. The Trust administers two scholarships:

- The Tony Godwin Award – open to all young people under the age of 35 who are UK nationals and working in the industry. The award is made biennially and provides the opportunity for the recipient to spend at least one month in America as the guest of a publishing house so as to learn about international publishing. A full report is published following the recipient's return to the UK.
- The Sir Stanley Unwin Travelling Scholarship – celebrates the life-long interest of Sir Stanley Unwin in the worldwide book trade. It creates opportunities for young booksellers and publishers (under the age of 35) to travel abroad in order to develop themselves as individuals and, by publishing a report, contribute to the continued success of the UK book trade through sharing their enhanced knowledge and experience. It is awarded biennially, alternating with the Tony Godwin Award.

The Worshipful Company of Stationers and Newspaper Makers
The Secretary, The Educational Charity of the Stationers' and Newspaper Makers' Company, The Old Dairy, Adstockfields, Adstock, Buckingham MK18 2JE.

- Stationers' Company Major Awards – assists young people in publishing, bookselling and related trades with development of their managerial and technological knowledge.
- Francis Mathew Stationers' Company Scholarships – enables management trainees in publishing and related trades to further their education by studying management methods, either in the UK or abroad.

NETWORKING OPPORTUNITIES

The following organizations provide excellent opportunities to mix with publishers and their staff, and hold open meetings at which non-members are welcome (a small entry charge may be made).

Childrens's Book Circle
c/o Kirsten Grant, Puffin Books, 27 Wrights Lane, London W8 5TZ. (020) 7416 3130.

Monthly evening meetings in London for everyone interested in children's books.

Independent Publishers Guild (IPG)
PO Box 93, Royston SG8 5GH. (01763) 247104.
www.ipg.uk.com; e-mail: sheila@ipg.uk.com

Occasional evening meetings in London for dynamic small and medium sized publishers.

Institute of Publishing
www.inst.publishing.org.uk

Fosters excellence in publishing and training, including occasional meetings.

Publishers Publicity Circle (PPC)
c/o Heather White, 65 Airedale Avenue, London W4 2NN. (020) 8994 1881.
e-mail: ppc-@lineone.net

Monthly lunch-time meetings in London at which high profile publicists from publishing houses and PR agencies share information and gossip.

Society of Freelance Editors and Proofreaders (SFEP)
(see above for address)

Local groups meet throughout the country, each with their own programme of events.

The Society of Young Publishers (SYP)
12 Dyott Street, London WC1A 1DF
www.thesyp.demon.co.uk

Monthly evening meetings in London and Oxford at which industry experts address the new generation of publishers.

Women in Publishing (WiP)
c/o The Publishers Association, 1 Kingsway, London WC2 6XF
www.cyberiacafe.net/wip

Monthly evening meetings in London led by women for women.

Electronic publishing

Most conferences and seminars aimed at professionals are very expensive to attend. However, the following organizations charge modest fees to members/non-members.

British Computing Society Electronic Publishing Specialist Group
www.bcs.org.uk

Regular day meetings throughout the year.

Electronic Publishers Forum
c/o The Publishers Association
www.publishers.org.uk

Occasional late afternoon meetings, with drinks afterwards.

See also **insidebookpublishing.com**

Further reading

Compiled by Iain D. Brown

The following is not intended to be a definitive book trade bibliography. Rather, it is a compilation of titles that will be of interest and use to readers, and should serve as a foundation for wider reading. (See also the Book Publishing Books *mail order catalogue issued by the Publishing Training Centre, Book House, 45 East Hill, London SW18 2QZ. 020–8874 2718. bpb@bookhouse.co.uk)*

PERIODICALS

The Bookseller (weekly, J. Whitaker & Sons, 12 Dyott Street, London WC1A 1DF). An essential source of information on publishing and book-selling, with regular special features and supplements. Advertisements for jobs in all fields, usually for people with previous experience see www.thebookseller.com.

Publishing News (weekly, 39 Store Street, London WC1E 7DB). Thinner and racier than *The Bookseller*, focusing more on consumer book publishing and personalities. Runs interesting articles and listings, but few job advertisements.

Publishers Weekly (weekly, 245 W. 17th Street, New York, NY 10011, USA). Bills itself as 'the international news magazine of book publishing and bookselling' but is essentially the American equivalent of the UK's *Bookseller* and *Publishing News* combined.

LOGOS (quarterly, Whurr Publishers, 19b Compton Terrace, London N1 2UN). More of an academic journal than a trade periodical. An impartial and useful source of information and analysis of 'the common causes of those engaged in writing, making, selling and disseminating books and journals throughout the world'.

Learned Publishing (quarterly, Association of Learned and Professional Society Publishers, South House, The Street, Clapham, Worthing BN13 3UU). Another academic journal well worth reading for the diversity of views.

Society periodicals

CopyRight (monthly, for members of the Society of Freelance Editors and Proofreaders). An excellent newsletter with many interesting and useful articles, tips and book reviews.

InPrint (monthly, for members of the Society of Young Publishers). General newsletter reporting the society's monthly speaker meetings and social events; runs occasional job ads, see also www.thesyp.demon.co.uk.

WiPlash (monthly, for members of Women in Publishing). The society's newsletter with news and information for women at all levels in publishing.

SIdelights (quarterly, for members of the Society of Indexers). Focuses on topics pertaining to this specialized book and journal production sector.

The Author (for members of the Society of Authors). A well-written periodical with contributions from well-known authors. Readable.

Other periodicals to note

Book Publishing Report, Bookselling, Editor and Publisher, Folio, Interactive Media International, New Media Age, Seybold Report on Internet Publishing.

DIRECTORIES AND REFERENCE BOOKS

Collin, P.H. (1997) *Dictionary of Printing and Publishing* (2nd edn), Peter Collin. Wondered what that word meant in an earlier chapter? Look it up in this specialized dictionary.

Directory of Publishing: UK, Commonwealth and Overseas, Cassell and the Publishers Association. Very useful for the names and contact details of mainstream and smaller publishers, literary agents, book packagers, trade societies and associations. Updated annually.

Turner, B. (ed.) *The Writer's Handbook,* Macmillan. Packed with interesting information for writers and publishers. Also contains information on bursaries and scholarships for publishers. Updated annually.

Writers' and Artists' Yearbook, A & C Black. Contains short entries on publishers and their subject areas, packagers, literary agents, societies, prizes, etc. Updated annually.

INTRODUCTION TO THE BOOK TRADE

Callenbach, E. (1989) *Publisher's Lunch: a dialogue concerning the secrets of how publishers think and what authors can do about it,* Ten Speed Press. Ah, the famous publishing lunch, over which the workings of the trade are discussed.

Curtis, R. (1998) *This Business of Publishing: an insider's view of current trends and tactics*, Allsworth Press. American in focus, but absorbing nonetheless.

Feldman, T. (ed.) (1988) *Pocket Glossary of Publishing Terms*, Pira International. Clear and concise explanations of publishing jargon.

Legat, M. (1998) *An Author's Guide to Publishing* (3rd edn), Robert Hale. The third edition of a useful book for anyone wanting information and advice on publishing.

Lines, J. (1994) *Careers in Publishing and Bookselling* (2nd edn), Kogan Page. A broad look at careers in the book trade, dispelling myths and correcting misinformation that many have about these industries.

Montagnes, I. (1998) *An Introduction to Publishing Management*, Association for the Development of Education in Africa. Do not be phased by the title. Written primarily for African publishers, this is a wonderful book that contains masses of information. All readers will learn something.

Norrie, I. (1998) *Mumby's Publishing and Bookselling in the 20th Century* (8th edn), HarperCollins. An in-depth analysis of the book trade and the changes that have happened in the past 100 years.

Owen, P. (ed.) (1988) *Publishing – The Future*, Peter Owen. Now rather dated, but still an interesting assortment of views by trade luminaries on publishing trends. Read this in conjunction with Owen's later publication.

Owen, P. (ed.) (1996) *Publishing Now* (revised edn), Peter Owen. Fascinating for the diversity of assessment of the present and future of the book trade by key people.

Page, G. (1997) *Journal Publishing*, Cambridge University Press. Excellent coverage of all aspects of journal publishing. Required reading if this publishing sector appeals as a career.

Stewart, D.M. (1992) *Bluff Your Way in Publishing* (revised edn), Oval Books. A humorous run-down on publishing. Contains some out-of-date information (not surprising really in an industry that changes weekly!), but a fun introduction to this industry.

Unwin, Sir Stanley (1982) *The Truth About Publishing* (8th edn), Academy Chicago. A new edition of the classic introduction to publishing written originally in 1926, a bygone era of pre-corporate publishing. Debunks many publishing mistruths.

Woll, T. (1999) *Publishing for Profit: successful bottom-line management for book publishers*, Kogan Page. How-to book on publishing business essentials by a US consultant. This European edition versioned by enduring independent publisher Philip Kogan and his team.

EDITORIAL AND INDEXING

Angelbeck, J. & Hughes, S. (1999) *Editing on Screen: effective working practice, a teach-yourself course*, EPE. Instruction on best practices for applying editorial skills to the electronic environment. Includes practical examples.

Butcher, J. (1992) *Copy-Editing: the Cambridge handbook for editors, authors and publishers* (3rd edn), Cambridge University Press. The indispensable and essential aid for authors, editors and publishers. Everyone should own a copy.

Davies, G. (1994) *Book Commissioning and Acquisition*, Blueprint/Routledge. Guidance and support for those involved in commissioning authors or titles, and advice on how to manage the whole acquisition process.

Foster, C. (1995) *Editing, Design and Book Production*, Pluto. All-round coverage of three integral parts of publishing.

Frewin Jones, A. & Pollinger, L. (1996) *Writing for Children and Getting Published*, Hodder & Stoughton. Don't be fooled by the title: this is an excellent and well-written introduction to both the general fiction market and the craft of writing by two prominent authors. Great fun!

Harris, N. (1991) *Basic Editing: a practical course*, Publishing Training Centre. A two-book self-tuition course that explains editorial techniques and offers 78 exercises for practical experience.

Horn, B. (1997) *The Effective Editor's Handbook*, Pira International. Written by a well-known and experienced editor, this book imparts a wealth of valuable information, tips and guidance.

Judd, K. (1995) *Copyediting: a practical guide*, Robert Hale. Useful as a refresher course and reference manual for the new editor or the old hand.

May, D.H. (1997) *Proofreading Plain and Simple*, Career Press. A detailed, step-by-step guide to an oft-misunderstood area.

Mulvany, N.C. (1994) *Indexing Books*, University of Chicago. The definitive text on how to index, including practical examples.

PRODUCTION

Bann, D. (1995) *Book Production Control*, Pira International. A useful guide to all the stages of print production. Also contains advice on how to survive in the production department.

Bann, D. (1997) *The New Print Production Handbook*, Little, Brown. The 'Butcher' for designers and production staff – and anyone else dealing with printers.

Barnard, M. (ed.) (1998) *The Print and Production Manual* (8th edn), Pira International. Used throughout the industry, this manual explains clearly the modern techniques used in the book and printing trades for digital processing, printing, colour origination and reproduction.

Barnard, M., Peacock, J. & Berrill, C. (1995) *The Pocket Print Production Guide*, Pira International. A ready source of information for the nontechnical. Useful for information that needs to be at one's fingertips.

Brunner, L. (1999) *First Steps in Digital Prepress*, Pira International. A new title that guides readers through the minefield of digital content creation and production.

Peacock, J. (1995) *Book production* (2nd edn), Blueprint / Routledge. The definitive reference book on all aspects of the production of books, updated to include technological developments.

DESIGN AND PICTURE RESEARCH

Campbell, A. (1993) *The New Designer's Handbook*, Little Brown. Another 'Butcher' for designers, editors and production staff – and anyone else dealing with clients and layouts.

Evans, H. (1992) *Practical Picture Research*, Pira International. Contains particulars on the techniques of picture research, from storage technologies through selecting materials to legal aspects.

Evans, H. & Evans, M. (1996) *Picture Researcher's Handbook* (6th edn), Pira International. An authoritative guide to sources for pictures and advice on using them.

Hughes, S. (1998) *Design and Typography in Easy Steps*, Computer Step. Handy distillation of tips on how to design for both print and online environments. Useful for editors.

Martin, D. (1989) *An Outline of Book Design*, Blueprint and the Publishers Association. A fascinating introduction to the whole subject.

Williams, R. (1994) *The Non-Designer's Design Book*, Peachpit. Another title that gives advice for the 'visual novice'.

MARKETING

Baverstock, A. (1993) *Are Books Different? Marketing in the book trade*, Kogan Page / Publishing Training Centre. When is a book not like a tin of beans?

Baverstock, A. (1999) *How to Market Books* (3rd edn), Kogan Page. Vital reading on how to make books sell. Used as a set text on training courses and in many universities.

Baverstock, A. (1997) *Commonsense Marketing for Non-Marketers*, Piatkus. Offers a good grounding in marketing, using clear language, examples and case studies.

Blake, C. (1999) *From Pitch to Publication*, Macmillan. One of the UK's leading literary agents talks about how books are sold and how the publishing process really works.

Brown, I.D. & Fletcher, J. (eds) (1997) *How Americans Publish Commercial Fiction: the reports of George Lucas and Richard Scrivener, 1996 Tony Godwin Award recipients*, The Tony Godwin Memorial Trust. A detailed look at how and why the American book trade differs from the British.

Brown, I.D. & Fletcher, J. (eds) (1999) *Superstores – Super News? The report of Fiona Stewart, 1998 Tony Godwin Award recipient*, The Tony Godwin Memorial Trust. An incisive examination of the impact American marketing and sales strategies are having on the American and British book trades.

Ellsworth, J. & Ellsworth, M. (1996) *Marketing on the Internet* (2nd edn), John Wiley. The internet is so large that knowing how to use marketing skills and tools to promote titles is essential.

Forsyth, P. & Birn, R. (1997) *Marketing in Publishing*, Routledge. Strategies for increasing book sales.

Millington, R. (1998) *Effective Copywriting for Publishers*, Pira International. How to produce effective sales copy for any publication.

Nair, C. (1991) *Book Promotion, Sales and Distribution: a management training course*, Publishing Training Centre and UNESCO. Covers a wide variety of topics on how to sell, promote and distribute books effectively.

ELECTRONIC PUBLISHING

Akeroyd, J. (1994) *Digital Books? On-demand printing and publishing*, Library Information Centre. A short overview of the possibilities offered by digital technology.

Blunden, B. & Blunden, M. (eds) (1994) *The Electronic Publishing Business and its Market*, Pira International. A weighty tome with useful and detailed information on the electronic publishing sector.

Blunden, B. & Blunden, M. (eds) (1997) *Electronic Publishing Strategies*, Pira International. Another weighty tome on the market, user behaviour and new paradigms for electronic publishing.

Dorner, J. (2000) *The Internet: a writer's guide*, A & C Black. Looks at how the internet can be used by and for publishers.

Earnshaw, R., Vince, J. & Jones, H. (eds) (1996) *Digital Media and Electronic Publishing*, Academic Press. Some parts of this book are now out of date but still a useful insight into the digital media.

Gates, B. (1996) *The Road Ahead* (revised edn), Penguin. The man from Microsoft speaks.

Moody, F. (1995) *I Sing the Body Electronic: a year with Microsoft on the multimedia frontier*, Hodder & Stoughton. An especially readable overview of the tribulations of multimedia publishing.

Negroponte, N. (1996) *Being Digital*, Hodder & Stoughton. Another readable account by the MIT guru of the opportunities and potential of digital technology.

Penfold, D. (1997) *EP, Multimedia and Communications Glossary*, Pira International. All those buzzwords explained!

Ressler, S. (1997) *The Art of Electronic Publishing: the Internet and beyond*, Prentice-Hall. The basics of electronic publishing.

Ward, G. (1998) *Publishing in the Digital Age*, Bowerdean. Introductory text to the new media.

RIGHTS AND CONTRACTS

Armstrong, C.J. (ed.) (2000) *Staying Legal: a guide to the issues and practice for users and publishers of electronic resources*, Library Association. A new guidebook to the 'electronic minefield'.

Cavendish, J.M. & Pool, K. (1993) *Handbook of Copyright in British Publishing Practice* (3rd edn), Cassell. A useful overview of the legislation and EU directives.

Clark, C., Owen, L. & Palmer, R. (1997) *Publishing Agreements* (5th edn), Butterworths. One of the essential reference works by three leading figures in this area.

Jones, H. (1996) *Publishing Law*, Routledge. Wondered how the law affects the publishing process? Find out from this guide.

Owen, L. (1997) *Selling Rights* (3rd edn), Routledge. A comprehensive and respected examination of the rights sector by a key figure in the industry.

Manches Media (1998) *Caught in the Web: law and the Internet* (2nd edn), Manches. A very readable explanation of a little-understood aspect of electronic communication. Used as a set text on some university courses.

See also insidebookpublishing.com

Index